THE GEORGE GUND FOUNDATION
IMPRINT IN AFRICAN AMERICAN STUDIES

The George Gund Foundation has endowed
this imprint to advance understanding of
the history, culture, and current issues
of African Americans.

The publisher and the University of California Press Foundation gratefully acknowledge the generous support of the George Gund Foundation Imprint in African American Studies.

The Black Reparations Project

The Black Reparations Project

A Handbook for Racial Justice

EDITED BY

William A. Darity Jr., A. Kirsten Mullen, and Lucas Hubbard

UNIVERSITY OF CALIFORNIA PRESS

University of California Press
Oakland, California

© 2023 by The Regents of the University of California

First Paperback Printing 2024

Library of Congress Cataloging-in-Publication Data

Names: Darity, William A., Jr., 1953– editor. | Mullen,
   A. Kirsten (Andrea Kirsten), editor. | Hubbard, Lucas
   (Freelance writer), editor.
Title: The black reparations project : a handbook for
   racial justice / edited by William A. Darity Jr., A.
   Kirsten Mullen, and Lucas Hubbard.
Description: Oakland, California : University of
   California Press, [2023] | Includes bibliographical
   references and index.
Identifiers: LCCN 2022040247 | ISBN 9780520383814
   (cloth) | 978052409828 (paper) | 9780520383821
   (epub)
Subjects: LCSH: African Americans—Reparations. |
   Racial justice—United States—Handbooks, manuals,
   etc. | Slavery—United States. | Racism—United States. |
   African Americans—Social conditions.
Classification: LCC E185.89.R45 B53 2023 |
   DDC 305.896/073—dc23/eng/20220902
LC record available at https://lccn.loc.gov/2022040247

Manufactured in the United States of America

32 31 30 29 28 27 26 25 24
10 9 8 7 6 5 4 3 2 1

Contents

Illustrations

Introduction

WILLIAM A. DARITY JR., A. KIRSTEN MULLEN,
AND LUCAS HUBBARD

During the 2019 phase of the US presidential campaign, a number of serious contenders for the Democratic Party's nomination actually invoked the term *reparations*, a few even indicating their support for restitution for black Americans. The leading voice at the time was Marianne Williamson, who recommended an outlay ranging from $100 to $500 billion as recompense for the many decades of racial injustice in the United States. And while they offered no specifics, both Julian Castro and Tom Steyer also endorsed black reparations.

The stresses of the COVID-19 pandemic coupled with the international protests in response to the highly visible police murders of unarmed black people, especially the killing of George Floyd, led to an additional dramatic surge in interest in black reparations in 2020. That interest has carried over to the present, in which more and more racial justice advocates and their allies are proclaiming a desire to pursue a program of redress on behalf of black America. It is, perhaps, an interest in reparations not witnessed since the Reconstruction Era.

However, not everyone means the same thing when referring to "reparations." Not everyone shares identical views about who should be eligible to receive reparations, what form reparations should take, how large the reparations fund should be, how reparations funds should be distributed, or who should pay the reparations debt. Moreover, this is truly a situation where the devil is in the details. While many Americans can agree, in principle, on the moral case for reparations, there are deep cleavages among reparations proponents over the substance of an actual program of restitution.

Many of us engaged in research on black reparations over the years have long been aware of these sharp differences in visions regarding the features of an act of redress. In 2019, two of the editors of this volume were anticipating the upcoming publication of their book *From Here to Equality: Reparations for Black Americans in the Twenty-First Century,* where, in the final chapter, they would offer a detailed plan for black reparations. They also were aware that others laboring in reparations research were trying to think through similar issues, and they knew that it was highly unlikely that the last chapter of *From Here to Equality* would be the final word.

Coupled with growing national interest in reparations, it was apparent that there would be tremendous value in bringing members of the reparations research community together to further refine and motivate the case and plan for reparations. The Reparations Planning Committee (RPC) assembled with the aim of producing a volume that would function as an extensive guide for designing and implementing a national black reparations initiative.

Financial support for the project came from an award from the William T. Grant Foundation to the Samuel DuBois Cook Center on Social Equity at Duke University given to aid the Cook Center in doing the research to further develop and consolidate an African American reparations plan.

Not all members of the RPC contributed chapters to the volume, but all provided advice and guidance on the path to the current edition. Nor is this a "consensus document" per se, although there is consistency in the shared vision of what black reparations should be among the contributors.

All of the essays in this collection have been written with the goal of pushing forward the black reparations project. These essays are working papers for African American reparations and hence working papers for a new America.

The chapters in this volume fall into two sections. The first section consists of chapters that interrogate and outline the case for reparations through the racial disparities observed across different areas—wealth, housing, education, and health—before highlighting potential and necessary paths to restitution that can be achieved as redress in each area. The second section considers the logistical elements of a reparations plan: potential pitfalls the plan should avoid, eligibility standards for reparations, methods of delivery of reparations, the parties responsible for delivering reparations, and the necessary next steps and timeline for effecting such a plan.

William A. Darity Jr. and A. Kirsten Mullen's opening chapter, "Where Does Black Reparations in America Stand?," provides an overview of the evolving terrain of an unfolding national conversation on black reparations. The authors examine the implications of the attempted coup d'état on January 6, 2021, for the black reparations movement and the policies that have made and sustained the immense racial wealth gap. They outline the four essential pillars of a sound plan for black reparations.

Calculation of the size of the bill for reparations starts in earnest in "Wealth Implications of Slavery and Racial Discrimination for African American Descendants of the Enslaved," by Thomas Craemer, Trevor Smith, Brianna Harrison, Trevon Logan, Wesley Bellamy, and William A. Darity Jr. These detailed estimates, ranging from $5 trillion to a fantastic $22 quadrillion, provide a grounding for the remainder of the volume, quantifying the costs of atrocities that later chapters—in particular, the three chapters that immediately follow, which highlight, largely, postslavery injustices—study in a more qualitative manner.

While the bulk of the chapter highlights various methods for estimating the economic losses black Americans have suffered from slavery times to the current moment, the authors settle on elimination of the racial wealth gap as the fundamental goal of a plan for reparations for black American descendants of US slavery.

This chapter previously was published in June 2020 in the *Review of Black Political Economy*. It is reprinted here with modest editing and data updates with the permission of the authors and the journal.

"Unequal Housing and the Case for Reparations," by Walter D. Greason, addresses the first area of qualitative consideration, studying inequitable housing policies in the US since the Civil War—particularly in the past century—as a basis for reparations. Greason identifies how the New Deal and civil rights eras, while transforming America's surface appearance, nonetheless failed to transform the racial hierarchy at the country's core.

In particular, Greason writes that "policies designed to promote black inclusion and equity were sabotaged" in favor of techniques that eradicated the small elements of wealth that black families had gathered during the Jim Crow years. Highlighting the effects in communities across the country, Greason shows the stagnation of progress that has defined the postslavery period, the obstacles to equity that black Americans (and well-meaning policy makers) have faced, and the missed opportunities that have warped the national trajectory.

Malik Edwards's chapter, "Education Inequities and the Case for Reparations," considers similar shortcomings in the education sphere. Providing a history of educational deprivation and its deleterious effects on black well-being, Edwards details the inequities long present in the educational system that persist to this day.

Focusing on the pre–Civil War period, the pre–*Brown v. Board of Education* era, and the lack of progress in the post–*Brown* era, Edwards highlights the disputes, debates, and objections to equal education that have defined each era of schooling in America. The most recent pattern of resistance dovetails neatly with Greason's discussion of contemporary residential segregation.

Edwards constructs a thoughtful through line between present-day disparities and those of centuries past, showcasing the inability to equalize opportunities for students across all schools—and the hesitancy of powerful entities (especially the Supreme Court) to set up and protect enforceable policies that might achieve such a goal.

The last chapter of Part I, written by Keisha Bentley-Edwards, focuses on the case for reparations from a health perspective. "The African American Health Burden: Disproportionate and Unresolved" looks at how a range of disparate health outcomes for black Americans can be traced back to a litany of policies and practices that have for centuries reduced the quality of—if not outright eliminated—medical care for this population. Bentley-Edwards describes how this arena, like many others described in this book, was long defined by outright subjugation and maltreatment of the black body. Moreover, when the Reconstruction era seemingly brought a flicker of opportunity, that hope was quickly squashed—most notably by the Flexner Report of 1910, which culminated in a shuttering of most black medical schools at the time. Finally, as universal policies like the Medicare Bill of 1965 came into being and tried to fix past injustices, they were built upon slanted ground in a discriminatory environment. Thus these attempts merely managed to create a newly unequal playing field for black medical professionals and, in turn, black patients.

The second section of the volume begins with "Learning from Past Experiences with Reparations," by A. Kirsten Mullen and William A. Darity Jr. Reiterating the focus on closing the racial wealth gap as the preeminent goal for reparations, the authors consider other efforts that have been undertaken—both in America and around the world—in response to previous atrocities. Mullen and Darity study the actions of five commissions that convened to study past atrocities (four of which awarded some form of reparations to victims and/or their families) to identify patterns and lessons for bringing black reparations to fruition.

The authors highlight myriad lessons: these commissions can be valuable even without significant popular support for reparations; indeed, a commission's report could prove valuable in increasing support for black reparations. They also determine that uniform payments, largely, are desirable; that the perpetrators of the atrocities should not benefit from having committed such actions; and that allies who support the push for reparations are valuable in swaying public opinion.

"Considerations for the Design of a Reparations Plan," by Trevon D. Logan, continues the strategic discussion of logistics for a reparations plan. Logan first notes, among other caveats, that estimates of the racial wealth gap may be less than the full debt owed to black Americans—both because of the outsized gains achieved by the enslavers and because of the intangible costs that the enslaved and their descendants have been forced to carry across generations.

Logan then proceeds to enumerate a bevy of concerns and considerations surrounding the administration of such a program of reparations. Among these he identifies the need for a committee to be established to study it, the need for the program to be national in scope, the need for it to be based on knowledge obtained from precedents (in parallel with Mullen and Darity), and various possibilities regarding the format of and funding of payments. Moreover, Logan emphasizes the need for a more factual treatment of American history and its record of racial atrocities, both as a necessary element of the process of restitution and as a means of engendering support for redress.

Lisa R. Brown's chapter, "Reparations and Adult Education: Civic and Community Engagement for Lifelong Learners," focuses on the role that adult education can play in the reparations push. Brown highlights the opportunity for this field, which has been at the forefront of numerous American social justice movements, to advance reparations by increasing general public knowledge and support.

The latter sections of the chapter explore Brown's adaptation of Clare Graves's ECLET (Emergent Cyclical Levels of Existence Theory) framework outlining stages of adult development in terms of individual and collectivist thinking. Brown posits that it could be a useful tool in identifying those adults most likely to become supporters of black reparations, as well as cultivating, through education, the kinds of collectivist thinking that are most likely to lead to reparations support. The framework, in conjunction with adult development provided by the educational systems Brown highlights, provides a path to forging the necessary broader coalition for this cause.

"The Children of Slavery: Genealogical Research and the Establishment of Eligibility for Reparations"—written by Evelyn A. McDowell—considers logistics in the process of delivering reparations to eligible individuals. Building off the qualifying criteria outlined by Darity and Mullen (2020), McDowell delineates a methodical process both for identifying relatives and for acquiring supporting evidence that establishes an ancestor's enslaved status.

McDowell walks readers through the types of source materials—census, federal, property, and other records—that can prove valuable in this research process. She presents a system for evaluating the strength of pieces of evidence, and she showcases this in two rich and nuanced examples. McDowell's chapter is a powerful rejoinder to critics who believe that it is impossible to establish a genealogical trail to one's enslaved ancestors.

Darity and Mullen's concluding chapter, "On the Black Reparations Highway: Avoiding the Detours," explores common complaints lodged against black reparations as well as alternative plans that have been suggested in lieu of a comprehensive form of targeted payments to black Americans. The chapter also argues that local initiatives labeled as "reparations," congressional legislation to form a study commission for black reparations, H.R. 40, the charge that reparations "must be more than a check," and an array of proposed universal or indirect measures to close the wealth gap, are diversions from an essential comprehensive national plan for reparations. The conclusion makes clear that nothing but reparations conducted at the federal level will alleviate the black-wealth gap and that if equality is the goal, then nothing but "true reparations" will suffice.

Taken as a whole, the chapters found in *The Black Reparations Project* provide a wide-ranging and emphatic argument for this long-overdue cause. The journey to get to this point has been arduous, and while there is some momentum currently, much ground still must be covered before redress becomes a reality. Our hope is that the contents of this book, and its presence in the nation's wider discourse in the coming years, will motivate, guide, and speed the final leg of the journey.

REFERENCES

Darity Jr., William A., and A. Kirsten Mullen. 2020. *From Here to Equality: Reparations for Black Americans in the Twenty-First Century.* Chapel Hill: University of North Carolina Press.

PART ONE

The Context and Cases for Reparations

1

Where Does Black Reparations in America Stand?

WILLIAM A. DARITY JR. AND A. KIRSTEN MULLEN

OF COUPS AND THE CONFEDERACY

On January 6, 2021, urged on by President Trump's false claim that the 2020 election had been stolen from him, a terrorist mob invaded the Capitol Building in Washington, D.C. The intent was to execute a coup d'état to maintain Trump's regime. Imperiling elected officials from both parties, the Capitol invaders brought with them the trappings and regalia of the Confederacy.

They also carried the full spirit and heritage of the Confederacy. In the aftermath of the Civil War, it was the defeated Confederates who violently sought to win the peace by a campaign of sustained terror directed against the freedmen. Time and again, they overthrew duly elected local governments co-governed by coalitions of newly emancipated blacks and pro-Union whites, including ousters of elected officials at St. Landry Parish in Louisiana in 1868; Colfax, Louisiana, in 1873; Coushatta, Louisiana, in 1874; Vicksburg, Mississippi, in 1874; Fort Bend County in Texas, in 1888; and Wilmington, North Carolina, in 1898.[1]

The January 6 assault on the national government runs in a straight line from the most concerted previous attempt to destroy the United States of America, the secession of the eleven states that formed the Confederate States of America 163 years ago. Indeed, the attempted coup on January 6 is symptomatic of the long-term failure to de-Confederatize American society. In contrast with Germany's active policy of de-Nazification, nothing similar has occurred with respect to the prominence of the Lost Cause narrative of the nation's history and the memorialization of the leaders of the southern secession.

We frequently hear the aphorism "The winners write the history," but this has not been the case with respect to US history. Via organizations like the United Daughters of the Confederacy (UDC) and the Daughters of the American Revolution (DAR), the Confederates and their ideological descendants crafted the story of the nation's past. In the United States, the losers—the losers of the Civil War—have faced little resistance as they have written the nation's history.

False images abound of kindly slaveholders generously conducting a civilizing mission on behalf of the Africans who were held as their human property, of the Civil War as motivated by the pursuit of "states' rights," of Reconstruction as a travesty of black misrule under the manipulation of scalawags and carpetbaggers, and of the Confederates as dignified patriots seeking to preserve the principles of the American Revolution. All of these lies are a product of the work of the UDC and the DAR. They have suppressed the accurate narrative of the formation of the Confederacy as a traitorous act born of insistence on maintaining an oppressive system of economic exploitation.

The Lost Cause narrative also has served as a powerful prop to hide an accurate story of the path taken toward white wealth accumulation and black wealth deprivation in the United States. Black Americans are characterized, collectively, as less intelligent, less motivated, more profligate, more likely to undervalue education, more likely to be ineffective parents, and/or more prone to criminality than whites. This characterization of black people as immature and largely dysfunctional, in the absence of white discipline and supervision, dates directly to the perspective taken by slavery apologists.

There is a striking commonality between the Democratic Party of the latter half of the nineteenth century and the Republican Party in the latter half of the twentieth century to the present. Both are parties of the Confederacy; both are parties that champion minority rule. Both raise the torch of the Lost Cause. Both are committed to erasure of an accurate presentation of the American story.

An accurate story of the divergence in wealth and general economic well-being between blacks and whites in the United States would aim directly at the national policies conducted by the federal government that have built white wealth while, simultaneously, inhibiting the growth of black wealth. Evidence of how public policy has been mobilized to create and sustain the black-white wealth gap provides a clear motivation for the use of public policy to develop a reparations program to eliminate the gap.

WEALTH, RACE, AND PUBLIC POLICY

The most recent survey conducted by the Board of Governors of the Federal Reserve on wealth in the United States was completed in 2019, prior to the onset of the COVID-19 pandemic. It indicated that the median white household had a net worth $164,100 greater than the median black household; at the mean, the average white household had a net worth $841,900 greater than the average black household (Bhutta et al. 2020).

It is routine for analysts to prefer to evaluate disparities at the median—the middle of the distribution—rather than the mean, since the median is not sensitive to outlying values and, presumably, provides a more accurate picture of the typical condition of members of each group. *But in the context of racial differences in wealth, the mean gap offers the superior measure for policy purposes.* This is so, one of us has argued, because

> wealth is so densely concentrated in the United States that 97 percent of white Americans' total wealth is held by households with a net worth above the white median. And white households with a net worth above the national median, which is approximately $100,000, hold close to 99 percent of white wealth. Twenty-five percent of white households have a net worth in excess of $1 million, in contrast with a mere 4 percent of Black households.
>
> Using the median figure would take an overwhelming share of white wealth off the table. (Darity 2021)

We propose that a true reparations plan, rather than taking that vast amount of wealth "off the table," must focus on elimination of the black-white wealth disparity at the *mean,* rather than the median.

Black Americans with ancestors enslaved in the United States constitute about 12 percent of the nation's population but possess less than 2 percent of the nation's wealth. To bring the share of wealth held by this segment of the black population—actually, about 90 percent of the black population in the United States—into consistency with their share of the population will necessitate a reparations plan setting the mean gap as its target for closure.

How did this enormous racial gulf in wealth come about? The gulf is the intentional effect of national policies that built white wealth at the expense of black American wealth accumulation. In an article we prepared for *The Economist,* we identified four periods of American public policy that contributed directly to the creation of the black-white wealth gap: the Wagon Train Period, the Bloodlust Period, the Picket Fence Period, and the Freeway Period.

The Wagon Train Period

In the immediate aftermath of the Civil War, a pledge was made to the formerly enslaved that they would receive forty-acre land grants as restitution for their years of subjugation. That pledge was never fulfilled.

President Lincoln's emissary, Secretary of War Edwin Stanton, and General William T. Sherman met in Savannah, Georgia, in January 1865 with a group of twenty representatives from black communities to chart the postwar agenda. When asked what they desired, the spokesperson for the black leadership group, Reverend Garrison Frazier, said the freedmen wanted "to have land, and turn it and till it by our own labor . . . until we are able to buy it and make it our own." He also said, with great prescience, that blacks preferred to live among themselves because "there is a prejudice against us in the South that will take years to get over" (Darity and Mullen 2020, 157–58). They wanted to be left alone to make their own tomorrow.

A few days later Sherman issued Special Field Orders No. 15, designating a 5.3-million-acre strip of land stretching from South Carolina's Sea Islands to the St. John's River in northern Florida as a territory to be set aside in forty-acre allotments to the formerly enslaved. This was supposed to be a first phase of a land reform that would have assigned at least forty million acres of land to the four million freedmen.

A process of settlement began with forty thousand freedmen taking over four hundred thousand acres of land. But in the aftermath of Lincoln's assassination, his successor, Andrew Johnson, simultaneously a Unionist and a white supremacist, rolled back all policies intended to give the newly emancipated full citizenship, including the land reform policy. Even the partial allotment of four hundred thousand acres was restored to the former slaveholders.

In contrast, the federal government introduced the Homestead Act in 1862 to complete its colonial settler project in the western territories by distributing 160-acre land allotments to 1.5 million white households, including recent European immigrants (Williams 2000). This was land the US government occupied that previously had been home to indigenous peoples.

While the projected allocation of forty acres to the freedmen was one-quarter of the size of the Homestead Act patents, ultimately the freedmen received nothing. Trina Williams Shanks has estimated that today at least forty-five million living white Americans are beneficiaries of the Homestead Act (Williams 2000).

The Bloodlust Period

Between the end of the Civil War and the end of World War II, white terrorists conducted upward of one hundred massacres of black communities with impunity (listed in Appendix A). Because of the recent attention drawn to it by the centennial commemoration and by a popular culture treatment in the television program *Watchmen*, the Tulsa massacre of 1921 probably is the most well known. In 1919 alone—the year of the Red Summer—upward of forty white attacks on black communities took place across the country in locations as far flung as Bisbee, Arizona; Chicago; Wilmington, Delaware; and Elaine, Arkansas.

The federal government either implicitly or explicitly sanctioned these acts of mob violence. Indeed, in the case of the Ocoee, Florida, massacre in 1920, Congress actually issued a commendation to the mobsters for "upholding 'law and order'" (Fussell 2016, 1915). In 1921, in Tulsa, incendiary devices were dropped from decommissioned World War I US Army airplanes on homes and businesses in the prosperous, black Greenwood district of the city. This, literally, was the firebombing of Greenwood.

In all these episodes, black lives were lost. Especially relevant to the creation of the racial wealth gap is the fact that, typically, black property was also seized by white terrorists to become their own. Frequently, the objective was to block black participation in electoral politics, but just as often the objective was to undermine black economic prosperity. In Ocoee, Florida, both objectives were plainly on display (Fussell 2016, 1915).

The Picket Fence Period

In the twentieth century, federal asset-building policy shifted from the provision of land to the promotion of homeownership. Here again, white Americans benefited and black Americans did not. Residential segregation, crystallizing with the development of restrictive covenants early in the century, drove a wedge between the values of black-owned and white-owned homes—independent of the residences' structural characteristics—that reduced the relative equity in black-owned homes.

Even after restrictive covenants were deemed illegal by the Supreme Court, a home-buying and home equity advantage was preserved for whites via redlining—a public-private partnership between the federal government and local banks that denied residents of black neighborhoods access to credit on the same terms as residents of white neighborhoods. The Federal Housing Administration, an agency created during the New Deal era, was an engine of discrimination against black home buyers.

Compounding matters further was the decentralized administration of the G.I. Bill—a condition for its passage through Congress to placate southern representatives—resulting in the discriminatory application of the legislation's home-buying and business development provisions. Local authorities, both north and south, used resources to support white veterans' home purchases and business start-up efforts, while excluding black veterans from equivalent benefits (Katznelson 2005).

The Freeway Period

Federal funding for an expanded national highway system, dating from the 1950s, became an additional mechanism for further destruction of black prosperity and community stability. Freeways were located at the heart of black business districts and residential neighborhoods.

The black business district of Durham, North Carolina, popularly known as a Black Wall Street, was shattered by the placement of North Carolina Highway 147, which connected Interstate 40 to Interstate 85, directly at its center. The Greenwood district of Tulsa, Oklahoma, also dubbed a Black Wall Street, undertook a concerted effort to rebuild the black business infrastructure after the 1921 white assault. The combination of an urban renewal ("slum clearance") program and construction of Interstate 244 erased the restoration effort nearly half a century after the massacre (Darity and Mullen 2020, 222; Graham 2021).

Nashville, Tennessee; Charlotte, North Carolina; New Orleans, Louisiana; Montgomery, Alabama; Birmingham, Alabama; Miami, Florida; Kansas City, Missouri; St. Paul, Minnesota; Tampa-St. Petersburg, Florida; Jacksonville, Florida; Orlando, Florida; Atlanta, Georgia; Columbia, South Carolina; Los Angeles, California; Camden, New Jersey; and Milwaukee, Wisconsin, are all cities where the location of interstate highways cleaved black business districts and communities

(Mohl 2002). The Freeway Period also took its toll on black wealth and well-being.

Given the history of the national government's direct role in creating the black-white gap in wealth, the federal government must take a direct role in eliminating that gap. This will require a plan for what we refer to as "true reparations."

TRUE REPARATIONS

We are convinced a plan for true reparations must have four basic pillars. First, it must designate those black Americans whose ancestors were enslaved in the United States as eligible recipients for reparations on the basis of two criteria. Drawing upon previous work and the information on black genealogical research in this volume (see chapter 9), one criterion is a lineage standard, requiring an individual to establish they had at least one ancestor enslaved in the United States. The additional criterion, an identity standard, requires an individual to demonstrate that for at least twelve years before enactment of a reparations plan or a study commission for reparations, they self-identified as black, Negro, African American, or Afro-American.

This is the community of descendants of the freedmen, those promised and then denied forty-acre land grants. This is the community that has borne the burden of the cumulative intergenerational effects of slavery, legal segregation, and white terrorist violence, as well as ongoing atrocities, including mass incarceration, discrimination, and police lynching.

In her review of *From Here to Equality* for the *New York Review of Books,* Shennette Garrett-Scott (2021) grumbles that we omit blacks who migrated to the United States more recently because, allegedly, we argue that they have not experienced American racism. In fact, we never make any such claim. For example, we are well aware that the police in the United States do not interrogate a black victim's ancestry before engaging in acts of brutality.[2]

What separates the recent black immigrants' case from that of black American descendants of US slavery is not the lack of exposure to racism. In part, the separation lies in the fact that they migrated to a racist country voluntarily, unlike the ancestors of the community that merits reparations from the US government.

Moreover, the wealth position that they bring with them upon arrival is not a product of US policies that led to white wealth accumulation and black wealth dispersion. Nor are they descendants of the persons newly emancipated who were victims of the unfulfilled promise of forty-acre land grants, the original source of the debt owed to today's descendants.

Virtually all black people across the African diaspora have a legitimate claim for reparations—but not on the US government. For instance, Jamaica has a claim on the United Kingdom, which it is making today. Colombia's claim is on Spain. The Congo has a claim on Belgium, which it also is making now. Haiti has a long-standing claim on France. Ironically, France compelled Haiti to pay reparations for the loss of enslaved property. Haiti should receive those monies back with interest—and more.

Neither Jamaica nor Belgium includes African Americans in their respective claims for restitution, nor should they.[3] In parallel, the claim for reparations made by black American descendants of US slavery should be lodged with precision on the US government, without any expectation that other blacks, who do not share the same historical background, be attached to the claim. The diaspora is diverse, and the culpable parties for each reparations claim are comparably varied (Mullen and Darity 2020).

Second, because the best economic indicator of the cumulative impact of the burden of America's antiblack history is the racial wealth gap, a reparations plan must provide, *at least,* adequate resources to raise average black wealth on par with average white wealth. Although there are many ways in which the size of a reparations bill might be calculated, we submit that suitable African American reparations must close the racial wealth gap.

Frequently, reparations advocates propose a measurement of the compensation made to living black Americans by the costs of bondage imposed on their ancestors. However, it is odd to use the financial toll of slavery to pay living descendants who never experienced that particular atrocity.

Perhaps the present value of a forty-acre lot affords a superior basis for the restitution sum. Denial of the land asset meant benefits were not transferrable to subsequent generations, thereby damaging the wealth position of living descendants now.

However, denial of land—at the same time that whites were receiving 160-acre land grants under the Homestead Act of 1862—was not the only federal policy producing the black-white gulf in wealth. As noted above, there also were the de facto sanctioning of white massacres from the end of the Civil War to World War II, the discriminatory application of policies to promote homeownership in the twentieth century, and the destruction of black homes and businesses courtesy of national highway construction.

The racial wealth gap is the best economic indicator that captures the aggregate, negative effects on black wealth today of this full array of federal policies. Eliminating the gap will require a national expenditure of no less than $14 trillion (in 2019 dollars).[4]

Still, we emphasize that closing the racial wealth gap sets the minimum size of the monetary account for reparative justice. As the essays in this volume indicate, there are many adverse effects of the nation's racial atrocities not consolidated in the black-white disparity in net worth. These include multigenerational harms to family well-being, individual health and longevity, educational opportunity, personal safety, and political participation.[5]

Third, reparations for black American descendants of US slavery must consist, predominantly, of direct payments. In other instances where communities subjected to collective harm have received reparations, direct payments went to eligible recipients. Primary examples include the German government's payments of restitution to the victims of the Holocaust and the US government's payments of restitution to Japanese Americans forced into mass incarceration during World War II.

Direct payments could take the form of cash transfers, but—in the interest of treating reparations as a black asset-building strategy—payments could take less liquid forms, like trust accounts or annuities. Regardless, individual recipients should have full discretion over the use of the payments, just as they have had in other cases.

Fourth, the US government must pay the debt. It is both the culpable and capable party. With respect to culpability, other entities—states, municipalities, churches, colleges and universities, and families with a history of slaveholding and other types of antiblack violence—certainly have engaged in immoral barbarity, but they have done so within the legal framework established by the federal government.

The federal government has sanctioned a past and present of American white supremacy. Therefore, the federal government bears the responsibility for the act of redress.

Moreover, with respect to capability, the combined budgets of all state and municipal governments in the United States amount to less than $5 trillion. It is infeasible for them to meet the reparations debt. And if a mix of private donors put $1 billion monthly donations into a reparations fund, it would take a millennium for them to reach even the $14 trillion threshold.

In contrast, the federal government's recent responses to the COVID-19 pandemic demonstrate that it can mobilize and spend huge sums of money virtually overnight, *without raising taxes*. In fact, the federal government is not tax revenue constrained.

The only barrier to additional federal spending is the risk of inflation, and, as we propose in the final chapter of *From Here to Equality: Reparations for Black Americans in the Twenty-First Century*, a reparations plan can be designed to inhibit triggering significant inflation (Darity and Mullen 2020, 264–67). The same issue is raised by Trevon Logan in chapter 7 of this volume. Still, even if the federal government chooses to finance its reparations plan by borrowing, there are a variety of ways to do this that are comparatively painless—methods examined in the final chapter of *From Here to Equality*.

Thus these are the four pillars of true reparations:

1. Eligible recipients must be black Americans who have ancestors who were enslaved in the United States.

2. The reparations plan must be designed to eliminate the black-white chasm in wealth.

3. The vast majority of the reparations fund should take the form of direct payments to eligible recipients.

4. The federal government must finance the reparations project.

The chapters that follow expand upon the foundation these pillars provide, describing the thoroughgoing nature of injustices perpetrated against black Americans in this country and unequivocally stating that any true reparations plan must be just as thoroughgoing.

NOTES

1. It is often asserted that the 1898 white massacre that took place in Wilmington, North Carolina, was the only successful municipal coup d'état in the history of the United States. The other instances listed here demonstrate this assertion is not true.

2. The police murder of Ahmadou Diallo is a case in point. On the other hand, we also are aware of anecdotes where black people have survived police encounters by speaking in English accented to suggest they are not American blacks. However, this may be sheer apocrypha.

3. The CARICOM Reparations Commission in advancing its claim to the UK for reparations for the former colonies of the British West Indies does not include black Americans, nor should it. In parallel, black Americans whose

ancestors were enslaved in the United States should not be expected to include blacks from all corners of the diaspora in their claim.

4. A detailed analysis of different approaches to estimating the dollar value of a reparations plan is found in Darity, Mullen, and Slaughter (2022).

5. Please see chapters 3, 4, 5, and 7 in this volume.

REFERENCES

Bhutta, Neil, Andrew C. Chang, Lisa J. Dettling, and Joanna W. Hsu. 2020. "Disparities in Wealth by Race and Ethnicity in the 2019 Survey of Consumer Finances." Board of Governors of the Federal Reserve System, FEDS Notes, September 28. www.federalreserve.gov/econres/notes/feds-notes/disparities-in-wealth-by-race-and-ethnicity-in-the-2019-survey-of-consumer-finances-20200928.htm.

Darity, William A. 2021. "The True Cost of Closing the Racial Wealth Gap." *New York Times*, April 30. www.nytimes.com/2021/04/30/business/racial-wealth-gap.html.

Darity, William A., Jr., and A. Kirsten Mullen. 2020. *From Here to Equality: Reparations for Black Americans in the Twenty-First Century*. Chapel Hill: University of North Carolina Press.

Darity, William A., Jr., A. Kirsten Mullen, and Marvin Slaughter. 2022. "The Cumulative Costs of Racism and the Bill for Black Reparations." *Journal of Economic Perspectives* 36 (2): 99–122.

Fussell, Melissa. 2016. "Dead Men Bring No Claims: How Takings Claims Can Provide Redress for Real Property Owning Victims of Jim Crow Race Riots." *William and Mary Law Review* 57:1913. https://scholarship.law.wm.edu/wmlr/vol57/iss5/7.

Garrett-Scott, Shennette. 2021. "What Price Wholeness?" *New York Review of Books*, January 17. www.nybooks.com/articles/2021/02/11/what-price-wholeness/.

Graham, Ginnie. 2021. "Interstate 244: 'It Took the Heart out of Greenwood.'" *Tulsa World*, July 6. https://tulsaworld.com/news/local/racemassacre/interstate-244-it-took-the-heart-out-of-greenwood/article_f61d48f4-ba7a-11eb-8e0e-67790e03b317.html.

Katznelson, Ira. 2005. *When Affirmative Action Was White: An Untold History of Racial Inequality in Twentieth-Century America*. New York: Norton.

Mohl, Raymond A. 2002. "The Interstates and the Cities: Highways, Housing, and the Freeway Revolt." Poverty and Race Research Action Council, PRRAC Report, May 16. www.prrac.org/the-interstates-and-the-cities-highways-housing-and-the-freeway-revolt/.

Mullen, A. Kirsten, and William A. Darity Jr. 2020. "How Much Is Owed to Afro-Descendants in the Americas?" *British GQ*, October 11. www.gq-magazine.co.uk/politics/article/reparations.

Williams, Trina. 2000. "The Homestead Act: A Major Asset-Building Policy in American History." CSD Working Paper No. 00-9. St. Louis, MO: Washington University, Center for Social Development.

2

Wealth Implications of Slavery and Racial Discrimination for African American Descendants of the Enslaved

THOMAS CRAEMER, TREVOR SMITH, BRIANNA HARRISON, TREVON D. LOGAN, WESLEY BELLAMY, AND WILLIAM A. DARITY JR.

"The American people owe a special debt to black Americans," wrote conservative reparations advocate Charles Krauthammer (2001). "There is nothing to compare with centuries of state-sponsored slavery followed by a century of state-sponsored discrimination." Of course, Krauthammer (2001) opposed affirmative action and believed reparations would be a better alternative. We, however, view these policies not as mutually exclusive alternatives but as mutually augmenting. Reparations address the present-day effects of past injustices like slavery and postslavery racial discrimination. In contrast, affirmative action is designed to prevent racial discrimination from going forward. It would be strange to allow part of the historical injustice, state-sponsored racial discrimination, to continue unchecked while paying reparations for past injustices. For closure to be achieved, not only slavery but racial discrimination must end, and their combined effects must be addressed by appropriate reparations.

Both injustices, slavery and postslavery racial discrimination, have profound wealth implications for African Americans living today. There is a substantial difference in the amount of wealth that whites and

This chapter previously was published in June 2020 in the *Review of Black Political Economy*. It is reprinted here with modest editing and data updates, with the permission of the authors and the journal.

blacks have today. If properly structured, reparations should suffice to close the black-white wealth gap.

Focusing on the wealth gap captures, better than any other disparity, the cumulative disadvantages visited upon the present generation. It embodies all of the effects of past atrocities: colonial slavery, US slavery, post–Civil War massacres, Jim Crow discrimination, New Deal discrimination, segregation during World War II, postwar discrimination, and post–civil rights discrimination.

This chapter outlines how to best estimate the historical economic losses to African Americans living today. Various formal and informal approaches have been devised to estimate aspects of the outstanding debt (e.g., America 1990; Craemer 2015; Darity 2008). Our estimates contribute a framework that is both *conservative* and *comprehensive.*

Conservatism refers to model parameters that can be arbitrarily set, such as the interest rate for compounding. At times, we use an interest rate of only 3 percent as a very conservative estimate of the historical annual return on an investment without consideration of inflation (see Darity and Mullen 2020). We compare this with corresponding estimates at 6 percent, the interest rate specified in the sales contract between Georgetown University and the Louisiana purchaser of 272 enslaved people in 1838 (Georgetown Slavery Archive 1838) and used also by Darity (2008) in his land-based estimation method (which we will explain below).

Arguments for much more generous interest rates can be made. For example, John Talbott recommends 9 percent, the average rate of return made by people who invested in the stock market from 1870 to the present (personal communication, January 7, 2020).

Comprehensiveness refers to the range of historical injustices we consider for compensation. Slavery resulted not only in lost incomes and, as a consequence, lost inheritances but also in lost opportunities to accumulate capital, lost freedom, and pain and suffering that, if compensated at the time, would have had major wealth implications for African American descendants of the enslaved living today. Racial discrimination after the abolition of slavery had similar wealth implications.

This chapter provides a number of estimates for some of these elements (e.g., lost incomes and inheritances, loss of freedom), points out how estimates for other elements could be obtained, and identifies gaps in the comprehensive framework that have yet to be filled by current research. Our task is to provide conservative but comprehensive estimates of the value that was lost to African Americans as a result of slavery and racial discrimination.[1]

At times, the assumptions we make may appear less than conservative: for example, when we count as billable all twenty-four hours of an enslaved person's day in our wage-based estimation method (explained below) rather than just the average twelve daylight working hours. This is another aspect of comprehensiveness; we take great care to ensure that our assumptions faithfully reflect the underlying economic theory. Nonworking hours were not negotiated between free agents; they were determined on the basis of the owner's self-interest alone and for the owner's exclusive benefit. Each day in the life of an enslaved person was stolen time. Therefore, we argue that nonworking hours do not represent "spare time" or "leisure time," in the free market sense of the terms, and should not be omitted from the outstanding bill.

This chapter also provides a number of rebuttals to reparations opponents who tend to argue against reparations by claiming that (a) tracing wealth over generations is too complex, (b) no original perpetrators or victims are alive today, (c) there is no precedent for compensating descendants for the losses of ancestors, and (d) abolition somehow provided compensation for slavery. We provide counterexamples for points (a) through (c) and argue regarding point (d) that *discontinuing an injustice is not the same as compensating for its lasting intergenerational effects.*

THE BLACK-WHITE WEALTH GAP AS A CONSERVATIVE REPARATIONS YARDSTICK

The current black-white wealth gap serves as a conservative yardstick to evaluate the success of a reparations program. According to Bhutta et al. (2020), the average net worth figure for white households in 2019 was US$983,400 and for black households was US$142,500. The average racial wealth gap amounted to US$840,900 per household in 2019.

The average white household (white alone, non-Hispanic) has 2.37 members and the average black household (black alone, non-Hispanic) 2.48 members, so the per capita wealth gap is somewhat more pronounced (US Bureau of the Census 2016). In average terms, white per capita net worth is $983,400/2.37 = $414,937, and black per capita net worth is $142,500/2.48 = $57,460, for a per capita average racial wealth gap of $357,477. Therefore, the minimum target we propose for African American reparations, in 2019 dollars, is a payment of US$357,477 per eligible recipient. If properly structured, reparations of that magnitude should suffice to achieve direct elimination of the black-white wealth gap.

One argument for focusing on the wealth gap as a target is that it captures, better than any other disparity, the cumulative disadvantages visited upon the present generation—so it can be viewed as embodying all of the effects of past atrocities of colonial slavery, US slavery, post–Civil War massacres, Jim Crow discrimination, New Deal discrimination, segregation during World War II, postwar discrimination, and post–civil rights discrimination. Darity and Mullen (2020, 263) view the racial wealth gap as *the most robust indicator of the cumulative economic effects of white supremacy* in the United States.

Economist Robert Williams (2017, 309) describes multiple mechanisms of intergenerational wealth transmission, from superior education, to cultural experiences, to social contacts that will translate for one's children into higher salaries and increased savings. In addition, wealthy parents can offer in vivo gifts at major life events (college admission, weddings, starter homes, schooling for grandchildren), and they can transmit their financial knowledge, giving their children greater exposure and comfort with different investments. Inheritance is only the most visible form of intergenerational wealth transfer but arguably not the most important, according to Williams (2017, 309).

These intergenerational wealth transfer mechanisms, which we will refer to here as "inheritances," result in missing wealth among African American descendants of the enslaved and extra wealth among the descendants of their ancestors' white enslavers. Williams (2017, 321–22) points to "wealth's unique role as a source of power, both within and across generations," and states that its intergenerational transmission, in all its varied forms, "create[s] an unequivocal link between the present and our racialized past of enslavement [and] . . . serves as a reminder of our White supremacist legacy." One effective way to neutralize this effect is a reparations program that, at minimum, should close the black-white wealth gap, with the size of the gap representing a yardstick to evaluate the success of the program.

An argument can be made that, because of compulsion by physical force, enslaved ancestors of African Americans living today worked harder than the ancestors of white Americans. Further, white Americans often were subsidized by federal or state-level policies from which African Americans were explicitly or implicitly excluded. On the basis of a conservative reckoning, African Americans living today may deserve a larger share of American assets than their proportion in the population, and a larger per capita amount in 2019 dollars than the $357,477 black-white wealth gap. A reparations amount aiming at closing the black-white wealth gap represents a bare minimum.

Another important question is why unpaid inheritances from distant ancestors should be paid directly to the descendants, especially when these amounts may go beyond eliminating the historically generated wealth gap. Conservative reasoning holds that the only form of morally acceptable unearned income consists of inheritances (as defined above). Unless specified differently, in a will, inheritances tend to go to immediate family members or direct descendants.

African American heirs have been systematically excluded from inheriting the fruits of their enslaved ancestors' stolen time and labor. Instead, the capital accumulated through slave labor has been handed down from generation to generation in the hands of families whose ancestors did *not* do the labor. This means that African American descendants of the enslaved living today continue to be affected materially by Article IV, Section 2, Clause 3 of the US Constitution, the Fugitive Slave Clause, which established permanent property rights in enslaved humans and which is considered unconstitutional today. We advance the legitimate case that payments should be made to the descendants of the enslaved living today to correct for this present-day injustice.

There are several methods to estimate the historical losses in wealth to African American descendants of the enslaved living today. Swinton (1990) provides formulas to compute the complete costs of slavery and postslavery racial discrimination. He writes,

> The cost during slavery not only included the value of appropriated labor services, but also the economic value of the lost freedom, as well as pain and suffering. The theoretically appropriate method of evaluating these costs would require determination of the amounts required to pay a free individual to submit to permanent slavery. . . . The costs of Jim Crow, discrimination, and segregation to the black population are similar to the costs of enslavement. The economic component consists of lost value from denied opportunities, both capital and labor. . . . In addition, there is lost value from restricted opportunities to acquire human and physical capital on the same terms and the same conditions as whites. (154–55)

Swinton (1990) provides two additive formulas, one for the costs of slavery to African Americans during each year t that the institution existed, CS_t (see formula 1), and one for the costs of postslavery discrimination for each year t up to today, CD_t (see formula 2).

$$CS_t = EL_t + LC_t + LF_t + PS_t \qquad (1)$$

$$CD_t = RL_t + RC_t + LC_t + PS_t \qquad (2)$$

where

CS = cost of slavery

CD = cost of Jim Crow, segregation, and discrimination

EL = value of labor expropriated

LC = value of lost opportunities to acquire capital

RL = reduced value of labor due to discrimination

RC = reduced value of capital due to discrimination

LF = value of lost freedom

PS = pain and suffering

t = year in which cost occurred

This would permit us to derive the present value of each year's cost PV_{COST},[2] and sum across all years, with interest rate i to obtain the total cost in the current year:

$$PV_{COST} = \sum_{t=1618}^{current\ year} (CS_t + CD_t)(1 + i)^{(t-1618)}$$

Swinton (1990, 155) writes, "As far as we know, no other estimates offer such a complete specification." We will be careful to indicate which aspects of each cost formula are used and which are omitted. Omission does not mean that a given component of reparations is unimportant— it may simply be difficult to determine with available data.

For example, the first subsection deals with colonial slavery without providing a cost estimate; instead, the cost estimates begin the subsection on US slavery but take only the value of expropriated labor (EL) and lost freedom (LF) into consideration. They do not consider lost opportunities to acquire capital (LC), or pain and suffering (PS), although all these items are worthy of further research, recognition, and reparation.

COLONIAL SLAVERY (1619–1775)

The United States inherited slavery from British colonial rule and enshrined it in Article IV, Section 2, of the new country's constitution. This raises the question whether reparations demands for colonial slavery should be directed at the British government or whether the United

States willingly inherited the moral debt resulting from colonial slavery. The founding generation could have abolished slavery (with compensation to the freed slaves). For example, George Washington freed his own enslaved in his will and made sure his will was published. Somewhat naively, he hoped to set an example for the voluntary abolition of slavery, which obviously did not materialize. He wrote, "it is my Will & desire that all the Slaves which I hold in my own right, shall receive their freedom," and charged his executors with "seeing that *a regular and permanent fund be established for their support* so long as there are subjects requiring it" (quoted in Ford 1893, 272–73, emphasis added).

Washington personally owned 124 enslaved, all of whom were freed in accordance with his will. According to his executors, more than $10,000 had been paid to Washington's formerly enslaved by 1833.

Although Washington's voluntary abolition scheme did not succeed, the fact that so many northern states managed to abolish slavery after the revolution suggests that abolition was practicable. The decision to inscribe slavery in Article IV, Section 2, of the US Constitution was a deliberate choice. It may be interpreted as the founding fathers' intention to accept slavery's moral debt from Great Britain.

To estimate the magnitude of the debt during the colonial period, we would need estimates from 1619 to 1775 for the slave populations in the colonies that later became the United States. This would allow us to estimate how many man-, woman-, and child-hours were available to slave owners in colonial North America. Further, we would need British statistics on historical free labor market wages in each North American colony. Similar data would be needed for establishing the compensation due for slavery in the Spanish, Dutch, and French colonies of the parts of North America that would become the United States.

Whether such data are at all available is unclear and necessitates further research. Of course, the possibility would have to be taken into consideration that the wage rate may have been depressed by the presence of enslaved labor because more labor was pressed from the enslaved than they would otherwise have offered in the labor market had they been free laborers. Any estimate obtained in this way would likely be very cautious. Obtaining this information would allow multiplying the available hours by then customary free labor wages, which, compounded with then customary interest rates, would yield possible estimates of the value of colonial slavery, not to the slave owners, but to the enslaved.

US SLAVERY (1776–1865)

Article IV, Section 2, of the US Constitution created a contradiction reconcilable, according to the Fifth Amendment, only through reparations (see Craemer 2015). Article IV, Section 2, referred to an enslaved person as a "Person held to Service or Labour," a euphemism that inadvertently recognized the personhood of the enslaved. As a consequence, the Fifth Amendment applies, for it states that "no person shall . . . be deprived of life, liberty, or property, without due process of law; nor shall private property be taken for public use, without just compensation." The Fifth Amendment does not say "no citizen," "no white person," or "no property owner"; it says, "no person." Just compensation for slave labor should have been rendered beginning in 1791 when the Fifth Amendment was ratified.

Republican Senate leader Mitch McConnell opposes slavery reparations simply because "it would be hard to figure out" (quoted in Kellman 2019). This is a common misconception in a country that prides itself on having landed on the moon—undoubtedly a feat that was hard to figure out. McConnell goes on to state, "I don't think reparations for something that happened 150 years ago, for whom none of us currently living are responsible, is a good idea." This view is also widely held, but it ignores the fact that although the individuals involved may be long dead, the institutions involved live on, as does the capital accumulated through slave labor. That capital continues to earn compound interest exponentially in the wrong hands, that is, in the hands of individuals whose ancestors did *not* do the hard work. Meanwhile, the individuals whose ancestors *did* do the hard work are excluded from their otherwise rightful inheritances. This present-day injustice demands a remedy.

Slavery reparations opponent Stuart E. Eizenstat (2019) casts doubt on the idea that heirs rather than the individuals who suffered harm should be eligible for reparations payments. He states, "Reparations in the form of cash payments for descendants of slaves are not the way to right this grievous wrong. I write this having spent decades of my life negotiating more than $17 billion in reparations for Holocaust survivors." He writes that the main difference between Holocaust reparations and slavery reparations is that Holocaust reparations went to the survivors, not their heirs.

However, he then explains that Holocaust reparations went not only to the survivors but to "their immediate relatives all over the world," the "direct heirs of victims," or "their spouses and children if they survived the war but died before our agreement." In Eizenstat's own words, "Restitution has . . . gone largely to those who directly suffered and survived, and, in some cases, their *direct heirs*" (emphasis added). By citing reparations programs that compensated not only survivors but also close family members and heirs, Eizenstat inadvertently makes a powerful moral argument in favor of, not opposed to, slavery reparations. The logical chain from victims to direct heirs does not break simply because the government withheld slavery reparations payments for more than a century and a half. Why should African American descendants of the enslaved forgo their rightful inheritances when the families, children, and heirs of victims of other historical injustices have received reparations payments?

Some reparations opponents point to the federal government's expenditures in blood and treasure to end slavery through the Civil War as a form of reparations already rendered. This argument suffers from two major problems. First, ending an injustice is not the same as making reparations for its enduring effects. Second, more than two hundred thousand black soldiers, including enslaved and free, fought and died disproportionately to earn the freedom of the enslaved. The moral credit for this self-liberation goes to them, not to the federal government that had permitted their enslavement for so long.

Land-Based Estimation

Reparations estimates based on land ("forty acres and a mule"), originally inspired by General Sherman's Special Field Orders No. 15 (1865) and Representative Thaddeus Stevens's Reparations Bill of 1867, take land values into consideration. General Sherman's Special Field Orders No. 15 (1865) provided "not more than (40) forty acres of tillable ground" designated "for the settlement of the negroes now made free by the acts of war and the proclamation of the President of the United States" (quoted in Darity 2008, 660).[3]

General Sherman's field order was a war measure that set aside 5.3 million acres of land for the freedmen as a first installment on, at least, a forty million acres commitment. However, only forty thousand freedmen were settled on four hundred thousand acres before President Andrew Johnson returned the land to the former slave owners.

Nevertheless, the promise of "forty acres and a mule" remained present in popular memory, especially among African Americans. It was the basis for Sojourner Truth's demand for land redistribution

(Araujo 2019). In the late 1960s, the Black Panther Party renewed the call for "forty acres and a mule," stating that "for slave labor and mass murder of Black people [w]e will accept payment in currency" (Allen 1998, 3). African American businessman Dempsey Travis developed the proposal for a new Homestead Act in 1970 as a form of reparations based on the current land value of forty-acre plots (Allen 1998).

William Darity (2008, 662) writes, "The unfulfilled promise of 40 acres per family . . . provides a means to gauge the magnitude of reparations owed to the descendants of those enslaved." He estimates the price of land in 1865 at about US$10 per acre (Mittal and Powell 2000) and notes that "an allocation of 40 acres to a family of four would imply 10 acres per person, hence a value of $100 per ex-slave in 1865. If we also take as a conservative estimate the total number of ex-slaves who had attained emancipation at the close of the Civil War as 4 million persons, 40 million acres of land valued at $400 million should have been distributed to the ex-slaves in 1865" (662).

Darity proposes to compound that sum of money from 1865 at 6 percent (5 percent for interest earned and 1 percent as an inflation adjustment) to the present. Using the formula for compound interest $R_y = R_{1865}(1 + i)^{(y - 1865)}$, whereby R represents reparations estimates in year y, and i the interest rate (here i = 0.06), the estimate for 2019 would be R_{2019} = $400,000,000(1 + 0.06)^{(2019 - 1865)}$ = approximately $3.156 trillion. Today's black American population who are descendants of persons enslaved in the United States amount to roughly forty-one million people (Tamir 2021). Therefore, per capita reparations based solely on the present value of the lost promise of forty acres amounts to $76,980.

One problem with taking "forty acres and a mule" as a baseline for estimating proper slavery reparations is that Sherman's Special Field Orders No. 15 (1865) and Thaddeus Stevens's Reparations Bill of 1867, albeit very progressive, were likely tainted by the antiblack prejudice of the time. For example, the Homestead Act of 1862 gave 160 acres to white settlers. Black families were promised only 40 acres, whereas white settler families were promised four times the amount.

Based upon an alternative 160-acre land grant, the reparations amount would be $12.6 trillion. Divided by forty-one million descendants of the enslaved in 2019, per capita reparations would amount to US$307,317. This is a sum still below the magnitude of the average black-white wealth gap of $357,477, but it is closer than the amount based on only forty acres.

Price-Based Estimation

Richard F. America's (1990) edited volume *The Wealth of Races: The Present Value of Benefits from Past Injustices* contains three proposals for calculating reparations on the basis of slave prices. Because the price was established through negotiations between the seller and the buyer of human property, and did not reflect the views of the enslaved, this price is likely to reflect only the value of slavery to the slave owner (what the owner gained during the twelve daylight hours during which the enslaved raised cash crops in the fields). It may not reflect the monetary equivalent of what the enslaved lost (control over all twenty-four hours of the day).

Price-based estimates range from $17.4 billion (Ransom and Sutch 1990) to $1.4 trillion (Neal 1990), up to $4.7 trillion (Marketti 1990), all in 1983 dollars. Further compounded at 3 percent interest to 2019, this would represent US$50.4 billion, US$4.1 trillion, and US$13.6 trillion, respectively. Compounded at 6 percent interest, it would represent US$141.8 billion, US$11.4 trillion, and US$38.3 trillion, respectively.

Ransom and Sutch (1990, 32) use the market value of the enslaved from historical records as "the buyer's calculation of the present value of the stream of income which the buyer could extract from the slave." With that expected income stream representing the difference of the enslaved person's productivity and the cost of feeding and housing the enslaved, according to Ransom and Sutch, "the price of a slave summarizes the capitalized value of the economic exploitation inherent in the slave system" (32). They define the term *economic exploitation* as "that part of labor's product which is not returned to the slave as food, shelter, and other consumption items" (32).

Using a rate of return of 6.6 percent, Ransom and Sutch "estimate the dollar value of exploitation from the crop output produced by slaves in each year using evidence on the slave population and the average price of slaves" (32–33) and arrive at a figure for the "*present value* of past exploitation in 1860," which they estimated in 1983 at US$17.4 billion (33); that amount further compounded at 3 percent would represent US$50.4 billion in 2019, or compounded at 6 percent US$141.8 billion.

The idea of subtracting the cost of slave consumption from the enslaved's productivity and treating only the difference as expropriated property for which reparations are due seems odd. Whatever food an enslaved person consumed was not his or her choice, nor was it for his or her benefit. Even when ingested, the calories remained the property of the slave owner, along with the work these calories produced.

The logical problem with this estimation method becomes even clearer in Neal's (1990) calculation of the current benefits of slavery. Neal follows Ransom and Sutch (1990) in using slave prices as a basis for estimating "slave wages." Neal (1990, 94) writes, "The empirical work involves three steps. The first estimates the market value of the unpaid net wages of slaves who lived at various times before emancipation. . . . The second estimates the number of slaves who labored without fair pay. . . . The third multiplies the amounts by the number of slaves . . . and aggregates them."

Neal (1990) arrives at a present-value estimate of diverted slave wages of $1.4 trillion in 1983, which further compounded at 3 percent represents $4.1 trillion in 2019, and at 6 percent, $11.4 trillion. Like Ransom and Sutch's (1990) method, Neal's method relies on the market price of the slave as the future income stream expected by the slave owner, not on the slave's actual time lost. Using a similar method, Marketti (1990) arrives at larger estimates, ranging from $2.1 to $4.7 trillion in 1983, which compounded further at 3 percent interest to 2019 would represent a range from $6.1 trillion to $13.6 trillion. Compounded at 6 percent, it would represent a range from $17.1 trillion to $38.3 trillion.

It is important conceptually and ethically to use historical records from the perspective of the enslaved, not the slave owner. Only from a slave owner's perspective would it seem necessary to "estimate the number of slaves who labored without fair pay" (Neal 1990, 94). From an enslaved person's perspective, "fair pay" is an obvious oxymoron. Slave prices resembled "wages" only from the perspective of a slave owner, who would have had the choice of hiring free laborers instead of purchasing enslaved workers.

From the perspective of the enslaved, upkeep costs did not resemble a "wage" (much less a fair one), because the enslaved had no (legal) choice in the matter. If unhappy with the "wage" (provisions), the enslaved could not choose a different "employer" (slave owner), ruling out any competition of "employers" (slave owners) for "employees" (enslaved). To circumvent this problem, we use historical data on hourly compensation for free labor, adding up the total hours of work that were available to slave owners and multiplying the two.

Wage-Based Estimation

Using historical data on wages for free labor raises the obvious question whether slaves, if freed, would have received the same compensation.

Racial discrimination might have led to lower wages for freed enslaved laborers in practice. However, discrimination cannot be legitimately used to reduce present-value reparations estimates. Racial discrimination itself is a historical injustice worthy of compensation. The only relevant consideration is the likelihood that wages could have changed, had an estimated four million forced laborers suddenly flooded the free labor market.

At least in theory, the addition of freed enslaved laborers might not have exerted a net effect on wages, as it would have increased not only the supply of labor but also, in rough proportion, the demand for free labor by former slave owners. These countervailing forces might have left the prices for labor in the free labor market roughly unaffected, justifying the use of free market hourly compensation records to estimate the earning potential of the enslaved, had they been free laborers at the time.

A better counterfactual may be what the wage rate would have been for an African who had migrated freely to the American colonies in a world without American slavery. In that world, voluntary African immigrants would have found higher wages because of a greater labor shortage. This consideration renders our estimation method very conservative.

To obtain reparations estimates, we use the work hours available in the enslaved labor force and multiply them by average free labor market wages at the time. The enslaved population is recorded beginning with the 1790 census (US Bureau of the Census 1975; see table 2.1). Information on production workers' hourly compensation (in nominal dollars) is provided online by Officer and Williamson (2019; see table 2.2). These wage data are available from 1790 to the present. Missing values before that time are estimated by linear extrapolation, using data on the cost of unskilled labor, which are available all the way back to 1774.

The extrapolation procedure assumes that production workers' hourly compensation in nominal dollars would have experienced swings up and down proportional to those of the cost of unskilled labor. The formula $w_t = w_{1790} / (C_{1790} / C_t)$ provides the extrapolated values, where w is production workers' hourly compensation, c the cost of unskilled labor, t the year, and 1790 the comparison year. Table 2.3 provides these figures rounded to four places after the decimal point. All numbers in regular print in table 2.3 are from Officer and Williamson (2019), and all numbers in italics have been estimated on the basis of the above formula.

We consider the period from 1776 to 1865 because this is the period when the United States could have abolished slavery but failed to do so. However, because estimates of the enslaved population from

TABLE 2.1   ENSLAVED POPULATION, 1790–1860

US census	Enslaved
1790	697,681
1800	893,602
1810	1,191,362
1820	1,538,022
1830	2,009,043
1840	2,487,355
1850	3,204,313
1860	3,953,760

SOURCE: US Bureau of the Census (1975, 14), footnote to Series A 91-104, "Population, by Sex and Race: 1790–1970."

TABLE 2.2   PRODUCTION WORKERS' HOURLY COMPENSATION IN NOMINAL DOLLARS

Year	Wage (US$)	Year	Wage (US$)	Year	Wage (US$)	Year	Wage (US$)
1790	0.02	1810	0.05	1830	0.06	1850	0.06
1791	0.02	1811	0.05	1831	0.06	1851	0.06
1792	0.02	1812	0.05	1832	0.05	1852	0.07
1793	0.03	1813	0.05	1833	0.06	1853	0.07
1794	0.03	1814	0.05	1834	0.05	1854	0.07
1795	0.03	1815	0.05	1835	0.05	1855	0.07
1796	0.04	1816	0.05	1836	0.05	1856	0.07
1797	0.03	1817	0.05	1837	0.06	1857	0.07
1798	0.04	1818	0.05	1838	0.06	1858	0.08
1799	0.04	1819	0.05	1839	0.06	1859	0.08
1800	0.04	1820	0.04	1840	0.06	1860	0.08
1801	0.04	1821	0.05	1841	0.06		
1802	0.04	1822	0.05	1842	0.06		
1803	0.04	1823	0.05	1843	0.06		
1804	0.05	1824	0.05	1844	0.06		
1805	0.05	1825	0.05	1845	0.06		
1806	0.05	1826	0.05	1846	0.06		
1807	0.05	1827	0.05	1847	0.06		
1808	0.05	1828	0.05	1848	0.07		
1809	0.05	1829	0.06	1849	0.06		

SOURCE: Officer and Williamson (2019).

TABLE 2.3   USING FLUCTUATIONS IN THE COST OF UNSKILLED LABOR TO
ESTIMATE PRODUCTION WORKERS' HOURLY COMPENSATION FROM 1776 TO
1789, IN NOMINAL DOLLARS

Year	Cost of unskilled labor (US$)	Production workers' hourly compensation (US$)
1776	0.0256	*0.0173*
1777	0.0280	*0.0189*
1778	0.0288	*0.0195*
1779	0.0248	*0.0168*
1780	0.0328	*0.0222*
1781	0.0344	*0.0232*
1782	0.0312	*0.0211*
1783	0.0288	*0.0195*
1784	0.0272	*0.0184*
1785	0.0352	*0.0238*
1786	0.0320	*0.0216*
1787	0.0384	*0.0259*
1788	0.0384	*0.0259*
1789	0.0336	*0.0227*
1790	0.0296	0.0200

NOTE: All numbers in regular font are from Officer and Williamson (2019). All numbers in italics are estimated based on the formula: $w_t = w_{1790} / (c_{1790}/c_t)$, where w is production workers' hourly compensation, c the cost of unskilled labor, t the year, and 1790 the comparison year.

the start until the end of the Civil War, that is, after the 1860 census, become unreliable, we estimate billable hours only for the period from 1776 to 1860. This means that we actually are underestimating the total.

The first step in estimating the debt using this method is to estimate annual enslaved population figures from the decennial figures provided by the US Census in table 2.1. We use linear inter- and extrapolation, although other estimation methods could be used as well. For the period from 1776 to 1789, estimates are obtained by linear extrapolation using the formula $p_t = p_{1790} - ((p_{1800} - p_{1790}) / 10) (1790 - t)$, where p_t is the enslaved population in year t, t is any year between 1776 and 1789, and p_{1800} and p_{1790} are the enslaved populations in the years 1800 and 1790, respectively. For years between decennial censuses, we employ linear interpolation, using the formula $p_t = p_d + ((p_D - p_d) / 10) (t - d)$, where p_t is the slave population in year t, t is any year between decennial censuses, d is the earlier decennial census year, and D the later decennial census year. The extra- and interpolated enslaved population estimates are represented in italic font in table 2.4, whereas census counts are printed in bold.

TABLE 2.4 ANNUAL TOTAL DEBT ESTIMATES AND CUMULATIVE DEBT ESTIMATES
AT 3 PERCENT INTEREST, 1776–1860

Year	Enslaved population	Hourly wage (US$)	Person-hours per year	Annual total debt (US$)	Cumulative debt at 3% interest (US$)
1776	423,392	0.02	3,708,910,416	64,154,126.11	66,078,749.90
1777	442,984	0.02	3,880,537,212	73,415,568.88	143,679,148.34
1778	462,576	0.02	4,052,164,008	78,852,921.24	229,208,031.66
1779	482,168	0.02	4,223,790,804	70,777,035.09	308,984,618.76
1780	501,760	0.02	4,395,417,600	97,411,957.62	418,588,473.67
1781	521,352	0.02	4,567,044,396	106,152,923.80	540,483,639.39
1782	540,944	0.02	4,738,671,192	99,896,311.62	659,591,349.54
1783	560,536	0.02	4,910,297,988	95,551,744.63	777,797,387.00
1784	580,128	0.02	5,081,924,784	93,397,536.57	897,330,771.27
1785	599,721	0.02	5,253,551,580	124,949,334.88	1,052,948,509.33
1786	619,313	0.02	5,425,178,376	117,301,154.08	1,205,357,153.31
1787	638,905	0.03	5,596,805,172	145,214,404.46	1,391,088,704.51
1788	658,497	0.03	5,768,431,968	149,667,424.03	1,586,978,812.40
1789	678,089	0.02	5,940,058,764	134,855,388.16	1,773,489,226.57
1790	**697,681**	0.02	6,111,685,560	122,233,711.20	1,952,594,625.90
1791	717,273	0.02	6,283,312,356	125,666,247.12	2,140,608,699.21
1792	736,865	0.02	6,454,939,152	129,098,783.04	2,337,798,706.72
1793	756,457	0.03	6,626,565,948	198,796,978.44	2,612,693,555.72
1794	776,049	0.03	6,798,192,744	203,945,782.32	2,901,138,518.18
1795	795,642	0.03	6,969,819,540	209,094,586.20	3,203,540,097.51
1796	815,234	0.04	7,141,446,336	285,657,853.44	3,593,873,889.48
1797	834,826	0.03	7,313,073,132	219,392,193.96	3,927,664,065.94
1798	854,418	0.04	7,484,699,928	299,387,997.12	4,353,863,624.95
1799	874,010	0.04	7,656,326,724	306,253,068.96	4,799,920,194.73
1800	**893,602**	0.04	7,827,953,520	313,118,140.80	5,266,429,485.60
1801	923,378	0.04	8,088,791,280	323,551,651.20	5,757,680,570.90
1802	953,154	0.04	8,349,629,040	333,985,161.60	6,274,415,704.47
1803	982,930	0.04	8,610,466,800	344,418,672.00	6,817,399,407.77
1804	1,012,706	0.05	8,871,304,560	443,565,228.00	7,478,793,574.84
1805	1,042,482	0.05	9,132,142,320	456,607,116.00	8,173,462,711.57
1806	1,072,258	0.05	9,392,980,080	469,649,004.00	8,902,405,067.03
1807	1,102,034	0.05	9,653,817,840	482,690,892.00	9,666,648,837.81
1808	1,131,810	0.05	9,914,655,600	495,732,780.00	10,467,253,066.34
1809	1,161,586	0.05	10,175,493,360	508,774,668.00	11,305,308,566.37
1810	**1,191,362**	0.05	10,436,331,120	521,816,556.00	12,181,938,876.04
1811	1,226,028	0.05	10,740,005,280	537,000,264.00	13,100,507,314.24
1812	1,260,694	0.05	11,043,679,440	552,183,972.00	14,062,272,024.83
1813	1,295,360	0.05	11,347,353,600	567,367,680.00	15,068,528,895.97
1814	1,330,026	0.05	11,651,027,760	582,551,388.00	16,120,612,692.49
1815	1,364,692	0.05	11,954,701,920	597,735,096.00	17,219,898,222.15
1816	1,399,358	0.05	12,258,376,080	612,918,804.00	18,367,801,536.93

(continued)

TABLE 2.4 *(continued)*

Year	Enslaved population	Hourly wage (US$)	Person-hours per year	Annual total debt (US$)	Cumulative debt at 3% interest (US$)
1817	1,434,024	0.05	12,562,050,240	628,102,512.00	19,565,781,170.40
1818	1,468,690	0.05	12,865,724,400	643,286,220.00	20,815,339,412.11
1819	1,503,356	0.05	13,169,398,560	658,469,928.00	22,118,023,620.32
1820	1,538,022	0.04	13,473,072,720	538,922,908.80	23,336,654,924.99
1821	1,585,124	0.05	13,885,687,116	694,284,355.80	24,751,867,459.21
1822	1,632,226	0.05	14,298,301,512	714,915,075.60	26,230,786,010.86
1823	1,679,328	0.05	14,710,915,908	735,545,795.40	27,775,321,760.45
1824	1,726,430	0.05	15,123,530,304	756,176,515.20	29,387,443,223.91
1825	1,773,533	0.05	15,536,144,700	776,807,235.00	31,069,177,972.68
1826	1,820,635	0.05	15,948,759,096	797,437,954.80	32,822,614,405.31
1827	1,867,737	0.05	16,361,373,492	818,068,674.60	34,649,903,572.30
1828	1,914,839	0.05	16,773,987,888	838,699,394.40	36,553,261,055.70
1829	1,961,941	0.06	17,186,602,284	1,031,196,137.04	38,711,990,908.53
1830	2,009,043	0.06	17,599,216,680	1,055,953,000.80	40,960,982,226.61
1831	2,056,874	0.06	18,018,217,992	1,081,093,079.52	43,303,337,565.3
1832	2,104,705	0.05	18,437,219,304	921,860,965.20	45,551,954,486.43
1833	2,152,537	0.06	18,856,220,616	1,131,373,236.96	48,083,827,555.09
1834	2,200,368	0.05	19,275,221,928	963,761,096.40	50,519,016,311.03
1835	2,248,199	0.05	19,694,223,240	984,711,162.00	53,048,839,297.22
1836	2,296,030	0.05	20,113,224,552	1,005,661,227.60	55,676,135,540.57
1837	2,343,861	0.06	20,532,225,864	1,231,933,551.84	58,615,311,165.18
1838	2,391,693	0.06	20,951,227,176	1,257,073,630.56	61,668,556,339.61
1839	2,439,524	0.06	21,370,228,488	1,282,213,709.28	64,839,293,150.36
1840	2,487,355	0.06	21,789,229,800	1,307,353,788.00	68,131,046,346.51
1841	2,559,051	0.06	22,417,285,008	1,345,037,100.48	71,560,365,950.40
1842	2,630,747	0.06	23,045,340,216	1,382,720,412.96	75,131,378,954.26
1843	2,702,442	0.06	23,673,395,424	1,420,403,725.44	78,848,336,160.09
1844	2,774,138	0.06	24,301,450,632	1,458,087,037.92	82,715,615,893.95
1845	2,845,834	0.06	24,929,505,840	1,495,770,350.40	86,737,727,831.68
1846	2,917,530	0.06	25,557,561,048	1,533,453,662.88	90,919,316,939.40
1847	2,989,226	0.06	26,185,616,256	1,571,136,975.36	95,265,167,532.20
1848	3,060,921	0.07	26,813,671,464	1,876,957,002.48	100,056,388,270.72
1849	3,132,617	0.06	27,441,726,672	1,646,503,600.32	104,753,978,627.17
1850	3,204,313	0.06	28,069,781,880	1,684,186,912.80	109,631,310,506.17
1851	3,279,258	0.06	28,726,297,452	1,723,577,847.12	114,695,535,003.89
1852	3,354,202	0.07	29,382,813,024	2,056,796,911.68	120,254,901,873.04
1853	3,429,147	0.07	30,039,328,596	2,102,753,001.72	126,028,384,521.00
1854	3,504,092	0.07	30,695,844,168	2,148,709,091.76	132,022,406,421.14
1855	3,579,037	0.07	31,352,359,740	2,194,665,181.80	138,243,583,751.03
1856	3,653,981	0.07	32,008,875,312	2,240,621,271.84	144,698,731,173.56
1857	3,728,926	0.07	32,665,390,884	2,286,577,361.88	151,394,867,791.50
1858	3,803,871	0.08	33,321,906,456	2,665,752,516.48	158,682,438,917.22

1859	*3,878,815*	0.08	*33,978,422,028*	*2,718,273,762.24*	*166,242,734,059.85*
1860	**3,953,760**	0.08	**34,634,937,600**	**2,770,795,008.00**	**174,083,934,939.88**
2019*					19,137,157,136,693.00

*Total in 2019: $R_{2019} = R_{1860} (1 + .03)^{(2019 - 1860)}$ = US\$19,137,157,136,693.00.

NOTE: Bold entries in columns 2 and 3 are based on historical records; italic entries in the same columns are estimated by linear extrapolation or interpolation (see text). Person-hours per year multiply population estimates with twenty-four hours a day times 365 days a year to obtain annual total person-hours available to slave owners.

These population estimates are multiplied by twenty-four hours a day times 365 days a year to obtain annual total person-hours available to slave owners. The enslaved were on call twenty-four hours a day, seven days a week, with no legal restrictions on their use. Practical limitations on the use of the enslaved were solely the owner's concern that working them to death might not be profitable—although in some instances, it might have been considered profitable, with severe consequences for the individual life expectancy of the enslaved. Round-the-clock compensation is what a slave owner would have had to pay a (white) worker to be on call in place of the enslaved person.[4] The slave owner would likely have had to pay overtime for nighttime hours, but for a conservative estimate we assume the same hourly wage for being on call around the clock.

The fourth column of table 2.4 shows what round-the-clock remuneration would have been at free labor market hourly wages. Column 5 in table 2.4 provides the total outstanding annual debt. This debt is compounded at 3 percent interest in column 6 of table 2.4. It should be mentioned that an interest rate of only 3 percent is extremely conservative. More typical of the time in contracts between sellers and purchasers of enslaved people is probably the 6 percent interest rate specified in the sales contract between Georgetown University and the Louisiana purchasers of 272 enslaved people in 1838 (Georgetown Slavery Archive 1838).

This is also the percentage Darity (2008) uses to estimate reparations based on the promise of "forty acres and a mule." Additional research would be required to determine the average interest rate commonly generated on investments during slavery. To keep the estimate conservative, we use the 3 percent rate in table 2.4. It should be noted that this low interest rate makes our already conservative reparations estimate even more conservative.

The first entry in the sixth column represents the annual total reparations debt R_{1776} in the year 1776, based on the formula $R_{1776} = T_{1776} +$

(T_{1776}) (i), where T_{1776} is the annual total debt in 1776 and i is the interest rate (0.03). To obtain the cumulative total at the given interest rate for any subsequent year between 1777 and 1860, the following formula is applied: $R_t = R_{t-1} + T_t + (R_{t-1} + T_t)$ (i), where R_t is the cumulative reparations debt in year t, T_t the annual outstanding debt for year t, and i the interest rate (0.03).

The total outstanding reparations debt at the beginning of the Civil War compounded at 3 percent interest amounts to $174 billion, which can be compounded to the present by applying the formula $R_y = R_{1860}(1 + i)^{(y - 1860)}$, where R_y is the total reparations debt at interest rate i (here 0.03) in year y after 1860. It amounted to $14.2 trillion in 2009 (see Craemer 2015) and $19.1 trillion in 2019.

This estimation method counts all twenty-four hours per day of an enslaved person's time as billable, accurately representing the role of downtime and sleep for a slave: it was restoration of energy for further forced labor. It was not spare time in the wage labor sense with choice of activities, and granting it or not was entirely up to the slave owner—no law required it. Granting or denying it was part of the economic calculation of the slave owner, and the life expectancy of the enslaved crucially depended on that utility calculation.

The total slavery debt figure for 2019 of $19.1 trillion can be divided by the estimated number of African American descendants of the enslaved, forty-one million, to arrive at the debt owed to each eligible recipient of black reparations. Here per capita reparations would amount to US$465,854. This is above the magnitude of the average black-white wealth gap figure of US$357,477 in 2019 dollars.

At 6 percent interest (the interest rate Darity [2008] uses and that Georgetown University charged the purchasers of its 272 enslaved persons), the numbers explode: the total debt in 2019 would exceed $6.6 quadrillion. Division by forty-one million black descendants of the enslaved would result in a staggering total reparations payment per descendant of US$161 million. This example illustrates how central the interest rate is in negotiating reparations over such long time spans. This line of reasoning also applies to estimates of the value of lost freedom.

Estimating the Value of Lost Freedom

So far we have focused only on various methods to estimate the value of labor expropriated. Another component we can consider is the value of lost freedom if we compare it with reparations for Japanese World War

II internment. The Civil Liberties Act of 1988 provided each surviving ex-internee US$20,000 per person and an apology letter from the US president (Craemer 2018) for the "enormous damages" due to "evacuation, relocation, and internment."[5] Internment lasted for three years, from 1942 to 1945, and did not involve slave labor (Encyclopedia Britannica 2019). Hence, reparations compensated for lost freedom at the rate of $20,000 / (3 years × 365 days × 24 hours) = $20,000 / 26,280 hours = $0.76 per hour in 1988 dollars.

In 1800, the earliest year for Friedman's (2019) inflation calculator, this would have represented roughly $0.11. The value for each year after 1800 is looked up on Friedman's inflation calculator (see column 3 in table 2.5) for years for which data are available (1800–1824), which is US$0.10. Because the calculator does not accept 0.76 as an entry, the amount of $76 in 1988 dollars is looked up, and the corresponding amount for 1800 to 1860 is divided by 100 to arrive at the estimated value of an hour of freedom in each of these years according to the same rate.

The years 1861 through 1865 are not considered because no clear estimates for the enslaved population are available, again rendering the total amount of reparations for lost freedom incomplete. The total amount in 1860 compounded at 3 percent is $326 billion, and at 6 percent $1.648 trillion. These amounts can be compounded to 2019 using the formula

$$R_y = R_{1860}(1 + i)^{(y - 1860)}$$

where R_y represents reparations for lost freedom in a given year, y the year, and i the interest rate. The 2019 values would be $35.8 trillion, at 3 percent interest, or US$874,139 for each of the estimated forty-one million African American descendants of the enslaved. At 6 percent interest, these numbers explode to a total of $17.4 quadrillion (see table 2.5), representing about $424 million per African American descendant.

The reparations estimate for lost freedom based on the hourly value of Japanese American World War II internment (US$0.76 per hour for three years of internment at a total of US$20,000 in 1988 dollars) far exceeds the estimate for lost wages and inheritances. This may seem surprising, since this estimate is compounded only at 3 percent interest rather than the more realistic 6 percent or more.

The purchasing power of US$0.76 in, say, 1800 (US$0.11) far exceeded the purchasing power of the nominal hourly wage for unskilled

TABLE 2.5 VALUE OF FREEDOM BASED ON JAPANESE AMERICAN WORLD WAR II INTERNEE REPARATIONS (US $20,000 per person in 1988 dollars for three years = US $0.76 per hour)

Year	Enslaved	Value per hour (US$)	Person-hours per year	Annual total (US$)	Annual total compounded at 3% interest (US$)	at 6% interest (US$)
1776	423,392	0.10	3,708,910,416	370,891,041.60	382,017,772.85	393,144,504.10
1777	442,984	0.10	3,880,537,212	388,053,721.20	793,173,638.87	828,070,118.81
1778	462,576	0.10	4,052,164,008	405,216,400.80	1,234,341,740.86	1,307,283,710.79
1779	482,168	0.10	4,223,790,804	422,379,080.40	1,706,422,445.90	1,833,442,558.66
1780	501,760	0.10	4,395,417,600	439,541,760.00	2,210,343,132.07	2,409,363,377.78
1781	521,352	0.10	4,567,044,396	456,704,439.60	2,747,058,998.82	3,038,031,886.42
1782	540,944	0.10	4,738,671,192	473,867,119.20	3,317,553,901.57	3,722,612,945.96
1783	560,536	0.10	4,910,297,988	491,029,798.80	3,922,841,211.38	4,466,461,309.45
1784	580,128	0.10	5,081,924,784	508,192,478.40	4,563,964,700.47	5,273,133,015.12
1785	599,721	0.10	5,253,551,580	525,355,158.00	5,241,999,454.22	6,146,397,463.51
1786	619,313	0.10	5,425,178,376	542,517,837.60	5,958,052,810.58	7,090,250,219.17
1787	638,905	0.10	5,596,805,172	559,680,517.20	6,713,265,327.61	8,108,926,580.55
1788	658,497	0.10	5,768,431,968	576,843,196.80	7,508,811,780.14	9,206,915,964.00
1789	678,089	0.10	5,940,058,764	594,005,876.40	8,345,902,186.24	10,388,977,150.82
1790	697,681	0.10	6,111,685,560	611,168,556.00	9,225,782,864.51	11,660,154,449.23
1791	717,273	0.10	6,283,312,356	628,331,235.60	10,149,737,523.11	13,025,794,825.92
1792	736,865	0.10	6,454,939,152	645,493,915.20	11,119,088,381.46	14,491,566,065.59
1793	756,457	0.10	6,626,565,948	662,656,594.80	12,135,197,325.55	16,063,476,020.01
1794	776,049	0.10	6,798,192,744	679,819,274.40	13,199,467,097.95	17,747,893,012.07
1795	795,642	0.10	6,969,819,540	696,981,954.00	14,313,342,523.50	19,551,567,464.04
1796	815,234	0.10	7,141,446,336	714,144,633.60	15,478,311,771.82	21,481,654,823.50
1797	834,826	0.10	7,313,073,132	731,307,313.20	16,695,907,657.57	23,545,739,864.90

1798	*854,418*	*0.10*	7,484,699,928	748,469,992.80	17,967,708,979.88	25,751,862,449.16
1799	*874,010*	*0.10*	7,656,326,724	765,632,672.40	19,295,341,901.85	28,108,544,828.85
1800	**893,602**	**0.11**	7,827,953,520	855,595,319.74	20,755,465,338.23	30,701,988,557.50
1801	*923,378*	**0.11**	8,088,791,280	866,309,546.09	22,270,428,130.85	33,462,395,989.81
1802	*953,154*	*0.09*	8,349,629,040	769,000,834.58	23,730,611,834.40	36,285,280,633.86
1803	*982,930*	*0.10*	8,610,466,800	830,048,999.52	25,297,480,658.93	39,342,249,411.38
1804	*1,012,706*	*0.10*	8,871,304,560	855,193,759.58	26,937,254,651.07	42,609,289,761.22
1805	*1,042,482*	*0.10*	9,132,142,320	880,338,519.65	28,652,120,965.84	46,099,005,977.72
1806	*1,072,258*	*0.10*	9,392,980,080	944,933,796.05	30,484,966,404.75	49,866,576,160.19
1807	*1,102,034*	*0.09*	9,653,817,840	909,389,640.53	32,336,186,726.63	53,822,523,748.77
1808	*1,131,810*	*0.10*	9,914,655,600	1,019,226,595.68	34,356,075,721.98	58,132,255,365.11
1809	*1,161,586*	*0.10*	10,175,493,360	1,023,654,632.02	36,441,122,264.62	62,705,264,596.96
1810	**1,191,362**	*0.10*	10,436,331,120	1,049,894,910.67	38,615,747,690.55	67,580,469,078.09
1811	*1,226,028*	**0.11**	10,740,005,280	1,150,254,565.49	40,958,982,323.72	72,854,567,062.19
1812	*1,260,694*	**0.11**	11,043,679,440	1,205,969,794.85	43,429,900,682.12	78,504,169,068.46
1813	*1,295,360*	*0.12*	11,347,353,600	1,409,341,317.12	46,184,419,259.22	84,708,321,008.71
1814	*1,330,026*	*0.13*	11,651,027,760	1,570,558,542.05	49,187,627,135.31	91,455,612,323.8
1815	*1,364,692*	*0.12*	11,954,701,920	1,407,068,415.98	52,112,536,417.83	98,434,441,584.18
1816	*1,399,358*	**0.11**	12,258,376,080	1,337,388,830.33	55,053,423,005.60	105,758,140,239.38
1817	*1,434,024*	*0.10*	12,562,050,240	1,290,122,559.65	58,033,851,932.21	113,471,158,566.97
1818	*1,468,690*	*0.10*	12,865,724,400	1,265,987,280.96	61,078,834,389.56	121,621,374,598.80
1819	*1,503,356*	*0.10*	13,169,398,560	1,295,868,818.30	64,245,944,304.10	130,292,278,022.13
1820	**1,538,022**	*0.09*	13,473,072,720	1,209,881,930.26	67,419,501,021.39	139,392,289,549.53
1821	*1,585,124*	*0.09*	13,885,687,116	1,187,226,248.42	70,664,929,087.90	149,014,286,745.83
1822	*1,632,226*	*0.09*	14,298,301,512	1,222,504,779.28	74,044,056,883.19	159,250,999,016.61
1823	*1,679,328*	*0.08*	14,710,915,908	1,132,740,524.92	77,432,101,330.35	170,006,763,914.01
1824	*1,726,430*	*0.07*	15,123,530,304	1,067,721,239.46	80,854,817,246.91	181,338,954,262.69
1825	*1,773,533*	*0.07*	15,536,144,700	1,129,477,719.69	84,443,823,815.60	193,416,537,901.32

(continued)

TABLE 2.5 *(continued)*

Year	Enslaved	Value per hour (US$)	Person-hours per year	Annual total (US$)	Annual total compounded at 3% interest (US$)	at 6% interest (US$)
1826	1,820,635	0.07	15,948,759,096	1,159,474,786.28	88,171,397,559.93	206,250,573,448.85
1827	1,867,737	0.07	16,361,373,492	1,189,471,852.87	92,041,695,495.19	219,886,448,019.83
1828	1,914,839	0.07	16,773,987,888	1,184,243,544.89	96,022,717,211.28	234,334,933,058.60
1829	1,961,941	0.07	17,186,602,284	1,177,282,256.45	100,115,999,451.77	249,642,948,233.96
1830	2,009,043	0.07	17,599,216,680	1,205,546,342.58	104,361,192,168.18	265,899,404,251.13
1831	2,056,874	0.07	18,018,217,992	1,234,247,932.45	108,763,303,303.65	283,161,671,314.60
1832	2,104,705	0.06	18,437,219,304	1,181,825,757.39	113,243,482,932.87	301,404,106,896.30
1833	2,152,537	0.06	18,856,220,616	1,169,085,678.19	117,844,945,669.39	320,727,584,128.96
1834	2,200,368	0.06	19,275,221,928	1,235,541,725.58	122,652,902,016.82	341,280,913,405.82
1835	2,248,199	0.07	19,694,223,240	1,305,727,000.80	127,677,387,888.16	863,141,838,831.03
1836	2,296,030	0.07	20,113,224,552	1,419,993,653.37	132,970,302,987.78	386,435,542,433.47
1837	2,343,861	0.07	20,532,225,864	1,492,692,820.31	138,496,885,682.34	41 1,203,929,369.01
1838	2,391,693	0.07	20,951,227,176	1,433,063,938.84	144,127,848,109.81	437,395,212,906.32
1839	2,439,524	0.07	21,370,228,488	1,461,723,628.58	149,957,258,890.54	465,188,352,726.99
1840	2,487,355	0.06	21,789,229,800	1,396,689,630.18	155,894,566,976.34	494,580,144,898.60
1841	2,559,051	0.07	22,417,285,008	1,484,024,267.53	162,099,948,981.19	525,828,019,316.10
1842	2,630,747	0.06	23,045,340,216	1,426,506,559.37	168,432,249,206.78	558,889,797,427.99
1843	2,702,442	0.06	23,673,395,424	1,415,669,046.36	174,943,355,800.73	593,923,794,462.81
1844	2,774,138	0.06	24,301,450,632	1,453,226,747.79	181,688,480,024.97	631,099,642,483.24
1845	2,845,834	0.06	24,929,505,840	1,490,784,449.23	188,674,642,408.43	670,545,852,548.42
1846	2,917,530	0.06	25,557,561,048	1,472,115,516.36	195,851,160,662.54	712,339,046,148.67
1847	2,989,226	0.06	26,185,616,256	1,565,899,852.11	203,339,572,330.09	756,739,242,760.83
1848	3,060,921	0.06	26,813,671,464	1,488,158,766.25	210,972,563,029.23	803,721,045,618.71

1849	3,132,617	0.05	27,441,726,672	1,465,388,204.28	218,811,089,770.52	853,497,619,852.37
1850	**3,204,313**	0.05	28,069,781,880	1,498,926,352.39	226,919,316,606.60	906,296,338,977.05
1851	3,279,258	0.05	28,726,297,452	1,533,984,283.94	235,306,899,917.25	962,300,142,656.64
1852	3,354,202	0.05	29,382,813,024	1,569,042,215.48	243,982,220,396.72	1,021,701,335,964.45
1853	3,429,147	0.05	30,039,328,596	1,604,100,147.03	252,953,910,160.06	1,084,703,762,278.17
1854	3,504,092	0.06	30,695,844,168	1,771,150,208.49	262,366,812,179.61	1,151,663,407,235.86
1855	3,579,037	0.06	31,352,359,740	1,874,871,112.45	272,168,933,790.82	1,222,750,575,049.21
1856	3,653,981	0.06	32,008,875,312	1,846,912,105.50	282,236,321,273.21	1,298,073,336,384.00
1857	3,728,926	0.06	32,665,390,884	1,953,390,374.86	292,715,402,997.52	1,378,028,330,364.39
1858	3,803,871	0.06	33,321,906,456	1,852,697,998.95	303,405,144,026.37	1,462,673,890,065.14
1859	3,878,815	0.06	33,978,422,028	1,960,554,951.02	314,526,669,946.70	1,552,512,511,717.13
1860	**3,953,760**	0.06	34,634,937,600	1,998,435,899.52	326,020,859,021.61	1,647,781,604,473.65
2019*				35,839,679,354,047.70		17,399,318,066,609,200.00

*Total in 2019: $R_{2019} = R_{1860}\,(1 + i)^{(2019 - 1860)}$, where i is the interest rate:
3% compounded interest: US$35,839,679,354,048.
6% compounded interest: US$17,399,318,066,609,200.

NOTE: Bold entries in columns 2 and 3 are based on historical records; italic entries in the same column are estimated by linear extrapolation or interpolation (see text). Person-hours per year multiply population estimates with twenty-four hours a day times 365 days a year to obtain annual total person-hours available to slave owners.

labor at the same time of only $0.04 (see tables 2.2 and 2.5). From the Civil Liberties Act of 1988, freedom is valued at a rate higher than merely an opportunity to earn an hourly wage. It represents the decision-making power and choice over one's own life denied to the enslaved.

Japanese American World War II internees were deprived of their freedom without enslavement, whereas the enslaved were deprived of freedom and experienced the theft of labor. This condition is embedded in Swinton's (1990) additive formulas. What is still missing from Swinton's total formula is the cost of lost opportunities to acquire capital and the intergenerational effect of compensation for pain and suffering. Further missing are estimates of the cost of slavery prior to 1776 and the cost of racial discrimination after 1865.

WHITE MASSACRES (1866–1961)

The Reconstruction period saw the adoption of the Reconstruction Amendments—the Thirteenth, Fourteenth, and Fifteenth Amendments, of which the Thirteenth declared slavery unconstitutional. However, this briefly worded amendment also contains a notorious exception clause: "Neither slavery nor involuntary servitude, except as a punishment for a crime whereof the party shall have been duly convicted, shall exist within the United States." Ratified in 1865, the Thirteenth Amendment formally ended the institution of chattel slavery in the United States but left the door open for continued enslavement of individuals who had been sentenced for a crime. The Thirteenth Amendment, arguably, was the genesis of the current pattern of mass incarceration, disproportionately affecting black Americans today.

The Reconstruction Amendments notwithstanding, state legislatures quickly began to craft ways to restrict black Americans' newfound freedom. For example, the Alabama legislature passed a law that allowed orphans of the formerly enslaved or "children of blacks deemed inadequate parents" to be apprenticed to their former masters (Smith 2015, 102). The sharecropping system that emerged shortly after the end of chattel slavery, where white landowners would lease land to black Americans in exchange for a share of the crop, was another economically exploitative system that allowed the landowners to continue to increase their wealth at the expense of black Americans.

These new exploitative economic arrangements were reinforced by rampant white violence. White southerners did everything in their power to ensure that the caste system remained in the South and that the black community was nestled at the bottom. In a 1984 essay published in the *Journal of Social History,* Barry Crouch labels the white violence that swept the South during the Reconstruction period a spirit of raw lawlessness.

Kenneth Hamilton (1999) analyzes the situation in Harrison County, Texas, where whites forced freedmen to work on former plantations and destroyed schoolhouses to prevent their education and empowerment. Violent actions directed against freedmen and their educational institutions would maintain a steady labor supply and allow whites to regain the income and wealth lost during the war (Hamilton 1999).

From the perspective of white southerners, typically Democrats, black advancement in the political realm threatened their control over the electoral landscape. Hennessey (1985) discusses the Reconstruction Era's race massacres and notes the political origins of the recurring violence. A third of the recorded massacres "occurred within two weeks of an election," and more than half of the riots "began with an attempt by whites to break up a black political meeting or to keep blacks from voting" (Hennessey 1985, 100).

For example, consider the origins of the 1866 massacre in New Orleans, Louisiana. A gang of ex-Confederates and New Orleans police attacked the Radical Republican Louisiana Constitutional Convention held at the Mechanics Institute (Stolp-Smith 2011b). The violence led to the deaths of 238 people and the wounding of another forty-six, including black Union war veterans and delegates who attended the convention (Stolp-Smith 2011b).

Black ownership of property and land represented rights as important as access to the franchise and education, and whites recognized this. The Memphis race massacre of 1866 deliberately destroyed property representing black advancement. More than forty blacks died, 285 blacks were wounded, and five rapes of black women were recorded. The massacre resulted in the destruction of more than one hundred houses and buildings used by blacks in Memphis (Lanum 2011).

Similarly, the 1873 race massacre in Colfax, Louisiana, also included deliberate destruction of black property and the murder of 150 blacks. The Hamburg, South Carolina, massacre of 1876 occurred in the year before the elections that brought Reconstruction effectively to an end, killing six black men and one white farmer (Stolp-Smith 2011a).

Meanwhile, legislative efforts attempted to limit effective black land-ownership, and heirs' property presented an obstacle to black American landowners during Reconstruction. Heirs' property included property passed down to descendants despite the lack of a clear title or will. During the postwar era, many freedmen did not have access to the proper legal channels and relied on the idea of heirs' property to bequeath property to the next generation. The absence of a title and an established will made black property vulnerable to whites who acquired the property for their own use (Presser 2019).

Through a combination of legislation and violence, whites limited black land ownership, black education, and black property more generally. This discouraged upward mobility and wealth creation for African Americans, with repercussions to this day. White violence that occurred during the post–Civil War era paved the way for further injustices that marked the Jim Crow era.

Methods to quantify the wealth implications of post–Civil War violence and their consequences in terms of missed education and lost wealth have yet to be developed. Estimation methods might be developed resembling those some scholars have developed for quantifying certain aspects of Jim Crow discrimination, discussed in the following section.

According to Bentley-Edwards et al. (2018), white mob violence against African American communities continued to set the tone during the Jim Crow era. During the 1883 Danville, Virginia, riot, four blacks and one white person were killed. During the 1898 riot in Wilmington, North Carolina, up to 250 black people were killed and the city's established black community was destroyed. The 1900 Robert Charles riot in New Orleans, Louisiana, cost twenty-eight lives and destroyed a black city school.

The Atlanta race riot of 1906 killed up to one hundred blacks, while that of Springfield, Illinois, in 1906 resulted in two recorded deaths but also destroyed an entire black neighborhood and business community by fire. In 1910, antiblack riots broke out in sixteen cities across the United States when blacks celebrated Jack Johnson's boxing victory over James Jeffries, and whites caused up to twenty-six casualties (see Bentley-Edwards et al. 2018). In 1917, a labor dispute over black strikebreakers in East St. Louis, Illinois, led to riots that cost up to two hundred black lives and cost, at the time, anywhere from $373,000 to $1 million in damages. This corresponds to losses ranging from $7.6 million to US$20.4 million compounded to 2019 at only 3 percent interest.

The Red Summer Riots of 1919 led to eighteen black and eight white deaths in Charleston, South Carolina; twenty-three black and thirteen white deaths in Chicago, Illinois; estimates running as high as one hundred deaths in Knoxville, Tennessee; three deaths in Omaha, Nebraska; and thirty-nine black and five white deaths in Washington, D.C. (see Bentley-Edwards et al. 2018). The Tulsa riots of 1921 in Oklahoma, also known as Black Wall Street Riots, cost about three hundred lives and destroyed thirty-five blocks in the black Greenwood community. The Rosewood Massacre in Florida in 1923 cost up to 150 lives and leveled a black town.

Present-value estimates of the damages from a limited number of these cases include an estimated loss of $10 million by black farmers in the 1919 white massacre that swept the small town of Elaine, Arkansas. Approximately a present value of $45 million was lost in the Chicago massacre, also in 1919, when white destruction of black property rendered one thousand black people homeless. And the present value of black property destroyed or seized during the Tulsa massacre of 1921 has been estimated to be at least $611 million (Darity, Mullen, and Slaughter 2022, 107).

In 1943, another wave of race riots swept the country from Mobile, Alabama, resulting in segregated shipyards, to Beaumont, Texas, where black-owned structures were burned. In Detroit, Michigan, the same year, thirty-four people were killed and $2 million in damage was caused ($40.8 million in 2019 dollars; see Bentley-Edwards et al. 2018). In 1961, in Anniston, Montgomery, and Birmingham, Alabama, white anger over the Freedom Rides caused riots.

In addition, a report by the Equal Justice Initiative (2017) cites 4,084 documented instances of racial terror lynching in twelve southern states between the end of Reconstruction in 1877 and 1950. Together, white antiblack race riots, mob violence, and lynchings set the tone for strict segregation laws during the Jim Crow era, mainly in the South but not exclusively there. This gave discriminatory laws their power to intimidate, discourage, and reverse black success. White violence must be viewed as an integral part of the system of Jim Crow discrimination that had massive intergenerational wealth implications for African Americans.

In Richard America's (1990) edited volume *The Wealth of Races*, David Swinton offered some estimates of the costs to blacks associated with employment discrimination. He referred to work by Udinsky, Chachere, and America, who calculated the cost of labor market discrimination to African Americans between the years 1929 and 1969. Their estimate in 1972 dollars was $363 billion, a figure that Swinton

(1990) compounded up to 1983 at a 6 percent interest rate to $689 billion, which, further compounded to 2019, would amount to $5.6 trillion.

This addresses only part of the Jim Crow era; the years from 1877 to 1929 are missing from this calculation. Further, it addresses only labor market discrimination. The impact of housing discrimination can be ascertained by looking at the value of housing stock available to African Americans compared with whites, as well as available (or unavailable) mortgages and interest rates that were often set discriminatorily by federal policy (see next section).

Kaplan and Valls (2007, 268) propose that "focusing on discrimination in housing allows us to quantify, at least in rough terms, the amount that is owed to African Americans: the differences in mean household wealth attributable to home ownership, multiplied by the number of African Americans." A source for the average household wealth attributable to homeownership would have to be located, and the corresponding figure of African Americans alive at that time could be obtained from the US Census Bureau.

The "separate but equal" doctrine that characterized the Jim Crow era also had major implications for the acquisition of education and with it intergenerational social capital. Quantifying the wealth effects of education discrimination could involve a look at the wealth effects of white versus black education in the southern states and could compound the difference up to the present as one aspect of the bill due for the harms of the Jim Crow era.

NEW DEAL DISCRIMINATION (1933–41)

At the time of the New Deal, the Democratic Party consisted of a liberal wing in the North (supporting the New Deal) and an overtly white supremacist wing in the South. New Deal measures could not pass Congress if they threatened Jim Crow laws in the South. Federally financed New Deal programs were allowed to be administered locally, and farmworkers and domestic workers (the typical employments of blacks in the South) were excluded from New Deal laws.

The National Labor Relations Act of 1935 (NLRA) explicitly stated that the definition of "employee . . . shall not include any individual employed as an agricultural laborer, or in the domestic service of any family or person at his home" (quoted in Katznelson 2005, 57). This had direct implications for intergenerational wealth generation among African Americans compared with white Americans.

Farmworkers and domestic servants were ineligible for new welfare policies (pensions, unemployment benefits, and poor assistance through the Federal Emergency Relief Administration [FERA] in 1933) and through the Social Security Act in 1935. Furthermore, workers' rights granted by New Deal legislation did not apply to farmworkers and domestic servants (see, for example, the National Industrial Recovery Act [NIRA] in 1933, the NLRA in 1935, and the Fair Labor Standards Act [FLSA] in 1938). How can this loss be quantified?

We would need to know the percentage of farmworkers and domestic servants in the black US labor force and the corresponding percentage of farmworkers and domestic servants in the white US labor force. This would allow us to estimate ineligibility for New Deal Era employee benefits for the two groups. Then we would need to know average or median benefits for "employees" (as defined by New Deal laws) and could determine the amount missing among black and white Americans due to the exclusionary definition of "employee" in New Deal labor laws.

Redlining and Its Effect on Homeownership

As part of the New Deal, the Home Owners' Loan Corporation (HOLC) was formed in 1933 (Rothstein 2017). It provided eligible prospective homeowners with zero percent down payments with low interest rate mortgages over twenty-five years instead of the then customary 50 percent down payments with seven years to complete payment. In 1934, the Federal Housing Administration (FHA) was formed and insured mortgages, covering 80 percent of the purchase price. The FHA appraised properties through its own agents to ensure low risk. Its Underwriting Manual of 1935 stated, "If a neighborhood is to retain stability it is necessary that properties shall continue to be occupied by the same social and racial classes. . . . A change in social or racial occupancy . . . leads to . . . a reduction in values. . . . Adverse influences . . . are infiltration of inharmonious racial or nationality groups" (Rothstein 2017, 65).

Risk was assessed on the basis of HOLC-generated maps. On these maps, "safe risk" zones were colored green, and "high risk" zones red. High-risk areas were by HOLC definition areas with African American residents or other "inharmonious" nationality groups. HOLC, FHA, and Public Works Administration (PWA) rules required restrictive covenants that prevented white homeowners from selling their property to African Americans or other "inharmonious" groups.

As a result, members of these groups could not qualify for government-insured home loans in desirable suburbs but had to stay in inner-city neighborhoods where they had to pay 50 percent down, rather than zero percent, for a seven-year instead of a twenty-five-year mortgage. They were therefore less likely to afford a home of their own unless they had significant wealth. Having significant wealth was less likely for African Americans because of the intergenerational wealth effects of slavery, government land distribution policies in the late nineteenth century, and the destruction and appropriation of black property during the waves of white massacres discussed above.

As a result, fewer African Americans sought to buy homes, and fewer of those who attempted to buy were successful because of the much higher monthly payments. The likelihood of default was much higher without the government insurance. The result was that African Americans paid more money for lower-quality housing stock and had less capital left over for upkeep, a fact that allowed many inner-city communities to fall into disrepair and to turn into slums. Nonetheless, slum housing was more expensive (whether to buy or to rent) than comparable suburban white housing.

To quantify the wealth effect of redlining, we would need to know the average black mortgage interest rate i_B in the New Deal Era, the average black home price P_B, the average black down payment D_B, and the average duration of black mortgages $Y_B(12) = N_B$. We would also need the corresponding figures for white mortgages, the white interest rate i_W, the average white home price P_W, the average white down payment D_W (whereby D_W would likely be $D_W = 0$), and the average duration of white mortgages $Y_W(12) = N_W$. These figures could then be plugged into the following general formula to determine the total price paid for a given home T_B and T_W, respectively:

$$T = D + Yi(12) \frac{(P - D)(1 + i)^{Y(12)}}{(1 + i)^{Y(12)} - 1}$$

where T is the total price paid for a given home, D is the down payment, and Y is the number of years. The interest rate i is the annual interest rate (APR) divided by the number of mortgage payments per year (here twelve months per year), so that $i = $ APR $/ 12$. P is the price for the home. The difference between the two would be the value of redlining discrimination: $\delta = T_W - T_B$.

To determine the overall reparations estimate for redlining discrimination, this difference could be calculated for each year between 1933 and 1977, when, finally, the Community Reinvestment Act required banks for the first time to apply the same lending criteria in all communities and thus ended redlining. The percentage of white households taking advantage of government mortgage subsidies in each year between 1933 and 1977 could be determined and the same proportion of African Americans computed. The difference in each year could then be multiplied by the estimated number of African Americans who would likely have qualified for government-subsidized mortgages, had it not been for de jure redlining discrimination.[6]

Each year's total then could be compounded to the present with an appropriate interest rate to compensate African American households for nonpayment in the years between the start of the New Deal in 1933 and the end of redlining in 1977. The total amount then could be divided by the number of African Americans in the current year (individual compensation) or by the number of African American households (for household-level reparations payments).

WORLD WAR II DISCRIMINATION (1941–45)

Black Americans played a crucial role throughout World War II and were affected deeply by its outcomes. By 1945, more than nine hundred thousand black people had enlisted in the war effort, and hundreds of thousands of others worked in the defense industry. Racial discrimination in the armed forces and in the labor market, specifically the booming defense industry of this time, highlighted the hypocrisy of America and its involvement in the war: fighting anti-Jewish racism abroad while practicing antiblack racism at home.

A. Philip Randolph and Walter White unsuccessfully lobbied President Roosevelt for the complete integration of the military and an end to discrimination within the defense industry (Wynn 2010). A countervailing memo from the War Department reached the president on October 16, 1940, stating, "The policy of the War Department is not to intermingle colored and white enlisted personnel in the same regimental organizations. This policy has been proven satisfactory over a long period of years, and to make changes now would produce situations destructive to morale and detrimental to the preparation for national defense. . . . It is the opinion of the War Department that no experiments should be tried with the organizational set-up of these units at this critical time" (quoted in Lee 1966, 76).

This policy cemented racial segregation in the armed forces for the duration of World War II. According to Katznelson (2005), about 10 to

11 percent of soldiers under arms during World War II were African American, roughly proportional to the black presence in the population in 1940. Black Americans were subject to segregated units and given the lowest-paying jobs.

On September 16, 1940, the United States issued the Selective Training and Service Act, creating the draft. However, black Americans who tried to enlist in the military were rejected at far greater proportions than their white counterparts. Whereas 18 percent of black Americans were rejected from serving in the war, only 8.5 percent of whites were rejected. Even though the US government played a crucial role in creating the educational disparities that existed between black and white Americans, it still excluded thousands of black applicants because of a lack in education.

In the army, black Americans were made to sleep, eat, and shower in separate facilities and were often passed over for promotions that would put them in command of any white soldiers. In the South, where many military camps were located and where more than 80 percent of black trainees were sent, black soldiers were the target of discrimination and violence at the hands of white civilians. Not only were black soldiers not given any of the special treatment that white soldiers received, they also were expected to follow the Jim Crow laws that ruled southern states at the time. Veterans challenging Jim Crow laws were brutally maimed, like Sgt. Isaac Woodard Jr., who was blinded by a police officer with a baton (Gergel 2019), or were killed, like Timothy Hood (Carr 2012).

Apart from the actual military, the defense industry was a significant economic factor throughout World War II. While unemployment among white Americans fell, it remained constant for black people. Of the 150,000 men placed in the defense industry between October 1940 and March 1941, only 4 percent were black (Wynn 2010). By 1945, almost 20 percent of the population was employed in the armed forces, but the National Urban League estimated that 75 percent of the defense industry was closed to black people (Institute for Economics and Peace 2011; Wynn 2010).

Across the country, local shipyards that were receiving government war contracts unashamedly proclaimed that they did not and would not hire a black American to work there (Wynn 2010). The aircraft industry displayed shocking statistics indicative of the degree of segregation in the American labor force at the time. Some of the largest carriers such as Boeing employed no black workers among forty-one thousand employees (Wynn 2010). Out of hundreds of thousands of aircraft workers nationally, it is estimated that only 240 black people worked in the aircraft industry (Wynn 2010).

The systematic denial of positions for black workers in the labor force, particularly the defense industry, prompted black organizers like Randolph to begin planning a large-scale march on Washington to end racial discrimination within the defense industry. As word of the march reached the White House, the Roosevelt administration scrambled to put an end to it. Executive Order 8802 (1941) emerged as a result, declaring that "there shall be no discrimination in the employment of workers in defense industries and in Government, because of race, creed, color, or national origin."[7] The march was called off, and the order was seen as one of the most significant wins for Black America since Reconstruction (Burns 2007). However, as often is seen when black Americans make any kind of political, social, or economic progress in America, there was intense white backlash.

On May 24, 1943, at the Alabama Dry Dock Shipping Company in Mobile, Alabama, twelve black workers were promoted to welding jobs, a position that had been exclusively for white men up until then (Nelson 1993). Thousands of white workers threatened and injured black people in the community. Army troops were called to restore order, and strict racial segregation was implemented in the shipyard.

Four separate shipways were created where black people were allowed to work in every position, except as foreman. The black-owned *Pittsburgh Courier* denounced the compromise as a victory for "Nazi racial theory and another defeat for the principles embodied in the Declaration of Independence" (quoted in Tsesis 2012, 278).

In the following months, there were similar violent racial confrontations in industrial areas across the country, such as Newark, New Jersey, and Harlem, New York. Perhaps the worst took place in Detroit, Michigan, where more than thirty people died and more than four hundred people were wounded, most of whom were black. Around the country, as black people tried to fill the president's executive order with substance, they were met by white antagonists who resorted to violence to achieve their goals. As a result, black Americans, systematically, were denied entry into the labor force throughout World War II, with intergenerational wealth implications to this day.

POSTWAR DISCRIMINATION (1945–65)

The Servicemen's Readjustment Act of 1944 (G.I. Bill) provided crucial benefits to returning war veterans: low-cost mortgages, low-interest loans to start a business, one year of unemployment compensation, tuition and living expenses to obtain education. It was defined in a color-blind manner. How, then, did it widen the black-white wealth gap?

Black people were underrepresented in qualifying functions during World War II as a direct result of de jure racial segregation. Rather than being centrally administrated by the federal government, the G.I. Bill was administered locally (states' rights), a measure that allowed both northern and southern states to discriminate against African American veterans.

The G.I. Bill's massive housing subsidies were also affected by de jure discrimination as a result of redlining (until 1977). Consequently, the G.I. Bill contributed to the emergence of a large white middle class in suburban subdivisions and a black underclass in urban ghettos. This was a direct result of de jure discrimination during the New Deal and after World War II, reinforced by the seemingly color-blind G.I. Bill. Federal policy interacted with private discrimination, where banks refused to give mortgages to eligible African American applicants (a policy required by the FHA).

Educational institutions openly discriminated on the basis of race in admissions. President Truman's Committee on Civil Rights stated in 1948: "It is clear that there is much discrimination, based on prejudice in admission of students to private colleges, vocational schools, and graduate schools. . . . In many of our northern educational institutions enrollment of Jewish students seems to never exceed certain fixed points and there is never more than a token enrollment of Negroes" (quoted in Katznelson 2005, 130).

How could the disparate effect of the G.I. Bill on white and black Americans be estimated and quantified? Discrimination in the provision of low-cost mortgages could be addressed through measuring the wealth costs of redlining (described above). The proportion of low-interest loans to start a business could be compared between whites and blacks and the shortfall for African Americans calculated.

If one were designing an itemized bill for black reparations, low-interest loans to start a business could be provided to African Americans in direct proportion to what was not received. The same procedure could be applied to compensate for each year of missing unemployment compensation for unemployed white and black Americans after the war. The exclusion of black people from the bill's educational opportunities could be addressed by providing qualifying African American students with tuition scholarships and grants for living expenses to complete their studies.

Educational institutions with low percentages of African American students could be required to offer scholarships to compensate for past explicit and implicit antiblack discrimination in admissions. These policies would have to go above and beyond existing affirmative action policies, as affirmative action is simply designed to prevent antiblack discrimination from going forward.

POST-CIVIL RIGHTS DISCRIMINATION (1965 TO TODAY)

The discrimination against African Americans under an ostensibly color-blind G.I. Bill demonstrates that seemingly egalitarian policies against the backdrop of explicit racial exclusion in the past can result in outcomes that are indistinguishable from outright racial discrimination in the present. The same phenomenon is observed today when we consider mortgage interest and property tax deductions in the federal tax code. Because African Americans consistently were discouraged from achieving homeownership while white homeownership was actively subsidized by the federal government between 1933 and 1977, tax benefits from homeownership go, disproportionately, to white Americans.

Other wealth implications of ongoing race-related inequities must be addressed by a comprehensive reparations program. These include the inequitable outcomes of the so-called War on Drugs, with its resulting excessive mass incarceration and ongoing cases of deadly police violence against unarmed black victims, coupled with the overwhelming unwillingness of grand juries to indict involved police officers. This leads to a hostile climate in many predominantly African American communities, impedes normal law enforcement activities (especially if witnesses to crime do not trust the police), and puts life and property of residents in these badly policed communities at risk. It also lowers property values in the affected neighborhoods, producing less intergenerational wealth accumulation.

Another form of ongoing racial discrimination is practiced in the nine states that, thus far, have banned affirmative action: California (1996), Texas (1996), Washington (1998), Florida (1999), Michigan (2006), Nebraska (2008), Arizona (2010), New Hampshire (2012), and Oklahoma (2012). In these states, the only instrument to address racial discrimination in college admission as well as in hiring and promotion has been rendered impotent, which means that racial discrimination (intentional or unintentional) can proceed unchecked.

Affirmative action is an important complement to a comprehensive reparations program, since it is designed to reduce (ideally to prevent) racial discrimination going forward, while reparations address the adverse effects of past discrimination. It would be odd to pay reparations for the intergenerational wealth implications of past discrimination, while allowing current discrimination to continue unchecked. Closure will not be achieved if the atrocity of discrimination persists.

We arrive at estimates of $19.1 trillion to $6.6 quadrillion in 2019 dollars for expropriated labor due to slavery and $35.8 trillion to $17.4 quadrillion dollars for lost freedom. Together these estimates would result in an outstanding debt between $54.9 trillion and $24 quadrillion in 2019 dollars. These estimates are massive, despite the conservative assumptions we are making.

Still missing from this total would be compensation for the reduced value of labor due to discrimination, the reduced value of capital due to discrimination, lost opportunities to acquire capital, and compensation due for generations of pain and suffering. According to Swinton's (1990) comprehensive formula, all these elements would need to be estimated and their current values established. Further research is required to estimate the outstanding magnitudes for a complete historical accounting.

While a complete accounting is necessary for historical accuracy, we propose minimum reparations as a *political compromise*. These minimum reparations should be sufficient to close the average per capita black-white wealth gap. In 2019, this gap amounted to $357,477 per person and could be paid to an estimated forty-one million African American descendants of the enslaved with an investment of $14.7 trillion (in 2019 dollars). We believe that this proposal has the advantage of resonating with the American political ideal of racial equality. The ultimate modalities of African American reparations remain to be negotiated between the descendant community and the federal government.

NOTES

1. At times, the goals of conservatism and comprehensiveness may appear to be at cross purposes: for example, when conservative estimation methods yield surprisingly large estimates, and when the comprehensive approach seems to double-count them. However, in reading subsequent sections of this chapter, it is important to note that no double counting is involved when we separately estimate the present value of unpaid wages, and the value of lost freedom based on reparations to Japanese American World War II internees. Lost freedom is about the inability to make decisions about one's own life and represents an injustice even if wages are paid, as they were for Japanese American World

War II internees. Unpaid wages are about just compensation for services rendered that should have been compensated at the time, as we will argue. Both historical injustices have major intergenerational wealth implications for African American descendants living today and are additive.

2. The original formula in Swinton's article is PV(COST) = (CS(t) + CD(t)) $(1 + 4)^t$. We inserted the "i" where the author had "4" and replaced the exponential t by $(t - 1618)$, where the year 1618 is the year before the arrival of the first enslaved Africans on later US soil. Finally, we added a summation sign ranging from 1619 to the current year to indicate that each year's debt has to be added up. In formula 2, we swapped out an equals sign for a plus sign and turned the index for the year into subscripts. The author wrote, "CD(t) = RL(t) + RC(t) = LC(t) + PS(t)" (Swinton 1990, 155).

3. Special Field Orders No. 15 (1865), https://en.wikipedia.org/wiki/Special_Field_Orders_No._15.

4. The working day for white workers was longer in the early nineteenth century than it is today. However, we do not limit our calculation to a white worker's typical workday, because white workers enjoyed spare time in the true free market sense with a choice of activities. The enslaved had no such choice.

5. H.R. 442, Civil Liberties Act of 1987, www.congress.gov/bill/100th-congress/house-bill/442, paragraph 1.

6. The term *de jure* refers to discrimination that is officially sanctioned by law, as opposed to *de facto* discrimination, which would mean discrimination due to custom but not inscribed in law.

7. Executive Order 8802 (1941), "Prohibition of Discrimination in the Defense Industry," www.ourdocuments.gov/doc.php?flash=false&doc=72, 1.

REFERENCES

Allen, Robert L. 1998. "Past Due: The African American Quest for Reparations." *Black Scholar* 28 (2): 2–17.

America, Richard F., ed. 1990. *The Wealth of Races: The Present Value of Benefits from Past Injustices.* New York: Greenwood Press.

Araujo, Ana Lucia. 2019. "The History of Black Women Championing Demands for Reparations." Truthout, June 1. https://truthout.org/articles/the-history-of-black-women-championing-demands-for-reparations.

Bentley-Edwards, Keisha L., Malik Chaka Edwards, Cynthia Neal Spence, William A. Darity, Darrick Hamilton, and Jasson Perez. 2018. "How Does It Feel to Be a Problem? The Missing Kerner Commission Report." *Russell Sage Foundation Journal of the Social Sciences,* 4 (6): 20–40.

Bhutta, Neil, Andrew C. Chang, Lisa J. Dettling, and Joanna W. Hsu. 2020. "Disparities in Wealth by Race and Ethnicity in the 2019 Survey of Consumer Finances." FEDS Notes, September 28. www.federalreserve.gov/econres/notes/feds-notes/disparities-in-wealth-by-race-and-ethnicity-in-the-2019-survey-of-consumer-finances-20200928.htm.

Burns, Ken. 2007. "Mobile Shipyards." Clip from Season 1 of *The War.* www.pbs.org/video/war-mobile-shipyards/.

Carr, Gregory L. 2012. "Timothy Hood: Reflections on a Soldier's Story and a Quest for Government Documents." Working document, Northeastern University School of Law. October 29. https://repository.library.northeastern .edu/downloads/neu:mo42t7767?datastream_id=content.

Craemer, Thomas. 2015. "Estimating Slavery Reparations: Present Value Comparisons of Historical Multigenerational Reparations Policies." *Social Science Quarterly* 96 (2): 639–55.

———. 2018. "International Reparations for Slavery and the Slave Trade." *Journal of Black Studies,* 49 (7): 694–713.

Crouch, Barry A. 1984. "A Spirit of Lawlessness: White Violence, Texas Blacks, 1865–1868." *Journal of Social History,* 18 (2): 217–32.

Darity, William A., Jr. 2008. "Forty Acres and a Mule in the 21st Century." *Social Science Quarterly* 89 (3): 656–64.

Darity, William A., Jr., and A. Kirsten Mullen. 2020. *From Here to Equality: Reparations for Black Americans in the 21st Century.* Chapel Hill: University of North Carolina Press.

Darity, William A., Jr., A. Kirsten Mullen, and Marvin Slaughter. 2022. "The Cumulative Costs of Racism and the Bill for Reparations." *Journal of Economic Perspectives* 36 (2): 99–122.

Eizenstat, Stuart. E. 2019. "What Holocaust Restitution Taught Me about Slavery Reparations." *Politico,* October 27. www.politico.com/magazine/story/2019/10 /27/slavery-reparations-holocaust-restitution-negotiations-229881.

Encyclopedia Britannica. 2019. "Japanese American Internment." www .britannica.com/event/Japanese-American-internment.

Equal Justice Initiative. 2017. *Lynching in America: Confronting the Legacy of Racial Terror.* 3rd ed. https://web.archive.org/web/20180510151602/https:// lynchinginamerica.eji.org/report/.

Ford, Worthington Chauncey, ed. 1893. *The Writings of George Washington.* Vol. 14, *1798–1799.* New York: G. P. Putnam's Sons.

Friedman, Morgan S. 2019. "The Inflation Calculator." *West Egg.* https:// westegg.com/inflation/.

Georgetown Slavery Archive. 1838. "Articles of Agreement between Thomas F. Mulledy, of Georgetown, District of Columbia, of One Part, and Jesse Beatty and Henry Johnson, of the State of Louisiana, of the Other Part." June 19. http://slaveryarchive.georgetown.edu/items/show/1.

Gergel, Richard. 2019. "An Account of the Blinding of Sgt. Isaac Woodard by the Police Officer, Lynwood Shull. A Decorated WWII Veteran Returns to the Jim Crow South." Literary Hub, January 22. https://lithub.com/an-account- of-the-blinding-of-sgt-isaac-woodard-by-the-police-officer-lynwood-shull/2.

Hamilton, Kenneth M. 1999. "White Wealth and Black Repression in Harrison County, Texas: 1865–1868." *Journal of Negro History* 84 (4): 340–59.

Hennessey, Melinda Meek. 1985. "Racial Violence during Reconstruction: The 1876 Riots in Charleston and Cainhoy." *South Carolina Historical Magazine* 86 (2): 100–112.

Institute for Economics and Peace. 2011. "Economic Consequences of War on the U.S. Economy." http://economicsandpeace.org/wp-content/uploads/2015/06 /The-Economic-Consequences-of-War-on-US-Economy_0.pdf.

Kaplan, Jonathan, and Andrew Valls. 2007. "Housing Discrimination as a Basis for Black Reparations. " *Public Affairs Quarterly* 21 (3): 255–73.

Katznelson, Ira. 2005. *When Affirmative Action Was White: An Untold History of Racial Inequality in Twentieth-Century America.* New York: Norton.

Kellman, Laurie. 2019. "McConnell on Reparations for Slavery: Not a 'Good Idea.'" Associated Press, June 18. www.apnews.com/e79abc3b64e7400 ea961f2fe99a73dc6.

Krauthammer, Charles. 2001. "How to Solve the Reparations Problem." *Jewish World Review*, April 10. www.jewishworldreview.com/cols/krauthammer 041001.asp.

Lanum, M. 2011. "Memphis Riot, 1866." Black Past, November 20. www .blackpast.org/african-american-history/memphis-riot-1866/.

Lee, Ulysses. 1966. *The Employment of Negro Troops.* Washington, DC: Office of the Chief of Military History, United States Army.

Marketti, James. 1990. "Estimated Present Value of Income Diverted during Slavery." In America, *Wealth of Races*, 107–23.

Mittal, Anuradha, and Joan Powell. 2000. "The Last Plantation." *Food First* 6 (1): 1–8.

Neal, Larry. 1990. "A Calculation and Comparison of the Current Benefits of Slavery and an Analysis of Who Benefits." In America, *Wealth of Races*, 107–23.

Nelson, Bruce. 1993. "Organized Labor and the Struggle for Black Equality in Mobile during World War II." *Journal of American History* 80 (3): 952–88.

Officer, Lawrence H., and Samuel H. Williamson. 2019. "Annual Wages in the United States Unskilled Labor and Manufacturing Workers, 1774-Present." MeasuringWorth. www.measuringworth.com/uswage/.

Presser, Lizzie. 2019. "Their Family Bought Land One Generation after Slavery. The Reels Brothers Spent Eight Years in Jail for Refusing to Leave It." ProPublica, July 6. https://features.propublica.org/black-land-loss/heirs-property-rights-why-black-families-lose-land-south/.

Ransom, Roger L., and Richard Sutch. 1990. "Who Pays for Slavery?" In America, *Wealth of Races*, 107–23.

Rothstein, Richard. 2017. *The Color of Law: A Forgotten History of How Our Government Segregated America.* New York: Liveright.

Smith, Andre L. 2015. *Tax Law and Racial Economic Justice.* Lanham, MD: Lexington Books.

Stolp-Smith, Michael. 2011a. "The Hamburg Massacre (1876)." Black Past, April 7. www.blackpast.org/african-american-history/hamburg-massacre-1876/.

———. 2011b. "New Orleans Massacre (1866)." Black Past, April 7. www .blackpast.org/african-american-history/new-orleans-massacre-1866/.

Swinton, David H. 1990. "Racial Inequality and Reparations." In America, *Wealth of Races*, 107–23.

Tamir, Christine. 2021. *The Growing Diversity of Black America.* Pew Research Center, report, March 25. www.pewresearch.org/social-trends/2021/03/25 /the-growing-diversity-of-black-america/.

Tsesis, Alexander. 2012. *For Liberty and Equality: The Life and Times of the Declaration of Independence*. New York: Oxford University Press.

US Bureau of the Census. 1975. *Historical Statistics of the United States. Colonial Times to 1970, Bicentennial Edition, Part 1*. Washington, DC: US Government Printing Office.

———. 2016. "Current Population Survey, 2016 Annual Social and Economic Supplement." https://www2.census.gov/programs-surveys/demo/tables/families/2016/cps-2016/tabavg1.xls.

Williams, Robert B. 2017. "Wealth Privilege and the Racial Wealth Gap: A Case Study in Economic Stratification." *Review of Black Political Economy* 44:303–25.

Wynn, Neil A. 2010. *The African American Experience during World War II*. Lanham, MD: Rowman and Littlefield.

3

Unequal Housing and the Case for Reparations

WALTER D. GREASON

At the peak of the New Deal coalition's power, urban development focused on the creation of public housing as a form of antipoverty policy. The Great Depression forged a legislative commitment to providing an unprecedented standard of living for the working and middle classes in the United States.[1] The divide between working and professional/managerial classes (based on occupation, not income) persists as the key division in a global service economy.

Two points of comparison help to clarify these transitions. Before 1930, the United States was an overwhelmingly rural nation with rapidly expanding urban industrial centers. These changes between 1880 and 1930 presented a "search for order"—a process where millions of people reimagined their lives and new generations invented unprecedented systems of knowledge. A similar process unfolded between 1970 and 2020: in a world of urban industrial networks, a global information society took root. Few anticipated the power of satellites and computers to completely transform human life, yet no similar structure for organizing this revolution has emerged. Progressive idealism about the power of scientific analysis in service to the public good continues to drive the creation of infrastructure on a scale unimaginable a generation earlier (Seligman 2005; Satter 2009; Vale 2018). Reparations offers one way to reject the chaos of antiblack racism, while creating a more just and inclusive world order by the start of the twenty-second century.

Snapshots of urban and rural life in 1925 and in 1965 would cause the casual observer to question whether the images depicted the same nation. For all of the failures of the New Deal's grand ambition—and the compromises with racial segregation at the local level stand first on that list— the underlying assumptions about the capacity of the federal government to mitigate the worst problems facing the nation hold bold promise for a more equitable and just world economy in the twenty-first century.

The most profound transformation of the American landscape in those forty years was the provision of massive financial subsidies for the creation of suburban communities on the fringes of every major urban center. The establishment of the Federal Housing Administration in 1937 opened the door to the widespread amortization of residential mortgages. These reforms were then compounded by discriminatory implementation of the G.I. Bill after 1946, which expanded patterns of antiblack racial segregation from local to regional and national scales (Jackson 1985; Cohen 2004). As a result, it became possible for professional and managerial households to purchase single-family homes at costs lower than urban apartment rentals (Wiese 2004; Nicolaides 2002; Michney 2017; Freund 2004).

For seventy years these policies evolved, creating thousands of suburban neighborhoods and underwriting the automobile culture that defined American life in the second half of the twentieth century. This suburban expansion carried a number of social costs. Most analysts examined the economic collapse of many American cities as the commuter class grew. Their suburban lifestyles eroded the revenue bases of many large cities (like Detroit, New York, and St. Louis), leaving the vast majority of low-wealth, African American household populations with no means to sustain local public services (Sugrue 1996; Kruse 2005; Pattillo 2007; Kusmer and Trotter 2009). Conversely, these suburban developments also displaced waves of rural residents (especially black Americans), who could no longer afford the cost-of-living increases that came with malls, highways, and office parks (Kahrl 2016; Freestone, Gournay, and Sies 2019; Wolcott 2012; Greason 2013; Connolly 2014; Armstead 1999). Suburbanization was a total transformation of American landscape design, and its consumer culture hollowed out any concept of shared civic community. The very idea of public space became a relic of an earlier generation (Sorkin 1992; Straus 2014; Hayden 2003; Cohen 2004).

New Jersey's Supreme Court, under the provisions of a stridently progressive state constitution, placed sharp limitations on the waves of suburban expansion from New York City and Philadelphia. In the Mount Laurel I and II decisions, municipalities had to resort to using zoning and land-use law to allow for affordable housing development in the suburbs (Massey and Denton 1993; Ammon 2016; Isenberg 2004; Baradaran 2017). The goal was the inclusion of working-class and lower-income families, especially families in communities defined by American Descendants of Slavery, in the benefits of the FHA's long-term largesse. Race remains a fluid social construction with profound material consequences. One of the most pervasive, and growing, effects of racism is segregation in housing markets— throughout the Anglophone world and beyond. In particular, black property continues to be undervalued, even rendered entirely worthless within real estate markets (NAREB 2020; Brown 2021). This specific intersection of race, space, and wealth reflects centuries of segregation for the explicit purpose of preventing material prosperity among black communities.

Consider Philadelphia: in the late eighteenth century, public expenditures multiplied around the celebration and preservation of the legacy of Benjamin Franklin. At the same time, African American residents meticulously saved and invested in the creation of a network of black churches that provided the only source of institutional financial stability within the local systems of Black Codes. Suppose that the city and state had invested in William Still, black chair of the Vigilance Committee of the Pennsylvania Anti-Slavery Society and leading agent of the Underground Railroad, in ways that it did for Franklin and other prominent white Philadelphians? The Vigilance Committee was one of the organizations most profoundly dedicated to human freedom in the antebellum United States, and Still created it with virtually no financial capital. How much larger would the regional markets have been had the barriers of race and space against black wealth been eliminated?

In New Jersey, private developers and local communities resisted the state Supreme Court's new legal requirements with enduring force. As a result, New Jersey became more segregated after 1990, not less. By 2010, its school systems were more segregated than they had ever been, surpassing the levels of displacement and exclusion seen in apartheid South Africa over the previous sixty years (Tractenberg, Orfield, and Flaxman 2013; Orfield, Ee, and Coughlan 2017). In the worst cases, the most suburban counties erased black communities wholesale, leaving abandoned, impoverished areas of black residents trapped in open-air ghettoes that denied social and economic opportunities in ways that the segregationists of the Jim Crow era never achieved (Rodriguez 2017).

How did this happen? The specific tools of legislative and judicial desegregation did not account for the resilience of white individuals and their communal commitments to inequality. Whereas in the South the Ku Klux Klan and White Citizens Councils used rallying cries like "massive resistance" and "segregation forever" to mobilize private-sector (and violent) defenses of white property, in metropolitan regions outside of the South the range of practices to maintain inequality have been described as *predatory inclusion* (Taylor 2019), or the opening of opportunities for homeownership and business creation to black people but on predatory terms. In nearly every town and neighborhood, policies designed to promote black inclusion and equity were sabotaged by banks, insurance companies, and real estate firms as they conspired to create systems of assessment and financing that undermined black access to credit (Weems 1998; Conley 1999; Logan and Parman 2017; Cook 2014; Darity and Mullen 2020). The fee-laden debt and the investment in substandard structures that resulted effectively eradicated the small amounts of wealth that black families had gathered during the Jim Crow years.

Since 1990, black communities in New Jersey have been under assault. Dozens of black towns have disappeared entirely from the landscape as the region grew into a paragon of suburban wealth. Places like Edison, Morristown, Moorestown, Colts Neck, and Rumson have fought fiercely in court to restrict equitable access to quality education. Despite the Mount Laurel decisions that required every community to provide affordable housing, the white, wealthy towns have subverted the ruling to prevent black families from gaining legal residence. As a consequence, the state's schools have become some of the most segregated in the United States: the one hundred whitest districts have fewer than 2 percent black students enrolled. Correspondingly, the twenty districts with the largest African American populations all have fewer than 2 percent white students enrolled. Without explicit reference to race, color-blind socioeconomic practices have expanded the racial inequities in an ostensibly liberal political jurisdiction.

During the decades of the nation's transformation from an industrial economy to the world's leading service provider, black households and communities were almost completely excluded from participation in the creation and expansion of private wealth through technology, health care, and professional service industries (Diamond 2019). Instead, they were targeted by predatory lenders, growing racialized patterns of debt that reinforced long-standing disparities in education, employment, occupational promotion, and health care.

The economic collapse, and subsequent Great Recession, between 2007 and 2009 further diminished the wealth that African American families had acquired over the previous decade. The Obama administration recognized the persistent discrimination that maintained higher levels of black poverty, but it could not enact an agenda that would substantially dismantle these historic barriers. Settling for limited forms of self-help programs (My Brother's Keeper) and other interventions that ignored antiblack racism (Building One America), it lost the opportunity to rebuild black communities that had been destroyed over the previous three generations (Building One America 2020, 2021).

In metropolitan areas nationwide, a clear and recurring pattern has emerged: the path to economic stability has never been secure in the United States. For native-born white Americans, the chance of achieving lifelong economic dignity has been difficult. Immigrant families have faced even greater challenges. However, for African American families, there have been unique and enduring obstacles to escaping the lowest levels of socioeconomic status. Since 1960, deindustrialization has had disparately high impacts on African American economic stability in places like Oakland, Detroit, Newark, Cleveland, Pittsburgh, Baltimore, St. Louis, New Orleans, Memphis, Minneapolis, Los Angeles, and Indianapolis.

Imagine the structure of the American economy like a ladder. Education, income, and occupation allow households to climb higher. Wealth enables access to the top of the ladder and prevents any chance of a sliding descent. Before 1960, African American families could rarely advance beyond the bottom two or three levels. Civil rights reforms allowed greater possibilities to access the middle portions of the ladder. As shown in chapter 2 of this volume, the racial wealth gap is the deepest, most persistent expression of antiblack racism in American history. Jobs, education, and access to public facilities were all difficult for black people to obtain, but wealth accumulation was beyond what white segregationists would allow. Likewise, as chapter 4 shows, the emphasis on equal access to public education would allow black Americans only to gain access to better jobs, stores, and neighborhoods. The most elite levels of business ownership and capital distribution remained out of reach. The only path to economic stability for African Americans—allowing them to achieve a position at the top of the ladder—is reparations.

African Americans have had their success and autonomy systematically thwarted by an economic system designed by nationalists and segregationists. Even as proverbially "color-blind" reforms emerged after 1994, the new laws created additional barriers to black wealth creation and permanence. Ironically, civil rights laws were adopted in ways that dismantled the black institutional infrastructure that made the political advancements possible. By 2010, the majority of African American communities across the southern United States had less access to financial capital, housing assets, and global investment than they had had in 1970. Worse, regional forms of racial segregation emerged that put new limits on affluent black communities in places like Charleston, Savannah, Montclair, Charlotte, Atlanta, Houston, and Prince George's County. A nationwide, federal plan for reparations is essential to reverse 245 years of dedicated law and private policy that have sabotaged black success.

Consider the massive community redevelopment funding attached to American military bases worldwide. For a century, these directed investments have sustained small towns across North America and around the world. In the shift from "Rust Belt" cities of the industrial Midwest to "Sun Belt" cities stretching from Los Angeles to Charlotte, the defining factor has been changes in the priorities for military investment in different states and local communities (Schulman 1994; Greason and Pratcher 2017). Between 1960 and 2010, nearly $11.2 trillion in new investment shifted from the Great Lakes region to the Sun Belt region as a result of private sector deregulation, deindustrialization, and shifts in federal military spending (Greason, Gorman, and Ziobro 2015). If a fraction of these funds helped to restore black communities in the century ahead, structural economic autonomy might become a reality.

Smaller, local attempts to achieve reparations through correcting the effects of an unequal housing market are insufficient. However, they might move the nation forward toward a federal and nationwide reparations law. Consider the New Deal interventions in public housing. These legislative actions transformed the housing landscape and dramatically reduced the levels of homelessness that were common before 1940. The only limitation on their success was the determination to slash the underlying public funding after 1970 (Kusmer and Trotter 2009). The marketplace fails to offer the basic human right to safe and secure homes for all people. Millions of Americans remain dependent on local and state partnerships with private philanthropy to access inadequate shelter. With a strong federal agenda for reparations in the housing market, black homelessness would be abolished. Veterans, single mothers, and Americans with disabilities would achieve new levels of dignity within twenty-four months of implementation.

One of the key areas of discussion is scale. Ongoing, public conversations through social media have raised engagement with research by Lisa Cook, Trevon Logan, and William Darity Jr. (Cook 2014; Logan and Parman 2017; Darity and Mullen 2020). These economists make essential contributions by grounding the claims of federal reparations in both historical research and stratification economics.

Urban and social historians have added important methodological and evidentiary elements to this policy framework. For a decade, Mary Sies and the Society for American City and Regional Planning History have organized regular studies of local, regional, and federal housing and economic development policy. This research has made it possible to teach ongoing, evolving patterns of racial discrimination in education, occupations, income, and wealth accumulation in works like *Planning Future Cities* (Greason and Pratcher 2017) and *Cities Imagined* (Greason and Chambliss 2018).

Planning Future Cities shows the ways that banks and state governments collaborated in limiting the conditions that permitted black participation in the regional and national economic structures. Even the National Association of Real Estate Brokers has been forced to confess its long-standing discriminatory practices that made much of the racial wealth gap grow (NAREB 2020). *Planning Future Cities* takes another step forward by showing promising advances in growing metropolitan areas that allow more opportunities for African American households to create and preserve wealth.

Still, these existing changes fall short of the necessary realities of a federal reparations law. For that work, greater imagination is essential. *Cities Imagined* explains the ways new teachers and students can engage with the models offered by stratification economics. By documenting past instances of wealth creation, especially in terms of housing and commercial enterprises, *Cities Imagined* examines untold stories of black affluence within the restrictions of Jim Crow. It advances the work of Juliet Walker (1998), Robert Weems (1998), and the *Journal of African American History*. More importantly, it examines the possibility for future economic autonomy by exploring the evolution of fictional places (like Wakanda) that energized the world's imagination about the concept of enduring black wealth.

In the early 1980s, writers thought that if the nation could see a professional black family as a success story on prime-time television, it would mean that civil rights laws might endure. Media producers began to offer images of a black president twenty years before it became a reality. And in the same way, Wakanda (and other black speculative spaces) created a generation that now has a vision of a black nation and economy unburdened by segregation and colonialism.

Once an idea has taken root, it becomes very difficult to prevent its manifestation. In 1881, Booker T. Washington and a host of black educators imagined a network of black churches and schools that would educate black people nationwide; such networks persist to this day. In 1901, T. Thomas Fortune organized networks of black businesses and political action groups that transformed the nineteenth-century literary club movement into a platform that produced Ida Wells-Barnett, W.E.B. DuBois, Marcus Garvey, Zora Neale Hurston, and William "Count" Basie. By 1935, Mary McLeod Bethune leveraged these networks to expand the work of the Second New Deal, inspiring the activist campaigns of A. Philip Randolph, Paul Robeson, Lena Horne, Jackie Robinson, and Adam Clayton Powell. Only in the last decade have researchers begun to appreciate how scientists like Walter McAfee and Katherine Johnson helped black families achieve new levels of professional success, housing equity, and political representation. McAfee and Johnson opened doors for new opportunities in public sector employment, especially within the US military and among a wide range of defense contractors. Between 1946 and 1981, this rising trend of professional employment dramatically expanded the black middle class in the United States (Katz, Stern, and Fader 2005).

These people all lived freedom dreams that made real versions of Wakanda possible in the twentieth century. What would a black utopia in the housing sector involve? To start with, it would abolish homelessness. In the next phase, it would guarantee renters' rights nationwide via protection from predatory landlords. For middle-class households, it would regulate the mortgage markets to lower interest rates and allow greater flexibility in forbearance over longer periods of time. At the top of the market, it would enable structural interventions in transportation, health care, and food access so that the best housing options would be more widely available at lower costs. Federal interventions to underwrite (and subsidize) black banks, insurance companies, and realtors for the next two centuries would correct the worst abuses of black people across every level of this sector. Indeed, subsidized housing cooperatives should become universal in every black community in the United States. The study of and engagement with these data are key in the development and implementation of a federal, nationwide reparations law.

Thus the outcomes of forthcoming national elections hold two versions of the United States in the balance. Should the conservative coalition force stagnation over the next decade, the erosion of metropolitan areas will accelerate with an economic system dedicated to the dominance of large, private firms at the expense of black households (Coates 2015; Darity and Mullen 2020). With victories for a moderate-left coalition, a renewed commitment to consumer globalization will unfold, still leaving most black Americans on the outside of any chance at real prosperity in the decades ahead. In the context of a commitment to a radical agenda of reparations, entirely new frameworks of land use and residential development must emerge (Greason and Pratcher 2017; Greason and Goldberg 2018). The subsidies for single-family residential development cannot continue. Local models of mixed-income, multiple-family housing have proven successful in pursuit of black economic justice in places like Seattle, Portland, and Nashville (Next City 2007–9). The demagoguery against building sustainable communities must be driven from every legislature.

Ultimately, it is an ethic of caring about all people, and especially black populations most injured by past public policy, that must prevail. In a system that derives wealth from predatory inclusion and ongoing segregation, it is impossible to achieve human dignity and economic autonomy. Without structural change in this moment, it will likely be another century before the next chance for change emerges.

NOTE

1. *Working class* here can be defined as household income 50 percent above the poverty line; *middle class* similarly can be defined as 100 percent above the poverty line (Conley 1999).

REFERENCES

Ammon, Francesca Russello. 2016. *Bulldozer: Demolition and Clearance of the Postwar Landscape*. New Haven, CT: Yale University Press.

Armstead, Myra B. Young. 1999. *Lord, Please Don't Take Me in August: African Americans in Newport and Saratoga Springs, 1870–1930*. Urbana: University of Illinois Press.

Baradaran, Mehrsa. 2017. *The Color of Money: Black Banks and the Racial Wealth Gap*. Cambridge, MA: Belknap Press of Harvard University Press.

Brown, Dorothy A. 2021. "Your Home's Value Is Based on Racism." *New York Times*, March 20. www.nytimes.com/2021/03/20/opinion/home -value-race-taxes.html.

Building One America. 2020. "Reimagining Opportunity: An Agenda for Racial Justice and Middle Class Opportunity for All Americans within a Metropolitan

Framework. Executive Summary." https://buildingoneamerica.org/sites/default/files/attachments/reimagining_opportunity2.pdf.

———. 2021. "Building One America: Create Inclusive Jobs; Support Inclusive Communities; Promote Sustainable Regions for an Inclusive and Expanded Middle Class." https://buildingoneamerica.org/sites/default/files/attachments/boa_infrastructure_0.pdf.

Coates, Ta-Nehisi. 2015. *Between the World and Me*. New York: Random House.

Cohen, Lizabeth. 2004. *A Consumers' Republic: The Politics of Mass Consumption in Postwar America*. New York: Vintage Books.

Conley, Dalton. 1999. *Being Black, Living in the Red: Race, Wealth, and Social Policy in America*. Berkeley: University of California Press.

Connolly, N.D.B. 2014. *A World More Concrete: Real Estate and the Remaking of Jim Crow South Florida*. Chicago: University of Chicago Press.

Cook, Lisa D. 2014. "Violence and Economic Activity: Evidence from African American Patents, 1870–1940." *Journal of Economic Growth* 19 (2): 221–57. https://doi.org/10.1007/s10887-014-9102-z.

Darity, William A., and A. Kirsten Mullen. 2020. *From Here to Equality: Reparations for Black Americans in the Twenty-First Century*. Chapel Hill: University of North Carolina Press.

Diamond, Michael L. 2019. "Middle Class in NJ: Where You Grow Up Determines If You Will Be Rich or Poor." *Asbury Park Press*, April 12. www.app.com/story/news/investigations/2019/04/08/where-you-grow-up-determines-if-you-rich-poor/3078143002/.

Freestone, Robert, Isabelle Gournay, and Mary Corbin Sies. 2019. *Iconic Planned Communities and the Challenge of Change*. Philadelphia: University of Pennsylvania Press.

Freund, David M. 2004. *Colored Property: State Policy and White Racial Politics in Suburban America*. Chicago: University of Chicago Press.

Greason, Walter. 2013. *Suburban Erasure: How the Suburbs Ended the Civil Rights Movement in New Jersey*. Madison, NJ: Fairleigh Dickinson University Press.

Greason, Walter, and Julian Chambliss. 2018. *Cities Imagined: The African Diaspora in Media and History*. Dubuque, IA: Kendall Hunt.

Greason, Walter, and David E. Goldberg. 2018. *Industrial Segregation*. Dubuque, IA: Kendall Hunt.

Greason, Walter, William M. Gorman, and Melissa Ziobro, eds. 2015. *The American Economy*. Dubuque, IA: Kendall-Hunt.

Greason, Walter, and Anthony Pratcher. 2017. *Planning Future Cities*. Dubuque, IA: Kendall Hunt.

Hayden, Dolores. 2003. *Building Suburbia: Green Fields and Urban Growth, 1820–2000*. New York: Vintage Books.

Isenberg, Alison. 2004. *Downtown America: A History of the Place and the People Who Made It*. Chicago: University of Chicago Press.

Jackson, Kenneth T. 1985. *Crabgrass Frontier: The Suburbanization of America*. New York: Oxford University Press.

Kahrl, Andrew W. 2016. *The Land Was Ours: How Black Beaches Became White Wealth in the Coastal South.* Baltimore: Project Muse.

Katz, Michael B., Mark J. Stern, and Jamie J. Fader. 2005. "The New African American Inequality." *Journal of American History* 92 (1): 75–108. https://doi.org/10.2307/3660526.

Kruse, Kevin M. 2005. *White Flight: Atlanta and the Making of Modern Conservatism.* Princeton, NJ: Princeton University Press.

Kusmer, Kenneth L., and Joe William Trotter. 2009. *African American Urban History since World War II.* Chicago: University of Chicago Press.

Logan, Trevon D., and John M. Parman. 2017. "The National Rise in Residential Segregation." *Journal of Economic History* 77 (1): 127–70. https://doi.org/10.1017/s0022050717000079.

Massey, Douglas S., and Nancy A. Denton. 1993. *American Apartheid: Segregation and the Making of the Underclass.* Cambridge, MA: Harvard University Press.

Michney, Todd M. 2017. *Surrogate Suburbs: Black Upward Mobility and Neighborhood Change in Cleveland, 1900–1980.* Chapel Hill: University of North Carolina Press.

NAREB (National Association of Real Estate Brokers). 2020. "Minorities and Mortgages: Black Leaders' Thoughts on Closing the Racial Divide." 2020. *National Association of Real Estate Brokers Blog,* June 16. www.nareb.com/minorities-and-mortgages-black-leaders-thoughts-on-closing-the-racial-divide/.

Next City. 2007–9. "Feature Archives." *Next City.* https://nextcity.org/features/archives/P20.

Nicolaides, Becky M. 2002. *My Blue Heaven: Life and Politics in the Working-Class Suburbs of Los Angeles, 1920–1965.* Chicago: University of Chicago Press.

Orfield, Gary, Jongyeon Ee, and Ryan Coughlan. 2017. "New Jersey's Segregated Schools: Trends and Paths Forward." Civil Rights Project, report, November 9. www.civilrightsproject.ucla.edu/research/k-12-education/integration-and-diversity/new-jerseys-segregated-schools-trends-and-paths-forward/New-Jersey-report-final-110917.pdf.

Pattillo, Mary E. 2007. *Black on the Block: The Politics of Race and Class in the City.* Chicago: University of Chicago Press.

Rodriguez, Robyn Magalit. 2017. *In Lady Liberty's Shadow: The Politics of Race and Immigration in New Jersey.* New Brunswick, NJ: Rutgers University Press.

Satter, Beryl. 2009. *Family Properties: Race, Real Estate, and the Exploitation of Black Urban America.* New York: Picador.

Schulman, Bruce J. 1994. *From Cotton Belt to Sunbelt: Federal Policy, Economic Development, and the Transformation of the South, 1938–1980.* Durham, NC: Duke University Press.

Seligman, Amanda I. 2005. *Block by Block: Neighborhoods and Public Policy on Chicago's West Side.* Chicago: University of Chicago Press.

Sorkin, Michael. 1992. *Variations on a Theme Park: The New American City and the End of Public Space.* New York: Hill and Wang.

Straus, Emily E. 2014. *Death of a Suburban Dream: Race and Schools in Compton, California*. Philadelphia: University of Pennsylvania Press.

Sugrue, Thomas J. 1996. *The Origins of the Urban Crisis: Race and Inequality in Postwar Detroit*. Princeton, NJ: Princeton University Press.

Taylor, Keeanga-Yamahtta. 2019. *Race for Profit*: Chapel Hill: University of North Carolina Press.

Tractenberg, Paul, Gary Orfield, and Greg Flaxman. 2013. *New Jersey's Apartheid and Intensely Segregated Schools: Powerful Evidence of an Inefficient and Unconstitutional State Education System*. Report, October 1. Newark, NJ: Rutgers University–Newark.

Vale, Lawrence J. 2018. *After the Projects: Public Housing Redevelopment and the Governance of the Poorest Americans*. New York: Oxford University Press.

Walker, Juliet E.K. 1998. *The History of Black Business in America: Capitalism, Race, Entrepreneurship*. Chapel Hill: University of North Carolina Press.

Weems, Robert E. 1998. *Desegregating the Dollar: African American Consumerism in the Twentieth Century*. New York: New York University Press.

Wiese, Andrew. 2004. *Places of Their Own: African American Suburbanization in the Twentieth Century*. Chicago: University of Chicago Press.

Wolcott, Victoria W. 2012. *Race, Riots, and Roller Coasters: The Struggle over Segregated Recreation in America*. Philadelphia: University of Pennsylvania Press.

4

Educational Inequities and the Case for Reparations

MALIK EDWARDS

When in 1954 Chief Justice Earl Warren wrote, "It is doubtful that any child may reasonably be expected to succeed in life if he is denied the opportunity of an education," the US Supreme Court affirmed educational opportunity as firmly implanted in the lexicon of fundamental rights upon which the American concept of democracy is based.[1]

Unfortunately, for far too many black and Latino students, that promise is not met. It is not met because many of those students are trapped in racially and economically isolated urban schools. This isolation is the continuation along what was defined in the Kerner Commission Report as a path toward two nations—one white and one black, separate and unequal (Kerner 1968). In fact, demographics shifts have exacerbated the effects of segregation identified in the Kerner Commission Report. When the postindustrial economy emerged in the US, there was a bifurcation of the middle class, such that the upper middle class and above became wealthier, while the rest of the nation became poorer; consequently income inequality grew and poverty deepened.

This matters in the context of reparations because, as Massey and Fischer (2000) have documented, "Stratification in the socio-economic sphere was accompanied by a growing spatial separation between classes." As a result, reformers cannot hope to narrow the educational achievement gap by addressing education alone. America's schools continue to be racially, ethnically, and economically segregated, and classrooms that used to be integrated are resegregating at a rapid pace.

Educational disparities are linked to intentional policy decisions that are documented throughout this text and that I will explore in the educational context below. The examination of policies and their effects on the unequal distribution of educational resources begins with Reconstruction and continues through the Jim Crow era and, finally, the post-Brown modern era.

RECONSTRUCTION

The Reconstruction period illuminates the power and effectiveness of the federal government to address structural barriers to educational equity, further reinforcing arguments of why the failure of the federal government to act creates a justification for remedies. The passage of the Reconstruction Amendments extended the promise of citizenship denied by the US Supreme Court in *Dred Scott v. Sandford* to people of African descent.[2] With passage of the Civil Rights Act of 1866 (42 U.S.C.A. §1981), Congress created the Freedmen's Bureau, funded by the Department of War, and granted it the authority, albeit without any appropriations, to establish public schools for the newly freed slaves (Williams 2006, 445).

From 1865 to 1870, the Freedmen's Bureau opened over four thousand schools, which were attended by more than 250,000 black people (see Du Bois (2002, 102)). It should be noted that the Freedmen's Bureau provided the first public schooling for blacks, as well as the first public schooling for whites in much of the South (Williams 2006, 445–46). The authorities who wanted to deny education to blacks also wanted to deny it to poor whites for similar reasons. It was understood that "a man's children should be educated by himself, in proportion to his social status. . . . The state should play no role, lest it might provoke unrest which could result only in disappointment. . . . Only when charity absolutely demanded it should the state intervene" (Pearson 1917, quoted in Williams 2006, 475). This understanding of charity and who was worthy was clearly colored by race and class. Money alone does not move one's social status; money may be lost and status retained. This phenomenon is indicative of an understanding that education supports social replication.

Former Confederate states were required to enact provisions guaranteeing the civil and political rights of all citizens of their states to gain readmittance into the Union (Beaubrun 2020, 209).[3] In *Black Reconstruction in America: 1860–1880*, W. E. B. Du Bois (1935/1992) examined the compromise required for readmission of southern states. The case of Virginia is illustrative.

In 1870, Virginia amended its constitution to require free public education for all children in the state, without respect to race.[4] Du Bois (1935/1992) writes that "the attempt to establish a public school system was vigorously opposed by the reactionaries, but with the backing of the Negroes, the Constitution provided for a uniform system of public schools to be established not later than 1876." Its support "was to be obtained from a corporation tax of $1 and a small property tax" (54). Du Bois notes that the issue of whether there should be two school systems, black and white, had been intensively debated at the 1867 constitutional convention: "The Negroes especially insisted upon mixed schools and the final report made no specific reference to whether the schools were to be mixed or segregated" (54). Neither did the 1870 constitution explicitly address this issue.

Du Bois writes that "the Constitution did not provide for separate schools, but the laws under it did" (54). The results were that "the first schools were opened in 1870, and by the end of the year, there were 2,900 schools, and 130,000 pupils, and 3,000 teachers. Of these, 706 were Negro schools, and 38,554 pupils. The Negroes were eager for the schools, but the whites were largely indifferent. There was a scarcity of Negro teachers and many white teachers were used" (54).

In some ways Virginia did the minimum required for readmission to the Union.[5] This process shows both the challenges to and promises of receiving an education on equal terms. Even at this moment the Radical Republicans refused to back a provision that would provide for integrated education as demanded by Virginia's black citizens (Du Bois 1935/1992, 542).[6]

The promise of a reversal of antiliteracy laws gave formerly enslaved people a newfound hope in obtaining an education. Nevertheless, their struggle for an adequate education, whether integrated or segregated, would continue to be a hard one, for literacy symbolized "a skill that contradicted the status of slaves" (Anderson 1988, 16).

The powers that be understood this, and the quest for education, as for all other civil rights, attracted their constant vigilance. The Freedmen's Bureau was disbanded by 1870 (Morgan 1991, 103). In Virginia, when the conservatives regained power in 1871, one year after the adoption of the new constitution, lawmakers enacted a measure establishing a state school board, the local members of which would be appointed by the state superintendent, the governor, and the attorney general (Williams 2006, 447). This structure ensured that only whites would lead the state system of schooling (McCrary 1995, 1281). During this white-led period, lawmakers formalized the system of segregated schools (Williams 2006, 448).[7]

In Virginia, as in much of the South, fortunes of black schooling changed with political administrations. The Republicans retook power from 1879 to 1883, resulting in the establishment of a Normal and Collegiate Institute, a postsecondary school for African Americans (Williams 2006, 448). This "Readjuster" period, however, was cut short by white terrorism in the Danville riots (Pearson 1917). Because the Readjusters were thwarted, they could not undo the damage caused by the earlier administration, and the continuation of a separate and unequal Jim Crow system of education was assured.[8]

JIM CROW

America's dual system of education and the concept of separate but equal had been introduced during the pre–Civil War period, not in the slaveholding states of the South, but rather in Boston. In *Roberts v. City of Boston*, suit was brought on behalf of Sarah Roberts, a black child who was denied admission to the elementary school nearest her home because it was an all-white school.[9] The Massachusetts Supreme Court considered whether, even though the applicable statutes were silent about race, each child was to attend the school nearest to his or her residence unless special provisions were made. The court justified requiring her to attend a school established for blacks even though it was further from her home because it was in all other respects "equal."

The Jim Crow system of American apartheid was given federal approval by the Supreme Court in *Plessy v. Ferguson*.[10] When *Roberts v. City of Boston* was decided, the Fourteenth Amendment had not yet been contemplated, and it was generally understood that the US Constitution did not apply to the states.[11] In fact the Bill of Rights was not held to apply to the states through incorporation until the 1940s. As discussed above, the Reconstruction Amendments, particularly the Fourteenth Amendment, were created to establish, unambiguously, citizenship to African Americans. The Fourteenth Amendment was made necessary by the Supreme Court's decision in *Dred Scott*, which denied claims of citizenship brought by persons of African descent.[12]

Plessy was a public accommodations case, examining a Louisiana statute requiring "equal but separate" passenger coaches for black and white train riders.[13] *Plessy* relied on *Roberts* to support its conclusion that "legal equality" meant equality in the sphere of politics and that the social sphere was beyond the reach of the court's authority.[14]

Justice Harlan, in a withering dissent, took his brethren to task for their failure to recognize the connection between the social and political spheres:

> In respect of civil rights, common to all citizens, the constitution of the United States does not, I think, permit any public authority to know the race of those entitled to be protected in the enjoyment of such rights. Every true man has pride of race, and under appropriate circumstances, when the rights of others, his equals before the law, are not to be affected, it is his privilege to express such pride and to take such action based upon it as to him seems proper. But I deny that any legislative body or judicial tribunal may have regard to the race of citizens when the civil rights of those citizens are involved. Indeed, such legislation as that here in question is inconsistent not only with that equality of rights which pertains to citizenship, national and state, but with the personal liberty enjoyed by everyone within the United States.
>
> The thirteenth amendment does not permit the withholding or the deprivation of any right necessarily inhering in freedom. It not only struck down the institution of slavery as previously existing in the United States, but it prevents the imposition of any burdens or disabilities that constitute badges of slavery or servitude. It decreed universal civil freedom in this country. This court has so adjudged. But, that amendment having been found inadequate to the protection of the rights of those who had been in slavery, it was followed by the fourteenth amendment, which added greatly to the dignity and glory of American citizenship, and to the security of personal liberty, by declaring that "all persons born or naturalized in the United States, and subject to the jurisdiction thereof, are citizens of the United States and of the state wherein they reside," and that "no state shall make or enforce any law which shall abridge the privileges or immunities of citizens of the United States; nor shall any state deprive any person of life, liberty or property without due process of law, nor deny to any person within its jurisdiction the equal protection of the laws." These two amendments, if enforced according to their true intent and meaning, will protect all the civil rights that pertain to freedom and citizenship. Finally, and to the end that no citizen should be denied, on account of his race, the privilege of participating in the political control of his country, it was declared by the fifteenth amendment that "the right of citizens of the United States to vote shall not be denied or abridged by the United States or by any state on account of race, color or previous condition of servitude."[15]

Although not an education case, *Plessy* reified the Jim Crow system, which resulted not only in enabling white supremacist policies but also in emboldening white supremacists themselves.[16]

Three years after Harlan's famous dissent in *Plessy,* he wrote for a unanimous court in *Cumming v. Richmond County Board of Education.*[17] In *Cumming,* the parents of black high school children sued the Georgia Board of Education for shutting down the only black high school in the area, as the board had argued that the black high school students could attend a private high school.

The court rejected the challenge and allowed a county to close its high school designated for African American students while keeping open its two high schools designated for white students.[18] The reasoning of the court, a justification still seen today, was that so long as citizens shared equitably in the financial burden of educating children, the federal courts had no power to interfere with the purely local educational judgments of the states:

> [The state court] rejected the suggestion that the board proceeded in bad faith or had abused the discretion with which it was invested by the statute under which it proceeded or had acted in hostility to the colored race. Under the circumstances disclosed, we cannot say that this action of the state court was, within the meaning of the Fourteenth Amendment, a denial by the state to the plaintiffs and to those associated with them of the equal protection of the laws or of any privileges belonging to them as citizens of the United States. We may add that while all admit that the benefits and burdens of public taxation must be shared by citizens without discrimination against any class on account of their race, the education of the people in schools maintained by state taxation is a matter belonging to the respective states, and any interference on the part of Federal authority with the management of such schools cannot be justified except in the case of a clear and unmistakable disregard of rights secured by the supreme law of the land.[19]

This argument invites the question of what meaning can be made of the equal provision of the "separate but equal" formulation if the complete deprivation of high school education to black children, in a town that provided two high schools for white children, could satisfy that condition. Gary Orfield (2005, 1051), the director of the Civil Rights Project, has noted that *Plessy v. Ferguson* was the law of the land for two-thirds of a century before *Brown* and that there is "no evidence of a school system that was separate and equal. No one has nominated a community at any point in time in American history where that condition existed."

BROWN AND BEYOND

As we think about what the Supreme Court's decision in *Brown* might have been, the understanding of reparations becomes even more important. *Brown* built upon not only the precedent above but also developments in social science research.[20] Myrdal's *An American Dilemma* (1944) became yet another in a long string of texts to identify racism as the continuing issue holding back American progress. Myrdal documented from the perspective of an economist "the vicious circle of cumulative causation" that existed in America (207). Blacks began at a disadvantage as a result not only of slavery but also of the caste system that followed it. This framework roots discrimination in a tradition of economic exploitation: "The very fact that the masses of Negroes, because of economic discrimination—partly caused by social inequality—are prevented from entering even the bottom of the occupational hierarchy, are paid low wages and, consequently, are poor gives in its turn motivation for continued social discrimination" (643).

Segregation laws were causal because they worked to institutionalize a system of exploitation. Such a construction contradicted the holdings of all of the courts since *Plessy* that viewed segregation as merely the preservation of the status quo. Charles S. Johnson's *Statistical Atlas of Southern Counties* (1941) documents the concentration of blacks in rural counties to support the agricultural economy. Of 551 cotton counties, only 37 had equal average expenditures for the education of black children.

The court in *Brown* overturned *Plessy*'s finding, quoting "a finding in the Kansas case [98 F. Supp. 797 (D. Kan. 1951)] by a court which nevertheless felt compelled to rule against the Negro plaintiffs":

> "Segregation of white and colored children in public schools has a detrimental effect upon the colored children. The impact is greater when it has the sanction of the law; for the policy of separating the races is usually interpreted as denoting the inferiority of the negro group. A sense of inferiority affects the motivation of a child to learn. Segregation with the sanction of law, therefore, has a tendency to [retard] the educational and mental development of negro children and to deprive them of some of the benefits they would receive in a racial[ly] integrated school system." Whatever may have been the extent of psychological knowledge at the time of *Plessy v. Ferguson*, this finding is amply supported by modern authority. Any language in *Plessy v. Ferguson* contrary to this finding is rejected.[21]

The framing of the Supreme Court's decision in *Brown* in some ways limits its effectiveness in support of arguments for reparations, a function of its misuse of the social science evidence and a continuing failure to heed Harlan's recognition of white supremacy as the primary justification for segregation. *Brown* is at its core a decision grounded in a deficit-based understanding of blackness. It was not the harm created by spending deficits but the need for proximity to whiteness that the court addressed, because the court's goal was to overturn *Plessy*.

Any examination of *Brown* and American educational policy more generally must be conducted with a full awareness of Derrick Bell's (1980) interest convergence theory. Interest convergence acknowledges that not only racist measures but seemingly antiracist reforms occur only when they advance the interests of the majority group—that is, white Americans (Delgado and Stefancic 2001).[22] An understanding of interest convergence helps us to understand why the remedial aspects of the *Brown* legacy are linked almost exclusively to the integration ideal. Wendy Scott (1994, 537) uses the terms *integrative* and *integrationism* to describe "the idea of according equality to racial and cultural minority group Americans through the process of increasing opportunities for racial mixing with white Americans. In its most radical form, integrationism results in the virtual assimilation of the minority group into the dominant culture."

While the integration ideal is consistent with the goals of Justice Marshall and the NAACP Legal Defense Fund in arguing *Brown I*, it is limited from a policy perspective and helps to explain why the harms requiring reparations are still accruing in the post-*Brown* era. The Supreme Court has made it clear that not every racial disparity within a school system is a constitutional violation. When deciding whether a particular racial inequality violates equal protection under *Brown*, courts consider if the inequality involves one of the six factors identified in *Green v. County School Board* or in a particular desegregation decree.[23] Using this limited reading, most federal courts examining the achievement gap have declined to consider it a vestige of past discrimination.[24]

The result of such a limited policy perspective is that almost seventy years after *Brown*, demographic shifts have left the majority of black youths in marginalized schools. They are politically abandoned in failing schools, and traditional desegregation remedies cannot address the educational deprivations.

The call for reparations does not require an argument as to the effectiveness of integration. The research, as we know, is mixed. While studies have found more positive than negative educational outcomes regarding black students, for the most part, no effect has been demonstrated on white achievement (Crain and Mahard 1982; Longshore and Prager 1985).

Crain and Mahard (1982) performed a meta-analysis of the early research that suggests two contextual features of desegregated schools. First, they found that achievement improves most when blacks are in schools that are mostly white and include students from higher socioe-conomic status backgrounds. Second, plans with metropolitan scope, including suburbs and not just isolated center cities, show greater black achievement gains. The success of metropolitan remedies has been linked to the ability to reach more middle-class whites (Kazal-Thresher 1993). This research has led to the conclusion that successful desegrega-tion remedies must address socioeconomic as well as racial issues (Kazal-Thresher 1993; Longshore and Prager 1985).

Regardless of the effectiveness of integration plans, the policy winds have shifted. In 1974 the Supreme Court began to abandon the promise of *Brown*; *Milliken v. Bradley* (*Milliken I*) marks the beginning of its retreat from attempting to achieve racial integration in America's schools.[25] *Milliken I* rejected a remedy that would have created a "met-ropolitan" school district encompassing Detroit, Michigan, and its sur-rounding suburbs. The court held that unless a constitutional violation on the part of one of the suburban districts leading to the segregation in the urban districts could be shown, interdistrict remedies were not allowed. With its ruling that residential segregation can be addressed only through unitary remedies, *Milliken I* signals the beginning of the end to federal supervision of desegregation plans.

In *Milliken II* (1977) the Supreme Court held that the state could pay for educational programs to repair the harm caused by segregation.[26] Although not framed as such, *Milliken II* supports a call for repara-tions. Orfield and Eaton (1996) called this a return to "separate but equal" because it allowed states to maintain segregated school systems as long as they attempted to address the underlying harm. The critique is grounded in the integration ideal and ignores the fact that there is a harm that must be compensated.

In *Board of Education of Oklahoma City Public Schools v. Dowell* (1991), the Supreme Court established a "good-faith" test allowing courts to relinquish supervision over desegregation orders once a dis-trict had shown a good-faith effort to comply with the order and to eliminate segregation "to the extent practicable."[27] Finally, in *Freeman v. Pitts,* the Supreme Court allowed courts to withdraw supervision of desegregation cases in incremental stages over those areas where the school district had complied if they met the good-faith standard from *Dowell*.[28] Once the standard was met, districts were declared unitary (nonsegregated) and were removed from court supervision.

After the US Supreme Court authorized a return to segregated schools with its decision in *Dowell,* the percentage of African American students attending majority nonwhite schools increased, from 66 percent in the 1991–92 school year to 73 percent in the 2003–4 school year. Latino students found themselves even more segregated, with 75 percent of them attending predominantly minority schools in the 2003–4 school year, an increase from 73 percent in the 1991–92 school year (Orfield and Lee 2006, 10–11). This resegregation was the result of white flight and actions taken by the state to appease white and middle-class families to keep them in school districts. The distinction between parental choice and state action is important for purposes of litigation but less so for crafting an argument for reparations.

Litigation addresses the termination of government oversight in districts found to be de jure segregated, or segregated by law. The Supreme Court has long held that de facto segregation, segregation not directly attributable to state action, such as that attributable to residential segregation, is not actionable.[29] The court has also made it almost impossible to establish de jure segregation. The court in *Columbus Board of Education v. Penick* required that the plaintiffs present direct, rather than circumstantial, evidence of intent to segregate: "Disparate impact and foreseeable consequences, without more, do not establish a constitutional violation."[30] Even the statutory cause of action for discrimination in education, created by Title VI of the 1964 Civil Rights Act, 42 U.S.C. § 2000(c), (d) (1970), requires proof of intent to segregate (Morgan 1991, 110).

Racial isolation tells only part of the story; as Orfield and Lee (2005) point out, segregation by race is "systematically linked to other forms of segregation, including segregation by socioeconomic status, by residential location, and increasingly by language." This segregation is more often than not found in urban centers that have been largely abandoned by white and middle-class flight to the suburbs. These urban centers are marred by poor housing stock, weak and failing infrastructure, poor job prospects, and municipal overburden, all of which work together to adversely affect educational success.[31]

Denise Morgan (1991, 109) eloquently explains why integration has been ineffective:

Integration failed to remedy the inadequacy of educational opportunity for several reasons. First, the litigation of the 1950s and 60s was only partially successful in getting Black children out of segregated schools and into integrated schools. In 1980, 33% of Black students in the United States attended racially-isolated schools, and almost 63% attended schools that were at least half non-white. The experience of integration was radically different in different areas of the country. In the South, less than 25% of Blacks were in racially isolated schools in 1980, as opposed to 77.8% in 1968. In the Northeast the trend was reversed; almost half of all Black children attended schools where less than one-tenth of the students were white, and the racial disparity was widening. More importantly, since students spend most of their time in classrooms, "on average, across the nation 5 percent more classrooms than schools have more than half non-Anglo students; 3 percent more classrooms than schools have over 90 percent non-Anglo students." Tracking programs tend to build another level of segregation into our school system: students of color are more likely to be tracked into lower academic ability groups than are their white counterparts.[32]

This harm must be a part of any examination of reparations for African Americans. Lucas and Paret (2005), in their article "Law, Race, and Education in the United States," explain the role of education in creating "structures of opportunity." "Students are allocated to schools, and within schools to courses, classrooms, and teachers. Educational opportunity is structured by these allocations" (205). They illustrate that characteristics associated with educational success are racialized across the board (as captured in table 4.1).

These disparities are clearly actionable. The issue can be framed in Denise Morgan's (1991, 117) terms of citizens having "a property interest in minimally adequate education." Morgan's argument is grounded in Charles Reich's (1964) New Property Theory. According to Reich, government benefits and services should be treated as property subject to the Due Process Clause of the Fourteenth Amendment ("Nor shall any State deprive any person of life, liberty, or property, without due process of law" [§ L]) and to the Just Compensation Clause of the Fifth Amendment ("Nor shall private property be taken for public use, without just compensation"), which applies to states through the Fourteenth Amendment. Reich argued that "'property' is a creation of the state": that "the concept of private ownership is only meaningful because the state recognizes the existence of private rights in wealth and enforces those rights. As a result of his conception of property, Reich questioned the distinction between traditional property—like land and money— and 'new property'—government distributed benefits and services. He claimed that land, welfare benefits, and government-provided services were all property, because without state support, citizens would not have a sense of entitlement to any of them" (Morgan 1991, 118).

In *Board of Regents v. Roth*, the Supreme Court articulated a test for determining which governmentally created property interests should receive protection under the Due Process Clause: "To have a property

TABLE 4.1 PROBABILITY OF HAVING CHARACTERISTICS ASSOCIATED WITH
EDUCATIONAL SUCCESS AND OPPORTUNITY

Characteristic	Student race / ethnicity					
	White	Black	Asian	Latino/a	Native American	Other
*Early childhood**						
Mastering addition and subtraction by the spring of first grade	78.0	56.0	74.0	68.0	—	64.0
Being able to "read words in context" by the spring of first grade	50.0	33.0	57.0	40.0	—	35.0
*High school***						
Achieving the NAEP highest math proficiency level, 17-year-olds, 1999	10.4	1.0	—	3.1	—	—
Taking a high-level combination of courses, 2000 high school graduates	31.5	28.9	37.8	28.4	16.2	—
High school or GED completion by 2000, NELS 1988 eighth grade cohort	94.0	91.0	99.0	87.0	—	—
High school dropout, 16- to 24-year-olds, 2001 (US degrees only)	7.3	10.9	—	27.0	—	—
*Postsecondary transition and completion****						
Postsecondary enrollment by 2000, if high school graduate, NELS 1988 eighth-grade cohort	82.0	80.0	95.0	82.0	—	—
Postsecondary credential by 2000, if college entry, NELS 1988 eighth-grade cohort	46.0	27.0	56.0	23.0	—	—
Bachelor's degree by 1992, 1980 high school sophomores	27.5	12.2	45.6	9.9	7.2	—
*Additional*****						
Special education placement for mental retardation, all grades, 1998	1.2	2.6	0.6	0.9	1.3	—
Placement in a gifted and talented program, all grades, 1998	7.5	3.0	10.0	3.6	4.9	—

Fear of being attacked or harmed at school in the last six months, 12- to 18-year-olds, 1999	3.9	9.0	—	8.1	—	4.2
Ever repeated a grade, all elementary and secondary students	9.0	18.0	7.0	13.0	18.0	—
Ever been suspended or expelled, all elementary and secondary students	15.0	35.0	13.0	20.0	38.0	—

SOURCE: Lucas and Paret (2005).
Abbreviations: NAEP = National Assessment of Educational Progress: NELS = National Education Longitudinal Study.
* Rathbun and West (2004, A-13, A-16).
** NCES (2004, tables 107, 122, 140; 2003a, 1–2).
*** NCES (2004, table 309; 2003a, 1–2).
**** Donovan and Cross (2002, 44, 51); Kaufman et al. (2001, table 12.1); NCES (2003b).

interest in a benefit, a person clearly must have more than an abstract need or desire for it. He must have more than a unilateral expectation of it. He must, instead, have a legitimate claim of entitlement to it. It is a purpose of the ancient institution of property to protect those claims upon which people rely in their daily lives, reliance that must not be arbitrarily undermined."[33]

Morgan (1991) argues that education satisfies all four prongs of the Roth Test.

1. As was clear to the then recently freed Black people who organized Black schools and desperately sought to become literate during the Reconstruction era, education is a prerequisite to political and social empowerment in a democratic society. Because functional literacy is essential to both the exercise of fundamental rights and the opportunity for economic advancement, students have more than "an abstract need or desire" for education (117).

2. The claim of entitlement to an adequate education is not unilateral, but arises from the states' provision of public schools and promulgation of compulsory school attendance laws. . . . Property rights in government benefits are most frequently derived from state law: Property interests, of course, are not created by the Constitution. Rather they are created and their dimensions are defined by existing rules or understandings that stem from an independent source such as state law—rules or understandings

that secure certain benefits and that support claims of entitlement to those benefits. Almost every state constitution mandates the establishment of a public school system and every state has compulsory attendance laws (120).

3. Although a state is not constitutionally obligated to establish a public school system, once it has done so and required its children to attend, "on the basis of state law, students plainly have legitimate claims of entitlement to a public education" (121).

4. Education is relied upon in daily life. The basics of reading, writing, and arithmetic are necessary to pay bills, to fill out job applications, to order food from a menu, and to perform many other routine tasks (121).

The Supreme Court explicitly stated, in *Goss v. Lopez,* that public education is a property right protected by the Fourteenth Amendment: "The State is constrained to recognize a student's legitimate entitlement to a public education as a property interest which is protected by the Due Process Clause and which may not be taken away for misconduct without adherence to the minimum procedures required by that Clause."[34]

The finding of a property interest matters because the deprivation then may be treated as a taking to be compensated under the Fifth Amendment. But the Supreme Court "has been unable to develop any 'set formula' for determining when 'justice and fairness' require that economic injuries caused by public action be compensated by the government."[35] The Penn Central Court identified three categories of government actions that adversely affect property rights that do not constitute "takings": "The first is the power to tax. The second is the class of cases where the 'taking' is of an interest that is not 'sufficiently bound up with the reasonable expectations of the claimant to constitute "property" for Fifth Amendment purposes.' The last group of non-'takings' cases are those where a 'tribunal reasonably concluded that "the health, safety, morals, or general welfare" would be promoted by prohibiting particular contemplated uses of land'" (Penn Central, quoted in Morgan 1991, 132).

Robert Westley (1998, 456) posits that the norm of reparations is best pursued through the legislative process, arguing that there is a moral principle that "when a State or government has through its official organs— its laws and customs—despoiled and victimized and murdered a group of its own inhabitants and citizens on the basis of group membership, that

State or its successor in interest has an unquestionable moral obligation to compensate that group materially on the same basis." Westley (1998) grounds his arguments in international human rights norms and not in American constitutional constructions of rights and harms (436).

Verna Williams (2006) examines the Brown Fund Act as a reparative measure.[36] The Brown Fund Act is intended to provide some measure of redress for persons harmed by school shutdowns. The scope of the remedy is limited, available only to someone currently "domiciled in Virginia" who

> resided in a jurisdiction in Virginia between 1954 and 1964 in which the public schools were closed to avoid desegregation and who (i) was unable during such years to (a) begin, continue, or complete his education in the public schools of the Commonwealth, (b) attend a private academy or foundation, whether in state or out of state, established to circumvent desegregation, or (c) pursue postsecondary education opportunities or training because of the inability to obtain a high school diploma; or (ii) was required to relocate within or outside the Commonwealth to begin, continue, or complete his K-12 education during such years because of public school closings to avoid desegregation. The Brown Fund Act makes tuition assistance available for pursuing a General Education Development program, a two-year program at the community college level, or a four- or five- year undergraduate degree program. The statute establishes a committee charged with developing criteria for the scholarships, reviewing applications and, ultimately, deciding upon the recipients. Resources for the scholarships are to be appropriated by the General Assembly and may be supplemented by "gifts, donations, bequests, or other funds." The initial appropriation for the scholarships was only $50,000, about one-fourth of what was necessary. However, after a private donor gave $1 million, lawmakers increased the amount to match the private grant. The Brown Fund Act expires in 2008. (435–36)

Funding provides the foundation upon which education systems are built. Three funding sources support schools: state, local, and federal (Robinson 2018, 942). The most recent data indicate that states provide 46.2 percent of funding, districts 45 percent, and the federal government 8.7 percent (NCES 2016a). The proportion of the state contributions varies widely, with a high of 89.8 percent in Vermont and a low of 26 percent in Illinois (NCES 2016b). Districts primarily raise their contributions through property taxes, an arrangement that exacerbates funding disparities because of the wealth differences between communities (Corcoran 2012, 85; Cox, Weiler, and Cornelius 2013, 34).

Linda Darling-Hammond's "Unequal Opportunity: Race and Education" (1998), though dated, provides insight into the source of the harm. Her examination of numerous state studies found that two-thirds of minority students still attended predominantly minority schools, mostly located in central cities and underfunded. On every tangible measure, "schools serving greater numbers of students of color had significantly fewer resources than schools serving mostly white students."

Addressing racialized educational disparities requires a reframing of how we view education. As Orfield and Lee (2005, 8) observe: "The civil rights movement was never about sitting next to whites, it was about equalizing opportunity." We know that high-poverty schools are systematically unequal and that segregated minority schools are almost always high-poverty schools (8). This economic reality results in a resource and opportunity gap that can be documented and must be addressed.

Ultimately, education funding is directly linked to the larger policy decisions discussed in the preceding chapters. We have a funding system where funding is directly linked to property wealth. Court challenges to these (legislatively created) problems have exacerbated the results of a dual system that still isolates the descendants of American slaves in failing schools. Federal courts, in rulings from *Brown* and beyond, have missed opportunities to address multigenerational spending disparities. They have placed systemic disparities outside of their remedial purview. By ignoring the demographic reality of American segregation and authoring deficit-based decisions, they have set education on a path that will never approach equality.

What Greason noted in the context of housing policy in chapter 3 is equally true in education: it is "impossible to achieve human dignity and economic autonomy" without an equitable educational system. The failures of policy makers to acknowledge this have established, maintained, and perpetuated inequities that, to be alleviated, will require a substantial infusion of resources. Said another way, the US education system, rather than leveling the playing field and providing a means of restitution, has only amplified the necessity of reparations for black Americans.

NOTES

1. Brown v. Board of Education, 347 U.S. 483, 493 (1954).
2. *Dred Scott v. Sandford*, 60 U.S. 393 (1857). The court held that "A free negro of the African race, whose ancestors were brought to this country and sold as slaves, is not a 'citizen' within the meaning of the Constitution of the United States." The Reconstruction Amendments are the Thirteenth, Fourteenth, and Fifteenth Amendments to the US Constitution. The Thirteenth abol-

ished chattel slavery; the Fourteenth gave birthright citizenship, and the Fifteenth extended the right to vote to African American men.

3. See also Williams (2006, 446).

4. Virginia Constitution of 1870, article VIII, §§ 3, 4.

5. See Williams (2006, 446): "Congress had to approve the 1870 Constitution in order to put an end to federal military occupation of Virginia. In keeping with the constitutional guarantee of 'equal civil and political rights and privileges.'"

6. This proposal "failed to get the support of enough Radicals to be adopted, in spite of the efforts on the part of the Negro delegates" (Du Bois 1935/1992, 542).

7. See also 1876–77 Virginia Acts, chap. 38 (providing for the establishment of free public schools as long as "white and colored persons [were] not taught in the same school, but in separate schools under the same general regulations as to management, usefulness, and efficiency").

8. It should be recognized that segregation in education was not limited to the South. Stephenson (1910) noted that only three states never required segregation in schooling: Arizona, Rhode Island, and Colorado.

9. Roberts v. City of Boston, 59 Mass. (5 Cush. 198 (1850)).

10. Plessy v. Ferguson, 163 U.S. 537 (1896).

11. See Barron v. City of Baltimore 32 U.S. 243 (1833). The court held that the Bill of Rights applied to the federal government and not to the states. Also see 60 U.S. 393 (1857).

12. Dred Scott v. Sandford, 60 U.S. (19 How.) 393 (1857).

13. *Plessy*, 163 U.S. 537.

14. *Plessy*, 163 U.S. at 543–45.

15. *Plessy*, 163 U.S. at 554–56 (Harlan, J., dissenting).

16. See Darity and Mullen (2020, 174), identifying the rise of "dismemory" campaigns following the court's decision in *Plessy*.

17. Cumming v. Richmond County Board of Education, 175 U.S. 528 (1899).

18. *Cumming*, 175 U.S. at 544–45.

19. *Cumming*, 175 U.S. at 545.

20. In footnote 11 in *Brown,* the court presents the social science research to establish the detrimental effects of segregation and support the decision.

21. *Brown I*, 347 U.S. at 494–95.

22. For the landmark statement of this position, see Bell (2001).

23. Green v. County School Board of New Kent County, VA, 391 U.S. 430 (1968). Green held that "racial identification of the systems was complete, extending not just to the composition of the student bodies at the two schools but to every facet of school operations—faculty, staff, transportation, extracurricular activities and facilities."

24. Hampton v. Jefferson County Board of Education, 102 F. Supp. 2d 358, 366 (2000).

25. Milliken v. Bradley, 418 U.S. 717 (1974).

26. Milliken v. Bradley, 433 U.S. 267 (1977).

27. Board of Education of Oklahoma City Public Schools v. Dowell, 498 U.S. 237, 249–50 (1991).

28. Freeman v. Pitts, 503 U.S. 467 (1992).

29. See *Milliken I*, 418 U.S. 717.

30. Columbus Board of Education v. Penick, 443 U.S. 449, 464 (1979), reh'g denied, 444 U.S. 887 (1979).

31. See also Rothstein (2004).

32. See also Chunn (1989).

33. Board of Regents v. Roth, 408 U.S. 564, 577.

34. Goss v. Lopez, 419 U.S. 565.

35. Penn Central Trans. Co. v. New York City, 438 U.S. 104, 124 (1978).

36. Va. Code Ann. §23–38.53:22C (2004).

REFERENCES

Anderson, James D. 1988. *The Education of Blacks in the South, 1860–1935.* Chapel Hill: University of North Carolina Press.

Beaubrun, Gelsey G. 2020. "Talking Black: Destigmatizing Black English and Funding Bi-dialectal Education Programs." *Columbia Journal of Race and Law* 10:196–244.

Bell, Derrick A. 1980. "*Brown v. Board of Education* and the Interest-Convergence Dilemma." *Harvard Law Review* 93 (3): 518–33. https://doi.org/10.2307/1340546.

———. 2001. *Race, Racism, and American Law.* 3rd ed. Boston: Little, Brown.

Chunn, Eva. 1989. "Sorting Black Students for Success and Failure: The Inequity of Ability Grouping and Tracking." In *Black Education: A Quest for Equity and Excellence,* edited by Willy DeMarcell Smith and Eva Chunn, 93–106. London: Routledge.

Corcoran, Sean P. 2012. "The Role of Local Revenues in Funding Disparities across School Districts." In *The Stealth Inequities of School Funding: How State and Local School Finance Systems Perpetuate Inequitable Student Spending,* by Bruce D. Baker and Sean P. Corcoran. Washington, DC: Center for American Progress.

Cox, Betty, Spencer C. Weiler, and Luke M. Cornelius. 2013. *The Costs of Education: Revenue and Spending in Public, Private and Charter Schools.* Lancaster, PA: ProActive Publications.

Crain, Robert L., and Rita E. Mahard. 1982. *Desegregation Plans That Raise Black Achievement: A Review of the Research.* Santa Monica, CA: RAND Corporation. www.rand.org/pubs/notes/N1844.html.

Darity, William A., Jr., and A. Kirsten Mullen. 2020. *From Here to Equality: Reparations for Black Americans in the Twenty-First Century.* Chapel Hill: University of North Carolina Press.

Darling-Hammond, Linda. 1998. "Unequal Opportunity: Race and Education." Brookings, March 1. www.brookings.edu/articles/unequal-opportunity-race-and-education/.

Delgado, Richard, and Jean Stefancic. 2001. *Critical Race Theory: An Introduction.* New York: New York University Press.

Donovan, M. Suzanne, and Christopher T. Cross, eds. 2002. *Minority Students in Special and Gifted Education.* Washington, DC: National Academy Press,

National Research Council Committee on Minority Representation in Special Education.

Du Bois, W. E. B. 1935/1992. *Black Reconstruction in America: 1860–1880.* New York: Touchstone Books.

———. 2002. "The Freedman's Bureau." In *Du Bois on Education,* edited by Eugene F. Provenzo Jr., 95–110. Walnut Creek, CA: AltaMira.

Johnson, Charles S. 1941. *Statistical Atlas of Southern Counties.* Chapel Hill: University of North Carolina Press.

Kaufman, Philip, Xianglei Chen, Susan P. Choy, Katharin Peter, Sally A. Ruddy, Amanda K. Miller, Jill K. Fleury, Kathryn A. Chandler, Michael G. Plany, and Michael R. Rand. 2001. *Indicators of School Crime and Safety: 2001.* NCES 2002-113/NCJ-190075. Washington, DC: US Departments of Education and Justice. https://files.eric.ed.gov/fulltext/ED457602.pdf.

Kazal-Thresher, Deborah M. 1993. "Merging Educational Finance Reform and Desegregation Goals." *Education Policy Analysis Archives* 1 (7): 1–21.

Kerner, Otto. 1968. *Report of the National Advisory Commission on Civil Disorders.* Washington, DC: Bantam Books.

Longshore, Douglas, and Jeffrey Prager. 1985. "The Impact of School Desegregation: A Situational Analysis." *Annual Review of Sociology* 11:75–91. www.jstor.org/stable/2083286.

Lucas, Samuel R., and Marcel Paret. 2005. "Law, Race, and Education in the United States." *Annual Review of Law and Social Science* 1 (1): 203–31. https://doi.org/10.1146/annurev.lawsocsci.1.041604.115931.

Massey, Douglas S., and Mary J. Fischer. 2000. "How Segregation Concentrates Poverty." *Ethnic and Racial Studies* 23 (4): 670–91. https://doi.org/10.1080/0141987005033676.

McCrary, Peyton. 1995. "Yes, but What Have They Done to Black People Lately: The Role of Historical Evidence in the Virginia School Board Case—Freedom: Constitutional Law." *Chicago-Kent Law Review* 70:1275–1305. https://scholarship.kentlaw.iit.edu/cklawreview/vol70/iss3/11.

Morgan, Denise C. 1991. "What Is Left to Argue in Desegregation Law? The Right to Minimally Adequate Education." *Harvard Blackletter Journal* 8:99–133.

Myrdal, Gunnar. 1944. *An American Dilemma: The Negro Problem and Modern Democracy.* With Richard Sterner and Arnold Rose. 9th ed. New York: Harper.

NCES (National Center for Education Statistics). 2003a. "The Condition of Education 2003." https://nces.ed.gov/pubs2003/2003067.pdf.

———. 2003b. "Percent of Elementary and Secondary Students Who Had Ever Repeated a Grade or Been Suspended/Expelled, by Race/Ethnicity: 1999." https://nces.ed.gov/pubs2003/hispanics/figures.asp?PopUp=true&FigureNumber=3_2.

———. 2004. "Digest of Education Statistics 2003." https://nces.ed.gov/pubs2005/2005025.pdf.

———. 2016a. "Digest of Education Statistics, 2016: Table 235.10." https://nces.ed.gov/programs/digest/d16/tables/dt16_235.10.asp.

———. 2016b. "Digest of Education Statistics, 2016: Table 235.20." https://nces.ed.gov/programs/digest/d16/tables/dt16_235.20.asp.

Orfield, Gary. 2005. "Why Segregation Is Inherently Unequal: The Abandonment of *Brown* and the Continuing Failure of *Plessy*." *New York Law School Law Review* 49:1041–52.

Orfield, Gary, and Susan E. Eaton. 1996. *Dismantling Desegregation: The Quiet Reversal of Brown v. Board of Education*. New York: New Press.

Orfield, Gary, and Chungmei Lee. 2005. *Why Segregation Matters: Poverty and Education Inequality*. Cambridge, MA: Civil Rights Project at Harvard University.

———. 2006. *Racial Transformation and the Changing Nature of Segregation*. Cambridge, MA: Civil Rights Project at Harvard University.

Pearson, Charles Chilton. 1917. *The Readjuster Movement in Virginia*. New Haven, CT: Yale University Press.

Rathbun, Amy, and Jerry West. 2004. "From Kindergarten through Third Grade: Children's Beginning School Experiences." *Education Statistics Quarterly* 6 (3): 7–15.

Reich, Charles A. 1964. "The New Property." *Yale Law Journal* 73 (5): 733–87. https://doi.org/10.2307/794645.

Robinson, Kimberly Jenkins. 2018. "Restructuring the Elementary and Secondary Education Act's Approach to Equity." *Minnesota Law Review* 103 (2): 915–98.

Rothstein, Richard. 2004. *Class and Schools: Using Social, Economic, and Educational Reform to Close the Black-White Achievement Gap*. Washington, DC: Economic Policy Institute.

Scott, Wendy B. 1994. "Justice Thurgood Marshall and the Integrative Ideal." *Arizona State Law Journal* 26:535.http://dx.doi.org/10.2139/ssrn.1626889.

Stephenson, Gilbert Thomas. 1910. *Race Distinctions in American Law*. New York: D. Appleton.

Westley, Robert. 1998. "Many Billions Gone: Is It Time to Reconsider the Case for Black Reparations?" *Boston College Third World Law Journal* 19 (1): 429–76. https://lawdigitalcommons.bc.edu/twlj/vol19/iss1/12.

Williams, Verna L. 2006. "Reading, Writing, and Reparations: Systemic Reform of Public Schools as a Matter of Justice." *Michigan Journal of Race and Law* 11:419–75.

5

The African American Health Burden

Disproportionate and Unresolved

KEISHA L. BENTLEY-EDWARDS

Across a broad spectrum of health indicators, African Americans carry a heavier burden of mortality and morbidity—even for diseases and conditions with effective standards of care. These poorer health outcomes can be seen throughout the life span. For example, black babies are more than twice as likely to die in their first year of life as white babies, typically because of low birth weight and prematurity. Black children, adolescents, and young adults are more likely to die from treatment-responsive cancers than their white counterparts (Siegel et al. 2020; Johnson 2020). Black men and women aged forty-five to sixty-four are at more than twice the risk of a fatal first-time heart attack as white people who are the same age (Colantonio et al. 2017).

As researchers and practitioners adopt a social determinants of health approach in understanding these disparities, they need to focus on the enduring effects of sociohistorical contexts that include slavery and *Dred Scott v. Sandford,* reconstruction, the de jure racist laws of the Jim Crow era, and contemporary racism (Duran and Pérez-Stable 2019). Ultimately, sociohistorical context matters. As noted by Darity (2008), the objectives of reparations include acknowledgment, redress, and closure.[1] Current health inequities can be traced to unresolved debts and harms that have diminished African American health; their acknowledgment needs to be included in the reparations discourse.

BLACK HEALTH AND ILLNESS, HISTORICALLY SPEAKING

What happened on that auction block centuries ago is still unfinished business for African-American women today.

—Wyatt (1999, 3)

During the American antebellum period, enslaved people were used for medical experiments that, if successful, meant they or their progeny would be unlikely to benefit. In her 2006 book *Medical Apartheid,* Harriet Washington writes of ongoing medical experimentation on black Americans from enslavement until contemporary times. Medical experiments that occurred during slavery typically involved insufficient or (more commonly) no anesthesia, even when it was readily available. Providing insufficient anesthesia to black people is based upon the false belief that black people do not experience pain similarly to whites. This perception that black people do not experience pain, or are faking the severity of their pain, was considered factual at the onset of formal medical training, and the consequences can be seen in modern practices today (Green, Baker, et al. 2003; T. Baker and Green 2005; Green, Anderson, et al. 2003; Badreldin, Grobman, and Yee 2019; Groenewald et al. 2018; Liao and Reyes 2018; Hoffman et al. 2016; Tipton 1886). In the antebellum era of medical experimentation, physicians acquired enslaved individuals with the expressed intent of medical experimentation (Washington 2006; Berry 2017).

J. Marion Sims, the physician noted for being the father of modern gynecology, is also noted for his medical experimentation on enslaved women (Badreldin, Grobman, and Yee 2019; Washington 2006; Ojanuga 1993). Sims is known for inventing the first iterations of the modern speculum and for perfecting a surgical procedure that corrected vesicovaginal fistulas, a severe complication of long and arduous childbirths. Sims himself acknowledged performing procedures on fourteen enslaved women, although this number may be underestimated. Three enslaved women were surgically experimented upon repeatedly: Lucy, Betsey, and Anarcha. Sims performed approximately thirteen surgeries on Anarcha over a four-year period, most times without anesthesia, and often with an audience (Ojanuga 1993).

Medical experimentation and training on enslaved people, whether they were alive or dead, were common practice for both private physicians and medical schools (Berry 2017; Washington 2006). Literally, from the womb to the tomb, black bodies were a key part of the education and innovation practices of American medical communities (Berry 2017).

Sympathizers argue that these practices were legal and acceptable by the standards of the time and that Sims and his colleagues cannot be critiqued with a contemporary lens (Wall 2006). However, this frame ignores the fact that some people at the time openly stated that this practice was morally wrong or, at the very least, fiscally irresponsible (Ojanuga 1993; Sausser 2017). Experimenting on enslaved people was seen as a waste of resources and property, since they needed to be fed, housed, and monitored, without the immediate financial benefit of their labor. Further, some white people were willing to participate in surgical experiments without compensation (Ojanuga 1993). But experimenting on white people required (informed) consent, and all the rights and care that come with consent when one is considered to be a person. Wall (2006) argued that the enslaved women were willing participants of the surgical experimentation provided by Sims because of their poor health and quality of life. Thus they were "willing" to participate in the extreme measures that Sims offered, painting a picture of benevolence.

However, being willing to participate is not the same as consenting to participate.[2] Even in its most elemental form, these women could not consent to medical experimentation. Informed consent requires volunteerism (absent of coercion), information disclosure, and decision-making capacity (Gupta 2013). On the basis of the Supreme Court's ruling in *Dred Scott v. Sandford*, black people in America, whether free or enslaved, were not considered citizens and had no rights to sue or hold a white person accountable for mistreatment.[3]

Once Sims perfected his surgical method for vesicovaginal fistulas, he stopped performing his experimentation, or any treatment, on enslaved women. His practice focused exclusively on white women; he became the president of the American Medical Association, cofounded the American Gynecological Society, and developed the first (white) women's hospital in America. It should be noted that Sims provided anesthesia to the white women who required surgery for vesicovaginal fistulas, because he understood the procedure was painful. Unfortunately for the enslaved women that served as test subjects, their humanity, suffering, and consent were not his concern; legally, their concerns had no recourse.

RECONSTRUCTION AND THE FREEDMEN'S BUREAU

After the Civil War, three amendments, often referred to as the freedom amendments, were ratified. The Thirteenth Amendment abolished chattel slavery; the Fourteenth Amendment afforded birthright citizenship to all black people, reversing the *Dred Scott* ruling; and the Fifteenth Amendment provided voting rights. Obviously, certain loopholes diminish or eliminate the rights provided by the freedom amendments, particularly to women and imprisoned people. However, these amendments were key for protections offered during Reconstruction and for black people today. The goal of Reconstruction was to offer remedies for some of the physical, political, legal, and financial problems caused by enslavement and the *Dred Scott* case.

Importantly, the Bureau of Refugees, Freedmen, and Abandoned Lands (commonly known as the Freedmen's Bureau) provided federal protection and services to formerly enslaved people and civil war veterans in the southern states and the District of Columbia.[4] The Freedmen's Bureau built schools, colleges, banks, and hospitals among other health, legal, and family services. The promised protections, as well as those that failed to be delivered, continue to have meaningful effects on today's health outcomes.

The Medical Division of the Freedmen's Bureau was created to address the health problems resulting from unattended war injuries, destitution, and disease outbreaks—especially smallpox (Pearson 2002). Often enslavers provided just enough care to ensure that the enslaved could work. As a result, those who were recently enslaved (freedpeople) often had long-neglected health concerns or injuries that needed care, especially the elderly or disabled. These needs were compounded with profound destitution, as many people left plantations without long-term provisions, if any provisions at all. Existing hospitals either were overburdened or excluded black people from care. The Medical Division of the Freedmen's Bureau was necessary, but it was insufficiently resourced to meet the needs of the people it served (Downs 2012).[5]

All activities related to the Freedmen's Bureau were controversial at the time, including the Medical Division. Racist tropes of freedpeople becoming too dependent on treatment and/or faking their medical needs in order to avoid work were a constant part of the political discourse (Pearson 2002; Downs 2012).[6] Calls for unity between the North and the South did not include the health concerns of, or the debt owed to, the freedpeople who were at the core of the Civil War.

DESTRUCTION/DISINVESTMENT OF BLACK HEALTH INSTITUTIONS

When Reconstruction ended in 1877, its Medical Division was also dismantled. The Freedmen's Hospital in Washington, D.C., was later reestablished as Howard University Hospital; it is the only remaining facility affiliated with the Medical Division of the Freedmen's Bureau. Several hospitals and health care training facilities for physicians, nurses, and dentists were created by and for black people in the late nineteenth and early twentieth centuries. Although hospitals dedicated to the care of black people were first founded in the 1830s in Georgia, Provident Hospital and Training School in Chicago was the first black-owned and operated hospital in America in 1891.[7] As black people used collective efforts to build towns or neighborhoods, hospitals and other health care facilities, as well as health training facilities, were part of the infrastructure building that occurred in these locations.

Hospitals and Health Care Facilities

Throughout the United States, black physicians and patients had limited access to predominantly white medical facilities. Black communities and white philanthropists invested in creating facilities that catered to black health care. During the racial terror campaigns of Reconstruction and the Jim Crow eras, black hospitals and clinics were included as targets for destruction (Bentley-Edwards et al. 2018; Wells-Barnett 1900; Parshina-Kottas et al. 2021). Despite these repeated assaults, black health facilities were rebuilt out of necessity because of de jure segregation in the South and exclusionary practices in the North (separate wards within facilities).

By 1944, there were 124 historically black hospitals where black patients could receive care and physicians could practice fully independently. Particularly in the 1950s and 1960s, pressure to desegregate was countered by southern states investing in historically black facilities to give the facade of "separate but equal" treatment as conditioned by the *Plessy v. Ferguson* (1896) Supreme Court ruling. Hospitals were included in these segregation efforts.

In 1965, the United States Congress passed the Social Security Amendments, officially known as the Medicare and Medicaid Act. A provision of Medicare was that only desegregated medical facilities were eligible to receive federal funds. This desegregation of health care facilities opened access to care and well-resourced facilities to black people, particularly those from rural communities. The desegregation provision was not only included but enforced with unannounced site visits, demonstrating the federal government's ability to influence state and private institutions' policies concerning race (Smith 2016).

An unintended consequence of the act's desegregation provision was that governments began to systematically disinvest in historically black hospitals. Although historically black hospitals had always been integrated (anyone could receive service regardless of race), no protections were put into place to preserve their continued operation. Additionally, black people began to seek services at both historically black and white health institutions, while white people continued to use these same white facilities, resulting in a significant drop in revenue in historically black hospitals. As the black facilities closed, black physicians and nurses were not hired into white hospitals, which often questioned their credentials. Today, only one historically black hospital remains, Howard University Hospital.[8]

The problem is not that there is only one historically black hospital in America. The key issue is that when these hospitals and health clinics were shut down in waves after the Medicare and Medicaid Act and again in the 1980s and 2010s, facilities were not built to replace them. As a result, predominantly black communities, whether urban or rural, once again face a shortage of local providers and accessible health care (Rau and Huetteman 2020; Whiteis 1992; Thomas, Holmes, and Pink 2016). Direct monetary reparations can provide the resources to access available hospital systems and the financial weight to demand better training of the providers at these facilities to improve African American health outcomes.

Medical Colleges

In 1910, there were fourteen medical schools that specifically trained black physicians and numerous others that trained health care professionals like nurses and dentists (Campbell et al. 2020; Harley 2006).[9] The American Medical Association (AMA) and the American Association of Medical Colleges (AAMC), in collaboration with the Rockefeller and Carnegie Foundations, were trying to standardize and regulate medical education in order to exclude institutions they deemed to be subpar (Brown 1979). Despite its long history of nonconsenting medical experimentation and training on black bodies, Johns Hopkins University was still seen as the standard bearer for medical training and innovation (Berry 2017; Washington 2006; Lederer 1995).

Commissioned by the Carnegie Foundation, the Flexner Report is often heralded as the turning point of modern medical training and thus modern medicine. Its author, Abraham Flexner, visited over 150 medical schools across the country, including seven black institutions. Unsurprisingly, he determined that five of the seven black institutions he visited were not suitable for medical education.[10] With regard to the two black medical colleges, Howard University College of Medicine and Meharry Medical College, that he recommended preserving, Flexner felt that these two institutions should remain in place to promote the training of sanitarians rather than black physicians. He famously stated that black physicians should be trained in "hygiene rather than surgery" to keep the broader white community safe from communicable diseases like tuberculosis (Campbell et al. 2020; Harley 2006).

The effects of the Flexner Report on black medical schools were immediate. Unable to acquire licensing, hospital privileges, and residents, those five medical schools, as well as others that were already struggling financially, were shuttered. The training of their students and alumni was not acknowledged, AMA membership was denied, and outside of historically black hospitals and institutions professional advancement was impossible (R. Baker et al. 2008).

The National Medical Association, an organization for black physicians and dentists, took up the charge to maintain the quality and status of the two remaining black medical schools and black physicians across the country. With the closing of their peer institutions, money was directed into Howard and Meharry's medical schools, especially by the Rockefeller Foundation. Support of Howard and Meharry ensured the availability of black physicians (with significant white oversight and provisions), while relieving pressure on white schools of medicine to enroll these students. It took more than fifty years before another black medical college, the Charles R. Drew College of Medicine and Science, was founded in 1966. Morehouse College of Medicine was founded in 1975. In 2008, the AMA commissioned a report that examined its harms to black physicians and institutions, resulting in an official apology but no plan of redress (R. Baker et al. 2008).

Campbell et al. (2020) determined that if the five medical colleges that were closed because of the Flexner Report had remained open, they would have produced over thirty thousand black physicians over the last hundred years. Further, they estimated that there would be almost 30 percent more black doctors currently available had those five medical schools remained in operation.[11] At the rate of enrollment for the top twenty residency specialty areas (between 2007 to 2018),[12] it would take between thirty-seven and seventy-seven years for these physician trainees to achieve the 13 percent representation found in the general population (Bennett et al. 2021).

The importance of black doctors goes beyond the concept of having a racially diverse workforce; it is also a key indicator for black health outcomes. Physician-patient racial concordance, or a doctor's sharing of a racial identity with their patient, has been associated with improved health communications, treatment adherence, and health outcomes in general (Shen et al. 2018; Konrad et al. 2005; Greenwood et al. 2020). One study examined racial concordance between black doctors and infants in Florida to determine its effects on infant mortality (Greenwood et al. 2020). The researchers found that black doctors who delivered black babies halved the infant mortality gap between black and white babies. Black doctors had even better outcomes with black babies during medically complex deliveries and in hospitals with a higher number of black patients. It should be noted that black physicians performed similarly to their white counterparts with white patients. These findings bring to light that equal access to health providers does not ensure equal care, at least not for black people. The loss of a strong black physician workforce has real life-and-death consequences—consequences that are the direct result of systemic racism and disinvestment in black health and its supporting institutions. Proposals for reparations must include both direct compensation and infrastructure support for medical training that focuses on African American physician and other health provider training.

BLACK HEALTH: A LEGACY OF HIGH RISKS AND LOW REWARDS

Poor health in the black community has been deemed endemic, with an ahistorical lens on the precursors and maintenance of these conditions. On the contrary, whether we are examining large public health data, health policies, or individual health experiences, it becomes clear that our past is ever present—sociohistorical contexts matter.

Black people have been involved as subjects and developers of scientific innovation in medicine, taking the greatest risks for science while reaping minimal rewards (Gamble 1997). We can point to Lucy, Betsy, and Anarcha; Henrietta Lacks; the men and their families in the Tuskegee Syphilis Study; and countless others who were not considered fully human enough to receive appropriate consent and available care during medical experimentation. Dr. Charles Drew, the physician-scientist who perfected large-scale blood banking, was not immune from racist health policies. As a black man, he was not initially eligible to donate or receive blood transfusions using the techniques that he created. Both then and now, there are policy makers and medical professionals who believe in the biological difference and/or inferiority of black people.

Race-based science is a part of the legacy of slavery and medical experimentation that allows race correction to exist today in obstetrics, nephrology, neuroscience, pulmonology, and other specialties (Norris, Eneanya, and Boulware 2021; Braun 2021).[13] Although race correction is being reevaluated and in some cases rescinded as a part of standards of care by several professional medical associations, such practices would be dismissed as unacceptable if race was understood as a social construct rather than a biological construct.

The heavy health burden faced by black people in America is not accidental, nor is it an act of God. Individual health behaviors can only function within the systems where they exist. Black people cannot wait another seventy-five years for the physician workforce to be representative of its population so that they can receive equitable, quality care. As seen by the Medicare and Medicaid Act, the federal government has the capability to intervene when discriminatory practices or policies that have disparate impacts are in place. Now is the time for the federal government to address and provide redress for these racial health disparities. Reparations closure is possible only when racial health and wellness gaps are also closed.

NOTES

1. Acknowledgment includes both a public recognition of egregious harm and a public apology for committing or allowing these harms to occur. Redress occurs when compensatory actions are taken to remedy the harms. Closure, which is a healing process, can be found only after acknowledgment and redress have been sufficiently implemented (Darity and Mullen 2020).

2. In the United States, informed consent became standardized and regulated in the twentieth century. However, physicians were expected to follow ethical standards of care and harm reduction for hundreds of years prior to the onset of these regulations. See Gupta (2013) for elegant definitions and components of informed consent.

3. In his infamous *Dred Scott v. Sandford* (1856) opinion, US Chief Justice of the Supreme Court Roger B. Taney (1860, 18) stated that black people "had for more than a century before been regarded as beings of an inferior order, and altogether unfit to associate with the white race, either in social or political relations; and so far inferior, *that they had no rights which the white man was bound to respect*; and that the negro might justly and lawfully be reduced to slavery for his benefit. He was bought and sold, and treated as an ordinary article of merchandise and traffic, whenever a profit could be made by it" (emphasis added).

4. The Freedmen's Bureau also provided care to poor white southerners, especially plantation employees and Confederate soldiers who were displaced in the aftermath of the Civil War.

5. In addition to the political controversy over whether freedpeople would become dependent on government aid, sufficient land was difficult to acquire in southern states. Former enslavers were recovering their land, and white townspeople sabotaged efforts to build resources dedicated to freedpeople.

6. These beliefs that black people exaggerate their pain or conditions to take advantage of systems, whether to be released from work duties or to gain access to disability-related Social Security benefits, persist and are reflected in today's racial disparities in health care.

7. Provident Hospital was founded by a black surgeon, Dr. Daniel Hale Williams, and remained open as a private hospital until 1987. It was reopened as Provident Hospital of Cook County in 1993.

8. At the turn of the twenty-first century, there were two historically black hospitals. However, Riverside General Hospital in Houston, Texas, originally called Houston Negro Hospital, was closed in April 2015. In 2018, Harris County commissioners agreed to reopen Riverside General Hospital in the future as an integrated primary and behavioral health facility, rather than a comprehensive care hospital (Zaveri and George 2018).

9. To be clear, a tradition of black healing and healers existed since long before the establishment of modern medical schools.

10. The five medical colleges Flexner identified as unsuitable for education were Flint Medical College of New Orleans University, Louisiana (1889–1911); Knoxville Medical College, Tennessee (1900–1910); Leonard Medical School of Shaw University, North Carolina (1882–1912); Louisville National Medical College, Kentucky (1888–1912); and University of West Tennessee College of Medicine and Surgery–Memphis (1907–23) (Campbell et al. 2020).

11. The percentage of physicians who were black in 1900 was 1.3 percent. In 2019, 2.6 percent of physicians were African American (Ault 2021; Association of American Medical Colleges 2020).

12. These twenty residency programs represent roughly 80 percent of all physician trainees.

13. Race correction, or race norming, is the practice of adjusting clinical guidelines on the basis of race or ethnicity, with white populations serving as the normative standard. Typically, these guidelines determine the point in which a medical intervention is necessary and typically require a greater threshold for black people. Race correction is rooted in Thomas Jefferson's writings of pulmonary structural differences in enslaved people that, in addition to purported biological, moral, and intellectual insufficiencies, represented one of many innate barriers to their freedom (Braun 2021).

REFERENCES

Association of American Medical Colleges. 2020. *The Complexities of Physician Supply and Demand: Projections from 2018 to 2033.* Washington, DC: Association of American Medical Colleges.

Ault, Alicia. 2021. "Percentage of Doctors Who Are Black Barely Changed in 120 Years." *Medscape Medical News,* April 21. www.medscape.com /viewarticle/949673.

Badreldin, Nevert, William Grobman, and Lynn Yee. 2019. "Racial Disparities in Postpartum Pain Management." *American Journal of Obstetrics and Gynecology* 220 (1): 1147–53.

Baker, Robert B., Harriet A. Washington, Ololade Olakanmi, Todd L. Savitt, Elizabeth A. Jacobs, Eddie Hoover, and Matthew K. Wynia. 2008. "African American Physicians and Organized Medicine, 1846–1968: Origins of a Racial Divide." *JAMA* 300 (3): 306–13. https://doi.org/10.1001/jama.300.3.306.

Baker, Tamara A., and Carmen Renee Green. 2005. "Intrarace Differences among Black and White Americans Presenting for Chronic Pain Management: The Influence of Age, Physical Health, and Psychosocial Factors." *Pain Medicine* 6 (1): 29–38.

Bennett, Christopher L., Maame Yaa A.B. Yiadom, Olesya Baker, and Regan H. Marsh. 2021. "Examining Parity among Black and Hispanic Resident Physicians." *Journal of General Internal Medicine* 36 (6): 1722–25. https:// doi.org/10.1007/s11606-021-06650-7.

Bentley-Edwards, Keisha L., Malik Chaka Edwards, Cynthia Neal Spence, William A. Darity, Darrick Hamilton, and Jasson Perez. 2018. "How Does It Feel to Be a Problem? The Missing Kerner Commission Report." *RSF: The Russell Sage Foundation Journal of the Social Sciences* 4 (6): 20–40. https:// doi.org/10.7758/RSF.2018.4.6.02.

Berry, Daina Ramey. 2017. *The Price for Their Pound of Flesh: The Value of the Enslaved from Womb to Grave in the Building of a Nation.* Boston: Beacon Press.

Braun, Lundy. 2021. "Race Correction and Spirometry." *Chest* 159 (4): 1670–75. https://doi.org/10.1016/j.chest.2020.10.046.

Brown, E. Richard. 1979. *Rockefeller Medicine Men: Medicine and Capitalism in America.* Berkeley: University of California Press.

Campbell, Kendall M., Irma Corral, Jhojana L. Infante Linares, and Dmitry Tumin. 2020. "Projected Estimates of African American Medical Graduates of Closed Historically Black Medical Schools." *JAMA Network Open* 3 (8): e2015220. https://doi.org/10.1001/jamanetworkopen.2020.15220.

Colantonio, Lisandro D., Christopher M. Gamboa, Joshua S. Richman, Emily B. Levitan, Elsayed Z. Soliman, George Howard, and Monika M. Safford. 2017. "Black-White Differences in Incident Fatal, Nonfatal, and Total Coronary Heart Disease." *Circulation* 136 (2): 152–66. https://doi.org/10.1161 /circulationaha.116.025848.

Darity, William A. 2008. "Forty Acres and a Mule in the 21st Century." *Social Science Quarterly* 89 (3): 656–64. https://doi.org/10.1111/j.1540-6237.2008 .00555.x.

Darity, William A., and A. Kirsten Mullen. 2020. *From Here to Equality: Reparations for Black Americans in the Twenty-First Century.* Chapel Hill: University of North Carolina Press.

Downs, Jim. 2012. *Sick from Freedom: African-American Illness and Suffering during the Civil War and Reconstruction.* New York: Oxford University Press.

Duran, Deborah G., and Eliseo J. Pérez-Stable. 2019. "Novel Approaches to Advance Minority Health and Health Disparities Research." *American Journal of Public Health* 109 (S1): S8-S10. https://doi.org/10.2105/ajph.2018.304931.

Gamble, Vanessa Northington. 1997. "Under the Shadow of Tuskegee: African Americans and Health Care." *American Journal of Public Health* 87 (11): 1773–78. https://doi.org/10.2105/ajph.87.11.1773.

Green, Carmen R., Karen O. Anderson, Tamara A. Baker, Lisa C. Campbell, Sheila Decker, Roger B. Fillingim, Donna A. Kaloukalani, Kathryn E. Lasch, Cynthia Myers, and Raymond C. Tait. 2003. "The Unequal Burden of Pain: Confronting Racial and Ethnic Disparities in Pain." *Pain Medicine* 4 (3): 277–94.

Green, Carmen R., Tamara A. Baker, Yuka Sato, Tamika L. Washington, and Edna M. Smith. 2003. "Race and Chronic Pain: A Comparative Study of Young Black and White Americans Presenting for Management." *Journal of Pain* 4 (4): 176–83. https://doi.org/ 10.1016/S1526-5900(02)65013-8.

Greenwood, Brad N., Rachel R. Hardeman, Laura Huang, and Aaron Sojourner. 2020. "Physician-Patient Racial Concordance and Disparities in Birthing Mortality for Newborns." *Proceedings of the National Academy of Sciences* 117 (35): 21194–200. https://doi.org/10.1073/pnas.1913405117.

Groenewald, Cornelius B., Jennifer A. Rabbitts, Elizabeth E. Hansen, and Tonya M. Palermo. 2018. "Racial Differences in Opioid Prescribing for Children in the United States." *Pain* 159 (10): 2050–57.

Gupta, Umesh Chandra. 2013. "Informed Consent in Clinical Research: Revisiting Few Concepts and Areas." *Perspectives in Clinical Research* 4 (1): 26–32. https://doi.org/10.4103/2229-3485.106373.

Harley, Earl H. 2006. "The Forgotten History of Defunct Black Medical Schools in the 19th and 20th Centuries and the Impact of the Flexner Report." *Journal of the National Medical Association* 98 (9): 1425–29.

Hoffman, Kelly M., Sophie Trawalter, Jordan R. Axt, and M. Norman Oliver. 2016. "Racial Bias in Pain Assessment and Treatment Recommendations, and False Beliefs about Biological Differences between Blacks and Whites." *Proceedings of the National Academy of Sciences* 113 (16): 4296–4301. https://doi.org/10.1073/pnas.1516047113.

Johnson, Kimberly J. 2020. "Disparities in Pediatric and Adolescent Cancer Survival: A Need for Sustained Commitment." *Cancer* 126 (19): 4273–77. https://doi.org/10.1002/cncr.33079.

Konrad, Thomas R., Daniel L. Howard, Lloyd J. Edwards, Anastasia Ivanova, and Timothy S. Carey. 2005. "Physician–Patient Racial Concordance, Continuity of Care, and Patterns of Care for Hypertension." *American Journal of Public Health* 95 (12): 2186–90. https://doi.org/10.2105/ajph.2004.046177.

Lederer, Susan E. 1995. *Subjected to Science: Human Experimentation in America before the Second World War*. Baltimore: Johns Hopkins University Press, 1995.

Liao, Lucia, and Lilia Reyes. 2018. "Evaluating for Racial Differences in Pain Management of Long-Bone Fractures in a Pediatric Rural Population." *Pediatric Emergency Care* 37 (7): 348–51.

Norris, Keith C., Nwamaka D. Eneanya, and L. Ebony Boulware. 2021. "Removal of Race from Estimates of Kidney Function: First, Do No Harm." *JAMA* 325 (2): 135–37. https://doi.org/10.1001/jama.2020.23373.

Ojanuga, Durrenda. 1993. "The Medical Ethics of the 'Father of Gynaecology,' Dr. J. Marion Sims." *Journal of Medical Ethics* 19 (1): 28–31. https://doi.org/10.1136/jme.19.1.28.

Parshina-Kottas, Yuliya, Anjali Singhvi, Audra D.S. Burch, Troy Griggs, Mika Gröndahl, Lingdong Huang, Tim Wallace, Jeremy White, and Josh Williams. 2021. "What the Tulsa Race Massacre Destroyed." *New York Times,* May 24.

Pearson, Reggie L. 2002. "'There Are Many Sick, Feeble, and Suffering Freedmen': The Freedmen's Bureau's Health-Care Activities during Reconstruction in North Carolina, 1865–1868." *North Carolina Historical Review* 79 (2): 141–81. www.jstor.org/stable/23522765.

Rau, Jordan, and Emmarie Huetteman. 2020. "Urban Hospitals of Last Resort Cling to Life in Time of COVID." KHN, September 17, 2020. https://khn.org/news/urban-hospitals-of-last-resort-cling-to-life-in-time-of-covid/.

Sausser, Lauren. 2017. "J. Marion Sims 'Savior of Women' or Medical Monster? The Fraught Legacy of South Carolina's Most Infamous Physician." *Post and Courier,* April 7.

Shen, Megan Johnson, Emily B. Peterson, Rosario Costas-Muñiz, Migda Hunter Hernandez, Sarah T. Jewell, Konstantina Matsoukas, and Carma L. Bylund. 2018. "The Effects of Race and Racial Concordance on Patient-Physician Communication: A Systematic Review of the Literature." *Journal of Racial and Ethnic Health Disparities* 5 (1): 117–40. https://doi.org/10.1007/s40615-017-0350-4.

Siegel, David A., Lisa C. Richardson, S. Jane Henley, Reda J. Wilson, Nicole F. Dowling, Hannah K. Weir, Eric W. Tai, and Natasha Buchanan Lunsford. 2020. "Pediatric Cancer Mortality and Survival in the United States, 2001–2016." *Cancer* 126 (19): 4379–89. https://doi.org/10.1002/cncr.33080.

Smith, David Barton. 2016. *The Power to Heal: Civil Rights, Medicare, and the Struggle to Transform America's Health Care System.* Nashville, TN: Vanderbilt University Press.

Taney, Roger Brooke. 1860. *The Dred Scott Decision: Opinion of Chief Justice Taney.* Introduction by John H. Van Evrie. Appendix by Samuel A. Cartwright. New York: Van Evrie, Horton.

Thomas, Sharita R., George M. Holmes, and George H. Pink. 2016. "To What Extent Do Community Characteristics Explain Differences in Closure among Financially Distressed Rural Hospitals?" *Journal of Health Care for the Poor and Underserved* 27 (4A): 194–203. https://doi.org/10.1353/hpu.2016.0176.

Tipton, F. 1886. "The Negro Problem from a Medical Standpoint." *New York Medical Journal,* May 22, 14. http://resource.nlm.nih.gov/101710951.

Wall, L.L. 2006. "The Medical Ethics of Dr. J. Marion Sims: A Fresh Look at the Historical Record." *Journal of Medical Ethics* 32 (6): 346–50. https://doi.org/10.1136/jme.2005.012559.

Washington, Harriet A. 2006. *Medical Apartheid: The Dark History of Medical Experimentation on Black Americans from Colonial Times to the Present.* New York: Doubleday Books.

Wells-Barnett, Ida B. 1900. *Mob Rule in New Orleans: Robert Charles and His Fight to the Death, the Story of His Life, Burning Human Beings Alive, Other Lynching Statistics.* Chicago: n.p.

Whiteis, D.G. 1992. "Hospital and Community Characteristics in Closures of Urban Hospitals, 1980–87." *Public Health Reports* (Washington, DC) 107 (4): 409–16.

Wyatt, Gail E. 1999. "Stolen Women: Reclaiming Our Sexuality, Taking Back Our Lives." *Cultural Diversity and Ethnic Minority Psychology* 5 (2): 167–68. https://doi.org/10.1037/1099-9809.5.2.167.

Zaveri, Mihir, and Cindy George. 2018. "Harris County Agrees to Buy Closed Riverside Hospital in Third Ward." *Houston Chronicle,* March 12. www.chron.com/politics/houston/article/Harris-County-seeking-to-turn-shuttered-Riverside-12747818.php.

PART TWO

The Path to Reparations and Related Considerations

6

Learning from Past Experiences with Reparations

A. KIRSTEN MULLEN AND WILLIAM A. DARITY JR.

Thus says the Lord, "Have you murdered and also inherited?"

—1 Kings 21:19 (Jeremiah Study Bible)

In the opening pages of *From Here to Equality,* we describe reparations as "a program of acknowledgment, redress, and closure for a grievous injustice" (Darity and Mullen 2020, 2). Acknowledgment is the recognition and admission of culpability on the part of the perpetrator of the atrocity. Redress is the act of restitution for heinous acts committed by the perpetrator. Closure is the victims' agreement that the perpetrator has met the debt owed and no further claims will be made, unless there is a renewal of the harm or infliction of a new harm.[1]

In the specific case of African American reparations, the objective is to achieve restitution for living black Americans. Black American descendants of persons enslaved in the United States bear the weight of damages produced by the cumulative, intergenerational effects of three phases of American history. These are the atrocities associated with the periods of slavery; legal segregation and white terrorism (blithely referred to as "Jim Crow"); and the era following passage of the Civil Rights Acts of the mid-1960s: mass incarceration, police executions of unarmed blacks, ongoing discrimination in access to employment, credit, and housing, and the black-white gulf in wealth.

With respect to the chasm between black and white wealth, in 2019 the Federal Reserve Board's Survey of Consumer Finances indicated that the average black household had a net worth approximately $840,000 *lower* than the average white household in the US (Bhutta et al. 2020). Correspondingly, black Americans constitute about 12 percent of the nation's population but possess less than 2 percent of the nation's wealth.[2]

This immense differential in wealth dramatically restricts black Americans' ability to survive and thrive. It denies black Americans the effective rights of full citizenship. An individual's or a household's wealth status, more powerfully than their income level, dictates the scope of opportunity to fulfill personal dreams and ambitions.[3] As Hamilton and Darity (2017, 59–60) explain:

> Wealthier families are better positioned to finance elite, independent school and college educations, access capital to start a business, finance expensive medical procedures, reside in neighborhoods with higher amenities, exert political influence through campaign financing, purchase better counsel if confronted with an expensive legal system, leave a bequest, and/or withstand financial hardship resulting from any number of emergencies. . . . Wealth provides financial agency over one's life. Simply put, wealth gives individuals and families choice; it provides economic security to take risks and shield against financial loss. . . .
>
> Finally, wealth is iterative: It provides people with the necessary initial capital to purchase an appreciating asset, which in turn generates more and more wealth, and can be passed from one generation to the next.

The disadvantages associated with lower wealth also are manifest in health disparities. While there is far more research that connects income and educational attainment with variations in health outcome, separate investigations using the Panel Study of Income Dynamics and the Health and Retirement Study suggest a key relationship between racial differences in wealth and racial difference in health (Duncan et al. 2002; Brown, O'Rand, and Adkins 2012). In the US, wealth disparities greatly influence access to adequate quality and quantity of health care; exposure to health hazards and diseases (especially evident in the COVID-19 crisis because of the overconcentration of black workers in low-wage personal services work deemed essential); and access to sound nutrition and opportunities for safe and health-promoting physical activities.

In sum, in *From Here to Equality* we argue that "wealth is the best single indicator of the cumulative impact of white racism over time" (Darity and Mullen 2020, 31). As a result, we propose that a primary objective of a reparations program for black American descendants of US slavery must be elimination of the racial wealth gap. Accomplishing that goal will require increasing black wealth in the United States by at least $14 trillion in 2019 dollars (Darity, Mullen, and Slaughter 2022).

Activation of a federally funded reparations project typically has involved establishing a study commission that charts the case for reparations and details a plan of action for execution of the program of restitution. Such congressional, parliamentary, ministerial, or presidential commissions, or their equivalent, have served as a prelude to reparations initiatives; they are neither new nor rare. They customarily document the scope and impact of the pertinent damages, assess a request or demand for redistributive justice, calculate the amount due to the injured parties, and design procedures for disbursement of payments to eligible recipients.

In what follows, we will focus on the records of five such commissions, four of which resulted in some form of reparations, and derive the lessons learned from each for future redress efforts. The five cases are the deliberations undertaken by the Conference on Jewish Material Claims Against Germany (Claims Conference), the National Advisory Commission on Civil Disorders in the United States, the Commission on Wartime Relocation and Internment of Civilians, the 9/11 Victims Compensation Fund, and the Iran Hostage Relief Fund.

Two of these victim groups—survivors of the World War II Holocaust and families who lost relatives during the events of 9/11—received some form of redistributive justice soon after the period of harm. Our discussion follows the chronology of the creation of the five panels.

REPARATIONS AGREEMENT BETWEEN ISRAEL AND THE FEDERAL REPUBLIC OF GERMANY

Reparations for victims of the Holocaust was proposed formally by the Conference on Jewish Material Claims Against Germany (the Claims Conference). The Claims Conference, established in 1951, still is very much active today. Among its key founders was Nahum Goldmann, then president of the World Jewish Congress. Goldmann, an ardent Zionist who years later would advocate, without success, peaceful resolution of the conflict between the Palestinians and the Israelis, joined with David Ben-Gurion, the first prime minister of Israel, to pursue the cause of reparations from Germany.[4]

By the 1940s, Goldmann already had secured his position as a provocative figure, having expressed enthusiasm for the failed 1937 British plan to partition Palestine into Arab and Jewish states. His insistence, following World War II, that the German government pay reparations both to Israel and to victims of the Holocaust was at least equally controversial.

Goldmann faced vehement, sustained opposition from many *within* the Jewish community who argued against contact or accommodation with a nation whose policy, just a few years earlier, had been outright genocide. But Goldmann felt it was his duty—and the right of the Jewish people—to make a claim for material restitution from Germany and establish the principle that states have a moral, if not legal, duty to make material amends for crimes committed in their name against a weaker people (Zweig 2009).

In 1945, after the Nazi regime was defeated and after the partition of Germany, the expectation grew that West Germany must pay reparations to support resettlement, primarily to Israel, of Jewish refugees displaced and impoverished by the Holocaust. Having the perpetrator meet the costs of resettlement was one of two reasons Ben-Gurion advanced for German material compensation for the atrocity. The second was axiomatic: in Ben-Gurion's words, reparations were required so that "the murderers do not become the heirs as well." If the murderers could not be tried for their crimes, they should, at least, be made to surrender, or pay an appropriate price for, the confiscated property of their victims (Auerbach 1991, 280).

Following six months of negotiations between Israel, the Claims Conference, and the German government, agreement was reached; monetary reparations would be paid by Germany. At the time, in 1952, Ben-Gurion said to Goldmann in a letter, "For the first time in the history of the *Jewish* people, oppressed and plundered for hundreds of years . . . the oppressor and plunderer has had to hand back some of the spoil and pay collective compensation for part of the material losses" (Taylor, Schneider, and Kagan 2009, 104). There was no stipulation that a formal apology also would be offered.

Subsequently, payments were (and still are being) made to the direct survivors of the World War II genocide and forced labor camps as well as to their heirs and descendants. In addition, payments went to the State of Israel, whose government had lobbied on behalf of reparations or *Wiedergutmachung*.[5] By the end of 2020, payments had exceeded 100 billion Deutsche Mark or US$61 billion, and an additional US$662 million has been paid since the beginning of the COVID pandemic.

In 1952, Konrad Adenauer, the West German chancellor, famously said, "In the name of the German people, unspeakable crimes were committed which create a duty of moral and material restitution" (Reinharz and Friesel 2009, 24). His resolute support for reparations proved decisive in gaining the affirmative decision from the Bundestag. This was no

small feat, given the extent of German popular opposition to reparations for Jewish victims of the Holocaust and the State of Israel. The late
historian Tony Judt (2006, 271–72) wrote the following:

> In making this agreement Konrad Adenauer ran some domestic political risk:
> in December 1951, just 5 percent of West Germans surveyed admitted feel-
> ing "guilty" towards Jews. A further 29 percent acknowledged that Ger-
> many owed some restitution to the Jewish people. The rest were divided
> between those (some two-fifths of respondents) who thought that only peo-
> ple "who really committed something" were responsible and should pay,
> and those (21 percent) who thought "that the Jews themselves were partly
> responsible for what happened to them during the Third Reich." When the
> restitution agreement was debated in the Bundestag on March 18th, 1953,
> the Communists voted against, the Free Democrats abstained and both the
> Christian Social Union and Adenauer's own Christian Democratic Union
> were divided, with many voting against any *Wiedergutmachung*. In order to
> get the agreement approved Adenauer depended upon the votes of his Social
> Democratic opponents.

The Claims Conference had succeeded in its aim of establishing a German reparations project, legislated by the German Parliament, despite
lack of support for the *Wiedergutmachung* from the German people.

URBAN UPRISINGS AND THE KERNER COMMISSION

In 1967 the National Advisory Commission on Civil Disorders, known
popularly as the Kerner Commission, after the commission's chair, Otto
Kerner, governor of Illinois from 1961 to 1968, was created under a state
of emergency. In the mid-1960s in over 150 cities, many black Americans, feeling powerless against wage and housing discrimination, a dual
school system that shunted worn and outdated materials and furnishings
to black schools, and unchecked police killings and brutality, took to the
streets and engaged in what were variously called "rebellions" and
"riots." The Chicago, Newark, and Detroit riots of July 23–28, 1967,
were described as among the most destructive in US history and conjured
images of apocalypse. In Detroit, at least forty-three people died, 1,189
were injured, 7,200 arrests were made, and nearly 1,400 buildings were
set on fire, most of them no longer habitable (National Advisory Commission 1968/2016, 92, 103). Over seven thousand National Guard and
US Army troops were called in to put down the insurgency.

Descriptions of the rebellion's destructiveness—the duration of the
mayhem; vast stretches of residential, municipal, and commercial real
estate that were destroyed; the loss of human life—and of the smoldering

divisiveness that lingered recalled earlier events: the New York Draft Riot nearly one hundred years before, in 1863, and the Red Summer of 1919. The New York Draft Riot had been sparked by President Abraham Lincoln's declaration of a mandatory draft to expand Union military forces. What started as a targeted attack on federal, state, and municipal strongholds by whites who opposed Lincoln's mandate expanded to become essentially a race riot: a coordinated attack on black residents and abolitionists (Harris 2004).

The Red Summer of 1919—not a single summer but a hellish eighteen-month period of vigilante rule—had been similarly racially directed: whites, unwilling to accommodate black World War I veterans' demands for equal rights, unleashed a torrent of sustained and horrific acts and laid ruin to black communities in at least thirty-six cities. No national commission was appointed in response to these earlier uprisings to study the root causes of the violence, and no reparations were paid to black American relatives for their loved ones who were killed, nor were the survivors compensated for their injuries or for loss of their property.[6]

What did the country's political landscape look like in the mid-1960s? Democrats maintained control of both the House and the Senate. On the heels of the assassination of President John F. Kennedy in 1963, his vice president and successor, Lyndon Baines Johnson, pushed through the Civil Rights Act in 1964, making it illegal to discriminate on the basis of race, color, creed, sex, or country of origin. In 1965, the Civil Rights Act was followed quickly by the Voting Rights Act, which made it illegal to discriminate in all levels of voting—essentially strengthening the provisions protecting the right to vote guaranteed in the Fourteenth and Fifteenth Amendments to the US Constitution.

While the Detroit riot still was raging, Johnson issued Executive Order 11365, creating the commission and directing its members to document the country's recent eruption of "race riots." The commission was charged with determining why they occurred and what must be done to prevent their recurrence in the future.

Over a seven-month period, the commission, whose members included several corporate CEOs known for their conservative beliefs, held public hearings across the country investigating the five previous turbulent years and, importantly, visited several black communities, becoming radicalized in the process. When the 426-page Kerner Report was published, in March 1968, five months before the deadline set by President Johnson, its unanimous findings became an instant bestseller—more than two million copies were sold.

The commission's key findings were the following: the riots resulted from black frustration at a blanket of discrimination covering every aspect of their lives with indignity and blocking access to economic security and opportunity. The central message conveyed was embodied in the famous sentence on the opening page of the report, "Our nation is moving toward two societies, one black, one white—separate and unequal." The commission report placed the blame for the conditions that had led to the black urban uprisings squarely at the feet of white society: "What white Americans have never fully understood but what the Negro can never forget—is that white society is deeply implicated in the ghetto. White institutions created it, white institutions maintain it, and white society condones it" (National Advisory Commission 1968/2016, 1–2).

While the Kerner Commission was not established to develop a black reparations program and did not create a blueprint outlining the scope of a redress plan, it did recommend a set of policies intended to target and improve the well-being of black America. Those remedies included large-scale investments in the creation of greatly expanded public service and private-sector employment for blacks, initiatives to confront and reverse de facto segregation in schooling, provision of decent housing, and expanded investments in institutions and services in urban black communities (National Advisory Commission 1968/2016, 420–77). Although the uprisings were executed by blacks, the Kerner Commission concluded that they were precipitated by the cumulative abuse heaped upon black Americans.

The Rev. Dr. Martin Luther King Jr. praised the report, calling it a "physician's warning of approaching death, with a prescription for life." A month later, in April 1968, King was assassinated and riots broke out in one hundred cities. Opinions vary regarding the extent of President Johnson's support for the commission's recommendations, and it is not clear, beyond persistent marginalization of black Americans, why they were shelved.

JAPANESE INTERNMENT AND REPARATIONS

Earl Warren, widely hailed as a stalwart defender of civil liberties on the basis of the record of the US Supreme Court while he was the chief justice during the last two decades of his life, had been a fierce and highly influential advocate of the relocation and confinement of California's Japanese American population during World War II. Warren, who served as California's attorney general from 1939 through 1943 and as the state's governor from 1943 through 1953, argued vehemently for Japanese American internment on three grounds.

First, in the aftermath of Japan's attack on the US military base at Pearl Harbor, he argued that Japanese American landholdings in California were in dangerous proximity to "sensitive areas such as power lines, railroads, military bases, and oil fields" (Niiya 2017). Claiming that this proximity was not coincidental, Warren said the location of Japanese Americans left them positioned to engage in acts of sabotage.

Second, Warren argued, echoing notions of the Yellow Peril, that Japanese Americans were sufficiently inscrutable that it was impossible to determine who among them were loyal to the United States and who were not (Niiya 2017).[7] In testimony before Congress, when asked by Rep. Laurence Fletcher Arnold (D-IL) if it were possible to determine which individuals among Japanese Americans were loyal to the United States, Warren responded:

> There is no way that we can establish that fact. We believe that when we are dealing with the Caucasian race we have methods that will test the loyalty of them, and we believe that we can, in dealing with Germans and Italians, arrive at some fairly sound conclusions because of our knowledge of the way they live in the community and have lived for many years. But when we deal with the Japanese, we are in an entirely different field and we cannot form any opinion that we believe to be sound. Their method of living, their language, make for this difficulty. Many of them who show you a birth certificate stating that they are born in this State, perhaps, or born in Honolulu, can hardly speak the English language because, although they were born here, when they were four or five years of age they were sent over to Japan to be educated and they stayed over there through their adolescent period at least, and then they came back here thoroughly Japanese. (Masaoka 1973)

For Warren, somehow, it was possible to identify the fifth columnists among German and Italian Americans but impossible to do so among Japanese Americans.

Warren's third, and final, argument to support Japanese American expulsion from civilian life was in response to the lack of evidence of subversive activities on their part. Warren offered "what historian Roger Daniels sarcastically dubbed the 'Invisible Deadline for Sabotage Theory': the idea that complete lack of espionage or sabotage activity by Japanese Americans was not an indication there wasn't going to be any, but rather a sign that some massive coordinated activity was coming at an unknown future date" (Niiya 2017).[8]

Earl Warren's position prevailed. On February 19, 1942, President Franklin Roosevelt issued Executive Order 9066, dictating mass eviction of Japanese Americans and their relocation to detention sites as far flung as Inyo County in California, Park County in Wyoming, La Paz County in Arizona, Jerome County in Idaho, Desha County in Arkansas, and Zavala County in Texas. While nearly half of the confinement sites were in California, including the repurposed Santa Anita Racetrack, it was clear that the objective of the US Army and the US Department of Justice was to widely disperse and isolate America's Japanese-ancestry population.

Between late February 1942 and March 1946, approximately 115,000 persons of Japanese descent, predominantly US citizens, were compelled to leave their homes, businesses, and farms on very short notice. Under the auspices of the Trading with the Enemy Act, the federal government confiscated financial records and assets of Japanese Americans and took control of Japanese American–owned banks, banks that accepted both yen and dollars. In 1945, Congress passed a bill making $10 million available for refunds to depositors, but it would take an additional twenty years and a US Supreme Court decision to resolve disagreements over the low exchange rates (Burton et al. 2000).[9]

In 1978, the Japanese American Citizens League (JACL) began a concerted campaign for restitution for the victims of domestic wartime incarceration. The JACL set three major goals for reparations: (1) a $25,000 payment to each internee, (2) a congressional apology, and (3) establishment of a trust fund to provide educational materials and projects of remembrance about the injustice. The premise underlying the JACL's proposed $25,000 figure was a base payment of $15,000 per person plus an additional $15 per average number of days of incarceration (Oyama 1981).

Strategically, while launching an intense media campaign to inform the American people about the compulsory relocation, JACL's leadership decided not to insist on immediate legislation for appropriation of funds for reparations. Instead, they argued for legislation to form "a blue ribbon federal commission to investigate the facts and circumstances surrounding the exclusion and incarceration of Japanese Americans." According to Japanese American redress architects John Tateishi and William Yoshino (2000), this was "not a popular decision" in the Japanese American community at the time, but it proved to be critical: "Although Japanese Americans knew well the extent to which they had suffered and been denied their rights, the American public and members of Congress knew little, if anything, about the incarceration."

In July 1980, Congress established the commission called for by the JACL, the Commission on Wartime Relocation and Internment of Civilians (CWRIC). The CWRIC held public hearings in eleven cities, taking testimony from 750 witnesses and publishing its findings only eighteen months later as *Personal Justice Denied* (CWRIC 1983).[10]

The CWRIC's report achieved two critical steps on the path to Japanese American reparations. First, the report established beyond a doubt that American officialdom had known the nation's Japanese citizens were not a national security threat. Intelligence reports from both the US Navy and the Federal Bureau of Investigation made it clear that the Japanese American fifth column was sheer fantasy. Second, *Personal Justice Denied* provided recommendations for legislation to provide compensation to Japanese American victims of wartime incarceration.

The commission's work was performed far more rapidly than the congressional response. Eventually, the CWRIC's recommendations were translated into the Civil Liberties Act, which became law five years later, in 1988.

Bipartisan support led to successful passage of the measure. Sponsorship across party lines came from Rep. Norman Mineta (D-CA) and Sen. Alan K. Simpson (R-WY), who, fortunately for the fate of the bill, had become friends during their preteen years at a Boy Scout Jamboree held at the Heart Mountain Relocation Center in Park County, Wyoming, where Mineta's family was confined (Beck 2019). The final version of the Civil Liberties Act of 1988 provided for $20,000 in payments to the living incarcerees, rather than the original $25,000 on the JACL's wish list.[11]

Still, it is worth noting what was *not* covered by legislation: additional costs associated with stigma of incarceration, psychological damage, lost earnings, injury, death, and resettlement. Property losses were covered only in part. Nonetheless, the US government payment of restitution to Japanese Americans must count as a signal moment in the nation's history.

SEPTEMBER 11TH VICTIM COMPENSATION FUND

The events on September 11, 2001, now referred to as 9/11, involved seven separate terrorist attacks on a single day: the World Trade Center buildings (2,388 casualties, 2,212 injuries), the World Trade Center streetscape and other spaces (209 casualties, 382 injuries), the Pentagon (114 casualties, 86 injuries), American Airlines Flight 11 (65 casualties),

United Airlines Flight 175 (46 casualties), American Airlines Flight 77 (33 casualties), and United Airlines Flight 83 (25 casualties). Restitution for the relatives of the victims and some victims who incurred nonfatal injuries was made possible by Congress's provision of the Title IV compensation fund, which resulted in $7 billion in public money being dispersed for 5,562 claims. There was no known precedent for a redress strategy in the face of a terrorist attack against Americans; the victims and families of the earlier 1993 attack on the World Trade Center, the 1995 Oklahoma City bombing of the Alfred P. Murrah Federal Building, and the 1998 embassy bombings in Kenya and Tanzania had never received such compensation.

After Kenneth Feinberg, an attorney, put his name in for consideration, Attorney General John Ashcroft named him "special master" and charged him with the administration of the fund (Kolbert 2002). Ashcroft famously declared that "the special master would not require any Senate confirmation" and that he alone, as attorney general, had the authority to select that individual (quoted in Berkowitz 2006). Critically, Feinberg also would be tasked with hearing the evidence, and, ultimately, he—and only he—would determine to whom and how much each claimant would receive.[12] Congress did not specify a total compensation sum, nor did it limit the amount to be received by any individual victim or victim's family.

Ashcroft told Feinberg that disbursements should reflect compassion and generosity but not profligacy. Though Feinberg and the Department of Justice worked together closely, what constituted profligacy was left up to Feinberg. "Congress had mandated that eligible families and victims should receive different levels of compensation depending on the level of financial hardship visited upon the survivors" (Feinberg 2005, 151). So the current incomes of the victims would be used "to calculate the economic loss the victim suffered—what the victims would have earned over a lifetime but for the terrorists—plus some amount for the noneconomic loss (the pain and suffering and emotional distress visited on the victim and their loved ones)" (Feinberg 2012, 47). At least 40 percent of the families had incomes under $100,000, 7 percent over $1 million, and eight individuals' incomes equaled or exceeded $4 million (Feinberg 2005, xxii, 21, 194; 2004).[13]

Feinberg's final report (2004), as well as his absorbing studies *What Is Life Worth? The Unprecedented Effort to Compensate the Victims of 9/11* (2005) and *Who Gets What? Fair Competition after Tragedy and Financial Upheaval* (2012), detail the innumerable decisions involved in administering the Victim Compensation Fund. Should claims be awarded to fiancées, same-sex partners, domestic partners, ex-spouses, infant children, estranged siblings? Would the calculations for individuals' restitution reflect only their base salary, or would commissions and bonuses be factored in? Would payouts be comparable to those specified in Public Safety Death Benefits Law, which provided $250,000 to families of police officers killed in the line of duty? (Feinberg 2005, 34). Unfortunately, the calculations for determining the magnitude of restitution necessarily baked in wealth and income inequality. But Feinberg exercised his discretion to narrow the gap between rich and poor and to discourage extravagant claims by the wealthy (Feinberg 2005, 165).

Early on, Feinberg became aware that the Bush administration had great reservations about the fund. The Director of the Office of Management and Budget mused to him "about the wisdom of singling out a small segment of American society for such generous treatment," worried about the precedent it could set, and asked if this was "sound public policy" (Feinberg 2005, 26). Further, Feinberg recognized that the public was skeptical about the fund's likely fairness and that expectations were "even lower. . . among the 9/11 families" (Feinberg 2005, 167). But he found that every small step he took to assist claimants and explain the fund's workings improved its reception.

He opted to administer the fund gratis, and his firm would donate over nineteen thousand hours to the initiative, the equivalent of $7 million. His priorities were to discourage litigation, avoid lengthy emotional testimonies, and encourage maximum participation in the fund (Feinberg 2005, 167). That meant consistency, transparency (they launched an extensive educational campaign), due process, a simple application process, and letting the claimants share their stories. The special master and his team were present for one hundred meetings and 1,600 hearings in nine months, and their credibility grew over time (Feinberg 2005, 43–48).

The core financial question for persons eligible for restitution was whether the eligible family member would prefer a guaranteed payment from the federal fund (ultimately, "each family that lost a loved one in the attacks received an average compensation of $2 million") or would prefer to take a chance on a judgment for a $10–20 million payment from the airline, the Federal Aviation Administration, or the Port Authority, knowing that the family attorney probably would take 50 percent off the top (Feinberg 2012, 55). Ninety-seven percent of claimants chose the first option, accepting direct payments from the Victim Compensation Fund, often because of less financial risk and more timely payment.

Feinberg required recipients who received payments from the federal fund to forgo lawsuits against any party ($6 billion was the maximum exposure for each airline, and $1.5 billion was the limit for the relevant insurance companies). The seventy-seven claims processed for individuals who had earned at least $1 million totaled $452.2 million, or 7.5 percent of the allocated funds. The lowest earners, the 180 individuals whose salaries were below $25,000, received a combined total of $193 million, or 3.2 percent of the allocated funds (Feinberg 2005, 194). Higher awards, of over $8 million, went to several burn victims "who suffered permanent disfigurement and months of hospital recuperation" (Feinberg 2005, 41).

The 3 percent of claimants who chose litigation were relatives of the wealthiest, most highly paid, victims of the attacks (Feinberg 2005, 34). By March 2009, ninety-three of the ninety-six claimants who had elected to pursue litigation had been awarded "an average of $5 million, [with] one [receiving] more than twice the average payment from the special fund" (Weiser 2009). Legal fees, along with the law's delays, did lessen the value of their awards, but at least one magistrate, US district judge Alvin K. Hellerstein of the Southern District of New York, "cap[ped] legal fees at 15 percent of settlements," setting a precedent for significantly reduced attorney compensation in these cases (Weiser 2009).

Feinberg (2006, xxiv) wrote that while administering the fund, he came to think it was less about giving money to grieving families than "an attempt to do the impossible—to provide for repayment for the sudden loss of a loved one and some degree of justice for the loss." But, he wondered, what would make the process and outcomes "fair" or "just"? In the end he concluded that his disbursement process was defective. If Congress could have a do-over, he would want each eligible claimant to "receive the same amount" (Feinberg 2005, 183). An individual's wealth or the economic circumstances of their families should not be included in the calculus. "Differences [in claimants' circumstances] are not necessarily inequities" (Feinberg 2005, 186). What was important, in response to the attacks, was the "expression of the collective cohesive spirit of the nation and its citizens"; the assertion of a "We'll show the world" attitude not only in pursuing the terrorists but also in comforting and helping the grieving. "The rest is window dressing, expensive window dressing . . . but window dressing nonetheless" (Feinberg 2005, 186).[14]

AMERICANS HELD HOSTAGE BY IRAN

For 444 days, beginning on November 4, 1979, and ending January 20, 1981, Iranian college student members of the Muslim Student Followers of the Imam Khomeini Line who were supporters of the Iranian Revolution occupied the US Embassy in Tehran and held fifty-two Americans hostage—primarily military and civilian Foreign Service diplomatic personnel. President Jimmy Carter enlisted the aid of Algeria to negotiate the hostages' release under the terms of the Algiers Accord, which included a commitment by the US to refrain from making any claim for compensation from Iran related to the hostage taking.

In 1980, while the fifty-two Americans were still being held hostage in the US Embassy, Congress passed legislation allowing the former captives to receive compensation amounts in line with those awarded to prisoners of war and service personnel missing in action during the Vietnam War. The Hostage Relief Act of 1980 did not include a cash payment; rather, it provided survivors and their families with benefits ranging from reimbursement for medical care and interest-bearing salary savings funds to college scholarships and training.[15] A proposal to make direct payments to the affected Americans in the amount of $1,000 per day of captivity using funds from confiscated Iranian assets was defeated by the State Department, which expressed concerns that such a measure would constrain the capacity of the US to negotiate the Americans' release.

When the hostages were released in 1981, President Carter created the President's Commission on Hostage Compensation and directed it to review precedents involving prisoners of war and make recommendations determining whether the US should make restitution to the former captives. Commissioners recommended the Americans be paid $12.50 for each day they had been held in captivity, an amount along similar lines (corrected for inflation) to what the government had paid prisoners of war in World War II, Korea, and Vietnam, as a "symbolic gesture" (President's Commission 1981/1985, 181, 173; Wright and Herron 1981). It also recommended that the US government through various civil service laws "assume the costs of restoring the hostages to health, provide disability compensation if their health cannot be restored, provide compensation for material losses and safeguard their employment rights and career prospects" (President's Commission 1981/1985, 190).

In 1986 the Omnibus Diplomatic Security and Anti-Terrorism Act raised the daily compensation rate to $50.[16] "Lawyers for the former hostages contended that in none of the precedents the commission cited had the United States surrendered the right of individuals to claim damages against a foreign government. They argued that the commission should consider what the hostages might have received through suits against Iran, conceivably as much as $1,000 a day" (Wright and Herron 1981).[17]

In 2003, the former hostages brought a lawsuit to have Iran's sovereign immunity annulled in *Roeder v. Islamic Republic of Iran*. When that effort was unsuccessful, the petitioners appealed directly to Congress for redress. Unsuccessful bill H.R. 3358 (proposed during the 108th Congress) would have provided $500 per day. Another failed measure, H.R. 6305/S3878, would have provided a total of $500,000 for the fifty-two former hostages. Several lawsuits followed, each of them defeated because of the courts' interpretation of the Algiers Accord.

Legislation proposed in the 113th (2013–15) and 114th (2015–17) congressional sessions called for the creation of the Senate Commission on Foreign Relations and American Hostages in Iran, which would provide for a compensation fund to be administered by the secretary of state with the instructions to pay $150,000 plus $5,000 per day, or $2.37 million per hostage or estate, subsequently increased to $6,750 per day of captivity ($3.14 million per hostage).

Finally, legislation passed in 2015 provided a reparations award to the released captives calculated at $10,000 per day of captivity, for an average of $4.4 million per person (Congressional Research Service 2015; Parvini 2019). Funds went to the former hostages or to their estates, and their spouses and children were authorized to receive lump sums of up to $600,000 (AFP 2015). Individuals who already had received $20 million or more from other lawsuits may not have been eligible to receive the entire $4.4 million award. Payments were to be made within a year.

Thus the ultimate award of $10,000 for each of the 444 days the captives had been held hostage, or $4.44 million for each estate of a former hostage, came after thirty-four years of failed legal challenges and legislative maneuvering. The unprecedented daily award appears to have been calculated to compensate for the long delay (Congressional Research Service 2015). The final payment amount should bode well for the community of African American descendants of US slavery, which has been waiting 156 years for redress.

Americans who were in the American Embassy in Kenya in 1998 when it was bombed were included in the legislation. Provisions were made for victims and their descendants to receive $3 million each as part of a State Department settlement with Sudan (out of the 224 people who were killed in the 1998 bombings in Nairobi and Dar es Salaam, 54 were embassy employees or contractors). The bill also provided an additional $2.8 billion for 9/11 victims and their families.

LESSONS LEARNED

We draw five major insights from the experiences of these five commissions. These insights could be highly informative for the deliberations of future reparations planning commissions, including a potential Commission to Study and Develop Proposals for Reparations for African Americans (CSDPR).

First, the German experience demonstrates that the efforts of a commission (or, in this case, the Claims Conference) can bear fruit even without significant popular support from the public for the government meeting the debt. Indeed, reparations for Japanese Americans, enacted by the US Congress, occurred without any groundswell of support from the American electorate.

Congressional debate and action on black reparations, however, are unlikely to proceed without significant support from white Americans. Moreover, the German case may not be an appropriate precedent on this score. The United States is not a defeated nation seeking to restore a measure of legitimacy in the international community. The closest parallel in the US context for an opportunity to enact a program of compensation for black Americans without massive support from the rest of the population was the period in the immediate days and weeks following the end of the Civil War:

> When Whitelaw Reid traveled along the Atlantic coast and spoke with a cross-section of residents, including shopkeepers, black artisans, farmers, and planters, Freedmen's Bureau agents and officers, and freedmen in urban and rural areas, and toured several cotton plantations, he observed, "It was manifest that if restoration of civil authority depended on negro suffrage it would be accepted." [Carl] Schurz's report to [President Andrew] Johnson concluded, "When the news of Lee's and [Joseph] Johnson's surrenders burst upon the Southern country, the general consternation was extreme. . . . The public mind was so despondent that if readmission at some future time,

under whatever conditions had been promised, it would have been looked upon as a favor." Here was the ideal moment to push forward for the full array of black rights. (Darity and Mullen 2020, 161–62)

According to Reuben D. Mussey, President Andrew Johnson's assistant, the period soon after the war's end would have been an ideal time to take the bold steps on behalf of those newly emancipated: "It seems to me that we had the opportunity when Lee surrendered and more than that when Lincoln was assassinated to make our own terms" (Darity and Mullen 2020, 164).

Nonetheless, there are grounds for optimism about the prospect of building adequate popular support in the United States for black reparations. Twenty-two years ago, when Dawson and Popoff (2004) asked, "Should the federal government pay monetary compensation to African Americans whose ancestors were slaves?" 96 percent of white respondents opposed such a measure. In a 2016 Marist Poll, the proportion of whites who opposed redistributive justice for black American descendants of slavery had fallen to 81 percent, about a one-percentage-point decline per annum (Marist Poll 2016). Furthermore, just under half of white millennials surveyed said they supported reparations for black Americans.[18]

During the summer of 2020, many across the globe were horrified by the police killing of an unarmed and subdued black man, George Floyd. A 2021 University of Massachusetts-Amherst poll found that white Americans' support for restitution for black Americans had reached 28 percent—a gain of nine percentage points—and that a majority of millennials indicated their support for redress (UMass Amherst 2021).

Hence the second lesson: depending upon its content, a report from a congressional or presidential commission could increase political support for black reparations. To achieve that outcome, the commission must do critical work on the nature of the nation's historical memory.[19]

A key contribution of the Commission on Wartime Relocation and Internment of Civilians—at least for congressional considerations—was to demonstrate, clearly, that American officialdom had carried out mass incarceration despite having extensive evidence that Japanese Americans did not threaten national security. And the stance of the Kerner Commission's report may have helped block a punitive, military response to black communities where urban uprisings occurred, even if the commission recommendations largely were ignored.

A report from the CSDPR must confront head-on the false narrative of the antebellum period, the Civil War, and the Reconstruction era that has been developed and propagated by proponents of the Lost Cause. The potential favorable impact on public opinion also expands the benefits associated with the prompt delivery of its report. In our view, the window from the start of a commission's operations to the release of its report must not exceed eighteen months.

A third insight is drawn from experience with the September 11th Victim Compensation Fund. Special master Feinberg concluded that one of the major problems with the administration of the fund was the practice of assigning payment amounts on the basis of the deceased's projected lifetime income—which necessarily would vary widely between persons with different types of occupations at the time of the attacks. The family of an investment banker who was killed received far more than the family of a person employed as a cashier in a World Trade Center coffee shop. The corresponding implication was that the life of the former was worth far more than the life of the latter.

Feinberg said that in the future he would recommend that restitution projects be designed, to the greatest extent possible, to provide uniform payments to all eligible recipients. In the case of the 9/11 fund this might have meant an identical payment of $5 million to each victim's relatives, instead of the vastly disparate payments actually made under the reparations plan. We modify Feinberg's recommendation to propose that the CSDPR form a plan to allot a substantial base amount to all claimants, while the option is reserved to provide additional support based upon need. This would precisely invert what took place with the September 11th Victim Compensation Fund: those with less would receive more, rather than those already with more receiving much more.

The fourth lesson is drawn from the principle that David Ben-Gurion invoked during the course of the pursuit of German reparations payments: the murderers must not inherit. This principle is particularly relevant to crafting the case for reparations for black American descendants of US slavery, since, generally, *the murderers have inherited.* Two examples are illustrative: Wilmington, North Carolina, and Ocoee, Florida.

According to LeRae Umfleet, who researched and wrote the definitive study examining the 1898 Wilmington massacre and its impact as a watershed moment in post-Reconstruction North Carolina politics, Wilmington before the massacre had been considered a mecca for African Americans. Blacks held roles in the management of the city and county and seats on the board of aldermen, in the state legislature, and in the US House of Representatives. Wilmington was also the largest and most prosperous city in North Carolina, largely because of its status as a critical deep-water port.

Umfleet explains in the film *Wilmington on Fire* (Everett 2015) that in the early 1890s, African American residents of the city experienced relative prosperity at every economic rung of society. Black shrimpers and fishers continued to pass down trade expertise in the Cape Fear River region; black literacy rates soared; African Americans served as police and firemen, practiced medicine and law, and owned an astonishing number of businesses on main streets, including restaurants.

After the November 1898 coup, only three of eighteen black-owned businesses remained. Once black magistrates "resigned," racist Democrats also ruled the courts, and when the state and federal government opted not to intervene, the newly empowered foreclosed on the homes of the dead, refinanced their own bad loans, inflated stock, lined their bloody pockets, and waited with shotguns at the polls.[20]

Wilmington on Fire draws a clear connection between political and social disenfranchisement and the scope of the generational wealth plundered from members of Wilmington's half-destroyed black community. Late in the film, Faye Chaplin, the great-granddaughter of Thomas C. Miller, a real estate developer who was one of the few "elite" African Americans in the city at the time of the massacre, cries as she reads aloud a letter he had penned detailing the impossibility of starting anew with no wealth. The mob had forcibly banished him by putting him onto a train headed north of the state line. She motions toward the window in her home through which she witnesses the construction of apartment buildings gentrifying the property her kin owned only a few generations ago (Everett 2015).

In Ocoee, Florida, the white riot that ensued after the lynching of Jule Perry, who had tried to exercise his right to vote on Election Day in 1920, led to the "legal" seizure of black property:

A committee of white Ocoee residents, together with the local court, distributed black residents' property to white citizens in the aftermath; the victims were uncompensated for the most part although some received a few dollars. Congress endorsed the actions of the Ocoee government and white citizens after the fact commending them for upholding "law and order." Cruelly the black cemetery in Ocoee—abandoned for eighty years after the riot—is located in a subdivision off of Bluford Avenue, named for Captain Sims, who took ownership of Perry's land. Adding insult to injury, every year the Ocoee government throws a festival celebrating the town's founders: former slave owners J. D. Starke and Captain Sims himself. In 2014 the city of Ocoee paid $302,000 to celebrate the founders. (Fussell 2016)

The fifth and final insight taken from this review of commissions designed to consider redress is the value of having a powerful ally or powerful allies who support the redress cause. Arguably the failure to adopt the recommendations in the Kerner Report was due to President Johnson's lack of enthusiasm for the findings of the commission that he himself had appointed. But in the case of the September 11th Victims Compensation Fund, national outrage and horror over the acts of terrorism meant that virtually all major political actors favored monetary restitution to the relatives of the victims. Both Congress and the executive branch supported a reparations plan. Similarly, when the Iran hostages testified in congressional hearings and described the horrors of their captivity and torture to a new generation of Americans, public opinion was swayed. Reparations for Japanese Americans were enabled by the serendipitous friendship between Norman Mineta and Alan Simpson, which served as a critical springboard for the enactment of the Civil Liberties Act of 1988. And Konrad Adenauer's determination to establish the *Wiedergutmachung* was patently a decisive factor in its establishment.

In his March 2020 State of the City Address, Steve Schewel, the mayor of Durham, North Carolina, called for Durham "to join a coalition to petition Congress to enact a comprehensive national program of reparations for all black American descendants of persons enslaved in the United States." Recognizing that in 2020 it would have required more than $10 trillion to eliminate the black-white wealth gap, Mayor Schewel advocated, "as an essential first step," that Congress pass a substantially revised version of HR40" (Schewel 2020). It was a courageous step, and we wait to see who else among the nation's leaders will bring their political capital to the movement.

NOTES

1. We thank Sandy Alexandre, associate professor of literature at Massachusetts Institute of Technology, for pointing out that acknowledgment, redress, and closure form the acronym ARC.

2. Calculation computed by one of the authors.

3. Of course, black household income levels also are markedly lower than white household income levels in the United States. Average white household income in 2019 was $123,400, while average black household income was $54,000, a large disparity but still dwarfed by the black-white wealth differential (see Bhutta et al. 2020).

4. See *JTA Daily News Bulletin* (1982/2015) and Sagi (1980).

5. By 1956 German transfer payments constituted close to 90 percent of Israel's annual revenue (Reiter 2019).

6. The year 1919 was not the only one in which white terrorists took brutal aim at black Americans. White massacres occurred with regularity from the Reconstruction Era well into the years of the Second World War. The most notorious, perhaps, were the Wilmington (North Carolina) massacre of 1898 and the Tulsa (Oklahoma) massacre of 1921. Again, in none of these instances was a national commission established to explore the causes of the assaults or to specify compensation for the victims. See Bentley-Edwards et al. (2018).

7. Niiya (2017) comments that Warren's expressed fears that Japanese Americans had located "near sensitive areas" ignored "the fact that coastal land was well suited for farming and the scraps of land along railroads and power lines were relatively undesirable—and thus available to [the] Japanese."

8. A 2012 National Park Service study reported, "No person of Japanese ancestry living in the United States was ever convicted of any serious act of espionage or sabotage during the war, yet the entire West Coast population of people of Japanese descent was forcibly removed from their homes and placed in relocation centers, many for the duration of the war" (Wyatt 2012).

9. The eventual rate specified in the US Supreme Court decision in *Honda v. Clark* (1947), over the advice of the Office of Alien Property custodian, was the prewar rate of 4.3 yen to the dollar and not the significantly reduced postwar rate of 361.55.

10. The commissioners were Joan Z. Bernstein (chair), Daniel E. Lungren (vice-chair), Edward W. Brooke, Robert F. Drinan, Arthur S. Flemming, Arthur J. Goldberg, Ishmael V. Gromoff, William M. Marutani, and Hugh B. Mitchell. The eleven cities where the commissioners held public hearings included Washington, D.C., Los Angeles, San Francisco, Seattle, Chicago, New York City, and Cambridge, Massachusetts.

11. Other provisions included $38 million authorized to preserve Japanese American internment sites. Federal agencies were directed to review "with liberality" all Nisei applications for restitution associated with the internment. A special foundation was created for the research and public education of "the causes and circumstances of" internment. See US Senate (2006).

12. A "special master" also played a key role in the determination that restitution was owed black victims of a white massacre in Rosewood, Florida, the first for any US state. In 1923, when a white woman alleged she had been attacked by an unidentified black man in her home, a white mob burned the black business district and residential neighborhood to the ground. Seventy years later, the Florida House of Representatives appointed Richard Hixson to lead an investigation. The special master concluded, "The claimants have met the test for an equitable claim bill by showing that a moral obligation exists to redress their injuries." Hixson recommended the state budget $7 million for the survivors. That figure was reduced first to $2.1 million and ultimately to $1.5 million. In the end, nine survivors received $150,000 awards, with $500,000 set aside for claimants who could prove they were direct descendants of victims who had lost property during the siege—only half of the 143 descendants who applied for the funds received more than $2,000—and a scholarship

fund for direct descendants was created. As of 2020, 297 eligible claimants have attended public state colleges and universities or vocational training institutions and been awarded scholarship funds of a maximum of $6,100. State reparations initiatives like this one are highly susceptible to manipulation by state lawmakers, making them less than ideal. Rosewood survivors who accepted the one-time reparations payment were declared ineligible for Medicare and were required to pay for their medical expenses. Direct descendants who left the state were not eligible to receive college scholarships. See Darity and Mullen (2020, 16); Associated Press (1994); and D'Orso (1996, 256–57). For details on Rosewood award recipients' loss of Medicare benefits, see Banks (2020). For the number of Rosewood descendants who have received scholarships to date, see Samuels (2020).

13. According to *New York Times* reporters Diana A. Henriques and David Barstow (2001), Ashcroft and Feinberg intimated that the disbursements "should put victims' needs ahead of the ultimate expense to taxpayers."

14. We were astonished to learn that Feinberg is an ardent opponent of black reparations. When one of the authors asked the arbitrator to weigh in on the topic, he responded fiercely, "Reparations for slavery? Terrible idea!" For Feinberg, a compensation program for black Americans was fraught with difficulty. "Who's eligible? If you say only descendants of slaves," Feinberg claimed, you eliminate those "thousands who cannot demonstrate a link" to enslaved ancestors. After this initial question about restitution for blacks who were victims of Jim Crow, Feinberg concluded that the case for black reparations is solely driven by the atrocity of slavery. He further postulated that slavery disadvantaged poor whites. In *From Here to Equality,* we discuss the benefits of slavery to whites generally and demonstrate the pervasiveness of slaveholding. In Mississippi and South Carolina, more than 55 percent of whites lived in slave-owning families. In Florida, George, Alabama, and Louisiana, "well above forty percent" of whites lived in slave-owning families. Across the Confederacy, at least one-quarter of whites lived in slaveholding families. Poor whites benefited from the system of black enslavement, principally, by being employees of the slaveholders, typically to perform the myriad tasks associated with the management of black bodies on the plantation, by trading with the slaveholders, by being hired to surveil and police the enslaved, by being slave auctioneers, and by engaging in allied activities like cotton brokerage and plantation clothing provision. Most important, in the aftermath of the war, the Homestead Act provided many landless whites with property, while the formerly enslaved, systematically, were denied access to property (Darity and Mullen 2020, 65–67).

15. Hostage Relief Act of 1980, Hearings and Markup of H.R. 7085 before the Subcomm. on International Operations of the H. Comm. on Foreign Affairs. 96th Cong. 28–29 (1980).

16. Victims of Terrorism Compensation Act §802, P.L. 99–399, Title VIII.

17. This contrast would be pointed up in 2008, when three of the US servicemen from the *USS Pueblo* who had been captured by North Korea in 1968 for alleged espionage successfully sued North Korea for $65 million for their 444-day captivity and torture—$16.75 million for each of the three crew members

and $15.6 million for the widow of the ship's captain. At the time we went to press, they were still awaiting payment out of US-held North Korean assets. See 28 U.S.C. ch. 97—Jurisdictional Immunities of Foreign States, Legal Information Institute, Cornell University Law School, www.law.cornell.edu/uscode /text/28/part-IV/chapter-97; Massie v. Government of Democratic People's Republic of Korea, 592 F. Supp. 2d 57 (D.D.C. 2008); and Wilber (2009).

18. While 59 percent of black respondents reported favoring monetary compensation for the victims of World War II domestic incarceration, a whopping 74 percent of white respondents expressed opposition. See also Russ (2019).

19. This is precisely the type of work that has been undertaken in Germany with respect to accounting for its Nazi past (see Neiman 2019). The United States must do similar work, finally, to achieve full de-Confederatization. For a description of what that process would entail, see Darity and Mullen (2020, 155, 354n30).

20. See the documentary film *Wilmington on Fire* (Everett 2015) and LeRae Umfleet's 2009 book *A Day of Blood: The 1898 Wilmington Race Riot*.

REFERENCES

AFP. 2015. "Americans in Iran Hostage Crisis to Receive Compensation—36 Years Later." *The Guardian*, December 24. www.theguardian.com/us-news /2015/dec/24/americans-iran-hostage-crisis-financial-compensation.

Associated Press. 1994. "Florida Urged to Compensate Victims of Racial Attack in '23." *New York Times*, March 22. www.nytimes.com/1994/03/22/us /florida-urged-to-compensate-victims-of-racial-attack-in-23.html.

Auerbach, Yehudit. 1991. "Ben-Gurion and Reparations from Germany." In *David Ben-Gurion: Politics and Leadership in Israel*, edited by Ronald W. Zweig, 274–92. New York: David Cass.

Banks, Adelle M. 2020. "Reparations after Rosewood Massacre a Model, Descendants Say." *Tampa Bay Times*, December 24. www.tampabay.com /news/florida/2020/12/24/reparations-after-rosewood-massacre-a-model -descendants-say/.

Beck, Julie. 2019. "Two Boy Scouts Met in an Internment Camp, and Grew up to Work in Congress." *The Atlantic*, May 29. www.theatlantic.com/family /archive/2019/05/congressmen-norm-mineta-alan-simpson-friendship -japanese-internment-camp/589603/.

Bentley-Edwards, Keisha L., Malik C. Edwards, William A. Darity Jr., Darrick Hamilton, and Jasson Perez. 2018. "How Does It Feel to Be a Problem? The Missing Kerner Commission Report." *RSF: The Russell Sage Foundation Journal of the Social Sciences* 4 (6): 20–40.

Berkowitz, Elizabeth. 2006. "The Problematic Role of the Special Master: Undermining the Legitimacy of the September 11th Victim Compensation Fund." *Yale Law and Policy Review* 24 (1): 1–41.

Bhutta, Neil, Andrew C. Chang, Lisa J. Dettling, and Joanna W. Hsu. 2020. "Disparities in Wealth by Race and Ethnicity in the 2019 Survey of Consumer

Finances." Board of Governors of the Federal Reserve System, FEDS Notes, September 28. www.federalreserve.gov/econres/notes/feds-notes/disparities-in-wealth-by-race-and-ethnicity-in-the-2019-survey-of-consumer-finances-20200928.htm.

Brown, Tyson H., Angela M. O'Rand, and Daniel E. Adkins. 2012. "Race-Ethnicity and Health Trajectories." *Journal of Health and Social Behavior* 53 (3): 359–77. https://doi.org/10.1177/0022146512455333.

Burton, Jeffery F., Mary M. Farrell, Florence B. Lord, and Richard W. Lord. 2000. "A Brief History of Japanese American Relocation during World War II." In *Confinement and Ethnicity: An Overview of World War II Japanese American Relocation Sites.* Washington, DC: National Park Service. www.nps.gov/parkhistory/online_books/anthropology74/ce3.htm.

Congressional Research Service. 2015. *The Iran Hostages: Efforts to Obtain Compensation.* EveryCRSReport.com, November 2. www.everycrsreport.com/reports/R43210.html.

CWRIC (Commission on Wartime Relocation and Internment of Civilians). 1983. *Personal Justice Denied.* Vol. 2. Washington, DC: Government Printing Office.

Darity, William A., Jr., and A. Kirsten Mullen. 2020. *From Here to Equality: Reparations for Black Americans in the Twenty-First Century.* Chapel Hill: University of North Carolina Press.

Darity, William A., Jr., A. Kirsten Mullen, and Marvin Slaughter. 2022. "The Cumulative Costs of Racism and the Bill for Black Reparations." *Journal of Economic Perspectives* 36 (2): 99–122.

Dawson, Michael C., and Rovana Popoff. 2004. "Reparations: Justice and Greed in Black and White." *Du Bois Review: Social Science Research on Race* 1 (1): 47–91. https://doi.org/10.1017/S1742058X04040056.

D'Orso, Michael. 1996. *Like Judgment Day: The Ruin and Redemption of a Town Called Rosewood.* New York: Boulevard Books.

Duncan, Greg J., Mary C. Daly, Peggy McDonough, and David R. Williams. 2002. "Optimal Indicators of Socioeconomic Status for Health Research." *American Journal of Public Health* 92 (7): 1151–57. https://doi.org/10.2105/ajph.92.7.1151.

Everett, Christopher, dir. 2015. *Wilmington on Fire.* Speller Street Films. http://wilmingtononfire.com/.

Feinberg, Kenneth R. 2004. Rep. *Final Report of the Special Master for the September 11th Victim Compensation Fund of 2001.* 2 vols. Washington, DC: Department of Justice.

———. 2005. *What Is Life Worth? The Unprecedented Effort to Compensate the Victims of 9/11.* New York: PublicAffairs.

———. 2012. *Who Gets What: Fair Compensation after Tragedy and Financial Upheaval.* New York: PublicAffairs.

Fussell, Melissa. 2016. "Dead Men Bring No Claims: How Takings Claims Can Provide Redress for Real Property Owning Victims of Jim Crow Race Riots." *William and Mary Law Review* 57 (5): 1913–48. https://scholarship.law.wm.edu/wmlr/vol57/iss5/7.

Hamilton, Darrick, and William A. Darity Jr. 2017. "The Political Economy of Education, Financial Literacy, and the Racial Wealth Gap." *Federal Reserve Bank of St. Louis Review* 99 (1): 59–76. https://doi.org/10.20955/r.2017.59-76.

Harris, Leslie M. 2004. "The New York City Draft Riots of 1863." See *In the Shadow of Slavery: African Americans in New York City, 1626–1863,* 279–88. Chicago: University of Chicago Press.

Henriques, Diana B., and David Barstow. 2001. "Mediator Named to Run Sept. 11 Fund." *New York Times,* November 27. www.nytimes.com/2001/11/27/nyregion/a-nation-challenged-the-special-master-mediator-named-to-run-sept-11-fund.html.

JTA Daily News Bulletin. 1982/2015. "Nahum Goldmann Dead at 87." August 31. www.jta.org/1982/08/31/archive/nahum-goldmann-dead-at-87.

Judt, Tony. 2006. *Postwar: A History of Europe since 1945.* New York: Penguin Group.

Kolbert, Elizabeth. 2002. "The Calculator." *New Yorker,* November 18. www.newyorker.com/magazine/2002/11/25/the-calculator.

Marist Poll. 2016. "Reparations for Slavery in the United States?" May 10. http://maristpoll.marist.edu/wp-content/misc/usapolls/us160502/Point%20Taken/Reparations/Exclusive%20Point%20Taken_Marist%20Poll_Complete%20Survey%20Findings_May%202016.pdf.

Masaoka, Mike M. 1973. "Introduction: Some Recollections of, and Reflections on, 1942." In *Japanese-American Relocation Reviewed,* vol. 1, *Decision and Exodus,* edited by James H. Rowe. The Earl Warren History Project. Online Archive of California. http://texts.cdlib.org/view?docId=ft667nb2x8&doc.view=entire_text.

National Advisory Commission on Civil Disorders. 1968/2016. *The Kerner Report.* Princeton, NJ: Princeton University Press.

Neiman, Susan. 2019. *Learning from the Germans: Race and the Memory of Evil.* New York: Picador.

Niiya, Brian. 2017. "Earl Warren." In *Densho Encyclopedia,* April 10. https://encyclopedia.densho.org/Earl_Warren/.

Oyama, David. 1981. "In 1942, Internment; in 1981, an Inquiry." *New York Times,* July 9. www.nytimes.com/1981/07/09/opinion/in-1942-internment-in-1981-an-inquiry.html.

Parvini, Sarah. 2019. "They Were Hostages in Iran for 444 Days. Decades Later, They're Waiting for Compensation." *Los Angeles Times,* November 3. www.latimes.com/world-nation/story/2019-11-03/iran-hostages-444-days-decades-later-waiting-compensation.

President's Commission on Hostage Compensation. 1981/1985. "Final Report and Recommendations of the President's Commission on Hostage Compensation." In *H.R. 1956 and H.R. 2019, Benefits to Federal Employees Who Are Victims of Terrorism,* by US Congress, 157–95. Washington, DC: Government Printing Office.

Reinharz, Jehuda, and Evyatar Friesel. 2009. "Nahum Goldmann: Jewish and Zionist Statesman—An Overview." In *Nahum Goldmann: Statesman without a State,* edited by Mark A. Raider, 3–62. Albany: SUNY Press.

Reiter, Bernd. 2019. "What US Slavery Reparations and Post-Holocaust Germany Have in Common." *Quartz*, April 2. https://qz.com/1680558/for-slavery-reparations-the-us-can-look-to-post-holocaust-germany/.

Russ, Valerie. 2019. "Most Americans Still Oppose Reparations, but That's Shifting with Younger Generations." *Philadelphia Inquirer*, July 1. www .inquirer.com/news/reparations-polls-slavery-african-americans-support -whites-2020-democratic-candidates-20190701.html.

Sagi, Nana. 1980. *German Reparations: A History of the Negotiations*. Jerusalem: Magnes Press.

Samuels, Robert. 2020. "Survivors of the Rosewood Massacre Won Reparations. Their Descendants Aren't Sure the Victory Was Enough." *Washington Post*, April 3. www.washingtonpost.com/graphics/2020/national/rosewood -reparations/.

Schewel, Steve. 2020. Mayor of Durham, North Carolina, State of City Address. March 3. https://durhamnc.gov/4002/State-of-the-City-Address.

Tateishi, John, and William Yoshino. 2000. "The Japanese American Incarceration: The Journey to Redress." *Human Rights Magazine*, April 1 (Spring). www.americanbar.org/groups/crsj/publications/human_rights_magazine_ home/human_rights_vol27_2000/spring2000/hr_spring00_tateishi/.

Taylor, Gideon, Greg Schneider, and Saul Kagan. 2009. "The Claims Conference and the Historic Jewish Efforts for Holocaust-Related Compensation and Restitution." In *Reparations for Victims of Genocide, War Crimes and Crimes against Humanity Systems in Place and Systems in the Making*, edited by Carla Ferstman, Mariana Goetz, and Alan Stephens, 101–13. Leiden: Martinus Nijhoff.

UMass Amherst. 2021. "New UMass Amherst / WCVB Poll Finds Majority Approval of Biden's First 100 Days, While One-Third of Americans Still See His Presidency as Illegitimate." Toplines and Crosstabs | Department of Political Science, April 26. https://polsci.umass.edu/toplines-and-crosstabs-april-2021-bidens-first-100-days.

Umfleet, LeRae. 2009. *A Day of Blood: The 1898 Wilmington Race Riot*. Raleigh: North Carolina Office of Archives and History and the African American Heritage Commission.

US Senate. 2006. *Preservation of Japanese American World War II Confinement Sites*. Report 109-314. 109th Congress. www.govinfo.gov/content /pkg/CRPT-109srpt314/html/CRPT-109srpt314.htm.

Weiser, Benjamin. 2009. "Value of Suing over 9/11 Deaths Is Still Unsettled." *New York Times*, March 12. www.nytimes.com/2009/03/13/nyregion/13lawsuits .html.

Wilber, Del Quentin. 2009. "USS Pueblo's William Massie Seeks Retribution from N. Korea." *Washington Post*, October 8. www.washingtonpost.com/wp-dyn /content/article/2009/10/07/AR2009100703890.html?sid=ST2009100703955.

Wright, Michael, and Caroline R. Herron. 1981. "Symbolic Gesture of $12.50 a Day." *New York Times*, September 27.

Wyatt, Barbara, ed. 2012. *Japanese Americans in World War II*. Report. Washington, DC: National Park Service, US Department of the Interior. https://

upload.wikimedia.org/wikipedia/commons/a/ao/Japanese_Americans_in_World_War_II%2C_a_National_Historic_Landmark_theme_study.pdf.

Zweig, Ronald W. 2009. "'Reparations Made Me': Nahum Goldmann, German Reparations, and the Jewish World." In *Nahum Goldmann: Statesman without a State,* edited by Mark A. Raider, 233–54. Albany: SUNY Press.

7

Considerations for the Design of a Reparations Plan

TREVON D. LOGAN

The design of a reparations plan is contingent on the goals of the program. It must be stressed that reparations have long been an objective of the formerly enslaved and their descendants, and political activity related to reparations has been met with active state resistance (Berry 2005). Although there is an emerging consensus around the goal of eliminating black/white disparities in wealth, it is important to note that such a goal may understate the size of a reparations program for several reasons.

First, it is not clear where in the white wealth distribution the descendants of enslavers fall. That is, the descendants of those who profited the most directly due to enslavement may be better positioned than whites generally. Therefore, equating at the mean or median of white wealth could understate the true size of a reparations program.

Second, equality of wealth works as reparations under the assumption that wealth functions as the realized profits from slavery and continuing discrimination against descendants of slaves in the United States. This method, too, underestimates the size of a reparations program. Violence under slavery, the sexual exploitation of women and men, and the emotional pain of family breakup, taken together or separately, would justify grounds for action and compensation. It is generally understood that enslavers did not explicitly include the human cost of these atrocities in their financial accounting. Violence, emotional terror, and psychological abuse were functional to maintaining the productivity of the system of slavery but, again, they were not incorporated in the enslavers' accounting ledgers.

Indeed, if violence was simply a part of the production process (where the enslaved were punished for effort deemed insufficient) it would be priced into the profits. The aim of a reparations program could extend beyond such an economic calculation to consider the totality of the injustices practiced under enslavement (cf. Swinton 1990).

It is a straightforward justification that a reparations program should account for the continued effects of enslavement and racial discrimination. For example, we know that pregnant enslaved women were worked in the fields up to the time of giving birth and placed back into the field shortly thereafter (Fogel and Engerman 1977). These women gave birth to exceptionally small children as a result, and these children were systematically malnourished until they reached an age at which they could be productive as agricultural labor (Steckel 1986).

Given what we know of the fetal origins of disease and intergenerational transmission of health, it is possible that the mortality and morbidity gaps by race seen today are a direct function of health conditions under enslavement (Fogel and Costa 1997). This is not a question of genetics but one of human physiology—the physical markers of enslavement, like wealth, are intergenerationally transmitted.

Moreover, a biological product of these women, their breast milk, was marketed and sold, and this submarket impeded the formation of mother-child bonds (Jones-Rogers 2019). Similarly, we know that the trade in enslaved individuals was related to dramatic differences in family structure (Logan and Pritchett 2018). These very real harms could be subject to reparations but fall outside of sufficiency for a program that aims to eliminate racial wealth inequality.

The considerations listed below are several options whose value is dependent on the range of history stipulated to be subject to reparations. For example, a reparations program that is limited to undistributed compensation under chattel slavery would likely require one set of payments, but it is unclear if the harms detailed above would be considered under the purview of such a reparations program.

Conversely, a program that sought to correct for historical discrimination after emancipation would require not only payment but also programmatic efforts directly tied to wealth building. Examples would include subsidized or tax-advantaged asset ownership or subsidized intergenerational transfers. With either goal, one would need to address the lingering impact of enslavement on a variety of outcomes that, like wealth, have been intergenerationally transmitted. An open question is how companies that profited from the enslavement regime should participate, since they profited privately from a system enforced by the federal government (Berry 2014). Similarly, reconciliation of the wealth that was stolen from African Americans falls outside of a goal of closing the racial wealth gap—but nevertheless could be one feature of such a system.

Dispelling myths about what a reparations program should be and should not be is the first matter of business. If the goal of eliminating the racial wealth gap is the object of a reparations program, then policies and programs that would directly build wealth among African Americans must be at its center. Programs designed to build human capital, reform criminal justice, develop entrepreneurs, cancel student loan debt, or give children endowments proportional to parental wealth—children whose parents had greater wealth would receive smaller endowments and those whose parents possessed less wealth would receive larger endowments—will prove insufficient to eliminate the black-white wealth gap (Darity 2019). At the same time, large transfers to African Americans could induce inflation, which would diminish the wealth African Americans would build in a program. It is important to remain cognizant of these macro-economic issues in considering the implications of a reparations program.

With these elements in mind, we briefly outline the fundamentals of the structure of a reparations program that would apply in any context.

1. The reparations program would need to be administered as a national program. State and local efforts are constrained by their size and limited population to address the problem (as shown in chapter 10 of this volume), and local policies by definition exclude some who should be eligible for reparations. Any program will require logistical support to identify all who qualify for reparations and to deliver services and/or payments to those who are eligible. Drawing on the framework outlined by Darity and Mullen (2020, 258), eligibility criteria could be based on two considerations and could comprise (a) people who have "at least one ancestor who was enslaved in the United States after the formation of the republic" and (b) people who have "self-identified as 'black,' 'Negro,' 'Afro-American,' 'African American,' or an equivalent for at least twelve years before the enactment of the reparations program or the establishment of a congressional or presidential commission 'to study and develop reparations for African Americans'—whichever comes first."

2. The reparations program would require the establishment of an administrative agency consisting of civil servants free from partisan pressure and influence.

To ensure that the agency's actions are consistent with the descendant community's interests, a supervisory board also should be established whose members will be elected by the adult eligible recipients of reparations payments. This proposal runs parallel with the one Darity and Mullen (2020) put forward in their book *From Here to Equality*.

Candidates should be experts, scholars, and activists with a proven track record of reparations research and activism; they could be nominated on the basis of suggestions from organizations dedicated to the reparations issue. To be clear, the board should be about its purpose, not composed of any members who see membership as a goal in and of itself or who seek to capitalize on board membership for personal gain.

3. The reparations program should have a limited number of concrete goals stated from the beginning: for example, a goal of eliminating the black-white wealth gap. Stated goals are important for clear delineation of what the program is supposed to accomplish and why. Benchmarks and goals should include greater wealth and income, dramatic declines in police violence and mass incarceration, improved health and health care, reduced discrimination in employment and housing, and other aspects of material, physical, and psychological well-being.

Establishment of these goals may require further study to determine the size of the program, but the committee must value thoroughness over expediency. Thus, an important component of a reparations program for the African American descendants of the enslaved is financing academic research (a) to determine eligibility, (b) to establish specific goals, and (c) to monitor goal achievement and evaluate program success.

4. The committee should draw from a wide range of domestic and foreign reparations programs that have been designed from the nineteenth to the twenty-first centuries, in order to determine both appropriate delivery and funding mechanisms. One prominent example is German Holocaust reparations, which, from 1952 to the present, have been provided to various recipients. Among the recipients are (a) the State of Israel for resettling five hundred thousand displaced Holocaust survivors; (b) the Conference on Jewish Material Claims, which received a compensatory lump sum for "heirless Jewish property" to be distributed to survivors in Israel and in the diaspora; and (c) individual survivors and their descendants and heirs, who were supplied with pensions on an individual basis beginning in 1953 and still ongoing (based on the Federal Supplementary

Law for the Compensation of Victims of National Socialist Persecution of 1953 and the Federal Compensation Terminal Law in 1965).

In addition, remaining Holocaust survivors received reparations payments in 1988, and surviving slave laborers received reparations through the public-private foundation Remembrance, Responsibility and the Future, which involved German companies that had profited from slave labor during World War II (Craemer 2018).

The most successful reparations program, thus far, in the United States may serve as another prominent example. The Civil Liberties Act of 1988 provided reparations to Japanese American World War II internees with a letter of apology from the US president accompanied by a check for $20,000 per survivor or their heir.

Reversed slavery reparations examples (reparations to slave owners for the abolition of slavery) from the nineteenth century may also serve as examples of how large reparations programs can be designed and administered. For example, the Haitian revolution of 1791–1804 that abolished French slavery there prompted France to demand an indemnity for the former slave owners in 1825.

With the aid of archivists, historians, and genealogists, the French government established a massive six-volume État Détaillé (Commission chargée 1828) containing the names of 7,900 former slave owners and their legal heirs as reparations recipients. Haiti financed these payments through loans it serviced from 1825 to 1947 (Craemer 2015).

In 1833, Great Britain indemnified its former slave owners to the tune of 40 percent of the Treasury's spending budget. British reparations to slave owners were paid in part on loans, and these loans were serviced for 182 years from 1833 to 2015 (Craemer 2019; Manjapra 2018).

A similar financing model could be used for slavery reparations in the United States. In fact, the US government has direct experience regarding slavery reparations. In 1862, the US government under President Lincoln ended slavery in the District of Columbia ahead of the Emancipation Proclamation, providing $300 in reparations per slave to enslavers. Kirsten West Savali (2014) writes, "The Board of Commissioners appointed to administer the act approved 930 petitions . . . from former owners for the freedom of 2,989 former slaves." Thus, the US government paid $896,700 in 1862 dollars (roughly $22.8 million in 2018 dollars) for emancipation of the enslaved population in Washington, D.C., to individual former slave owners.

Together, these historical examples suggest that reparations for African American descendants of the enslaved can be structured in multiple ways, with reparations going to individual heirs and/or community organizations (e.g., German Holocaust reparations), in the form of cash payments (US reparations to Japanese-American World War II internees) or pensions (German Holocaust reparations), and by extension via educational grants, public health initiatives, and housing programs.

The government can employ archivists, historians, and genealogists (see the Haitian example) to establish eligibility according to the criteria listed above. It can form public-private foundations (German Holocaust reparations) involving companies that benefited from slavery in the United States, and it can take up large loans, if it chooses to meet the expense of the plan by borrowing, to be paid off over the time span of centuries (see the Haitian and British examples).

5. Like the historical examples listed above, the reparations program could be delivered over several phases, some with direct compensation and others with the delivery of programs to address specific harms. If there are programs that address specific harms, there must be clear guidance on the duration, goals, and expectations of the programs, as well as means for review of goals and whether stated objectives are met. Failure to achieve goals within a given time frame should subject a program to revision, extension, or abolishment, with new programs designed to achieve the stated goals.

6. The reparations program should provide for the creation of a board to advise on the payments and on education for wealth management (including subsidies for wealth management so that reparations are not taken by fees from financial institutions). Members of the advisory board should be recruited by the committee primarily from African American financial experts.

7. The committee should recognize not only the symbolic importance of a direct payment but also the need to balance this against the goal of long-term asset building, which would be illiquid to a certain extent. To this end, it is important to recognize that policy could play a large role in a program, outside of taxes and transfers.

This would include tax-deferred or nontaxed accounts, creation of a class of stock or property ownership types specifically for eligible participants, abatements for property taxes for those eligible, policies to minimize exposure to real estate fluctuations, forbearance initiatives for current debt among the eligible, and subsidized interest rates for those eligible.

8. It should be within the committee's power to propose novel approaches to wealth building and transfer payments that would prevent inflationary pressure. These policies, like others, should have specific

goals to be achieved. The design of any reparations program should be informed by the needs of the intended beneficiaries. Information should be assembled on the functional consequences of racial wealth inequality. A representative survey of slave-descendants should be taken as part of a reparations project to ascertain how potential recipients view the purpose of a program. This would help to ensure that the program meets the expectations and desires of the recipients.

Designing a successful reparations program also requires building a national narrative based on a factual account of the United States' history of racial oppression and racially biased economic policy. Unfortunately, recent developments have revealed that many important events—such as the antiblack violence of the Reconstruction era, the white terror campaign of the Red Summer of 1919, and the white riot in Tulsa in 1921 and many other white-led massacres—have not been woven into the nation's historical narrative or properly contextualized as events of racial, political, and economic oppression of black people.

Similarly, the nation has yet to acknowledge let alone atone for these events and for the federal government's role in them. Preliminary work by scholars has begun to document not only the economic loss of direct racial violence but also the productivity and innovation losses due to racialized violence and economic capture of black wealth (Cook 2014; Darity and Mullen 2020).

A reparations project would address this problem not only through policy but also through education and historical analysis. Narratives can be gathered to gauge the national price paid for racially exclusive and discriminatory practices that potentially lower national productivity and misallocate resources (Hsieh et al. 2019). Indeed, the building of a narrative would make the moral, economic, and political case for reparations even more apparent.

Seizing the momentum of the reparations movement is critical for the United States to move forward as a multiracial, multiethnic society committed to the ideals of equal opportunity and equality before the law. These conditions have not been met in the American past, but reparations can begin the process of bringing that promise to fruition in a genuine way.

American history has attempted to address racial inequality and present and cumulative discrimination in fits and starts, but never before has there been a genuine opportunity for reparations that, if properly designed, could methodically address America's racial stain. Fulfilling that promise is critical if this nation is to live up to its creed and survive as a functioning democracy into the future.

REFERENCES

Berry, Mary F. 2005. *My Face Is Black Is True: Callie House and the Struggle for Ex-slave Reparations.* New York: Knopf.
———. 2014. "We Need a 'Reparations Superfund.'" *New York Times,* June 9.
Commission chargée de répartir l'indemnité attribuée aux anciens colons de Saint-Domingue. 1828. *État détaillé des liquidations opérées par la Commission chargée de répartir l'indemnité attribuée aux anciens colons de Saint-Domingue, en exécution de la loi du 30 avril 1828* [Detailed statement of the liquidations carried out by the commission in charge of distributing the indemnity attributed to the former colonists of Saint-Domingue, in execution of the law of April 30, 1828]. Paris: Imprimerie Royale.
Cook, Lisa D. 2014. "Violence and Economic Activity: Evidence from African American Patents, 1870–1940." *Journal of Economic Growth* 19 (2): 221–57.
Craemer, Thomas. 2015. "Estimating Slavery Reparations: Present Value Comparisons of Historical Multigenerational Reparations Policies." *Social Science Quarterly* 96 (2): 639–55.
———. 2018. "International Reparations for Slavery and the Slave Trade." *Journal of Black Studies* 49 (7): 694–713.
———. 2019. "Comparative Analysis of Reparations for the Holocaust and for the Transatlantic Slave Trade." *Review of Black Political Economy* 45 (4): 299–324. https://doi.org/10.1177_0034644619836263.
Darity, William A. 2019. "Running the Numbers on Closing the Racial Wealth Gap." Policy Brief, August. Samuel DuBois Cook Center on Social Equity. https://socialequity.duke.edu/wp-content/uploads/2019/10/Running-the-Numbers-8.4.19-FINAL.pdf.
Darity, William A., Jr., and A. Kirsten Mullen. 2020. *From Here to Equality: Reparations for Black Americans in the 21st Century.* Chapel Hill: University of North Carolina Press.
Fogel, Robert W., and Dora L. Costa. 1997. "A Theory of Technophysio Evolution, with Some Implications for the Forecasting Population, Health Care Costs, and Pension Costs." *Demography* 34 (1): 49–66.
Fogel, Robert W., and Stanley L. Engerman. 1977. "Explaining the Relative Efficiency of Slave Agriculture in the Antebellum South." *American Economic Review* 67 (3): 275–96.
Hsieh, Chang-Tai, Erik Hurst, Charles I. Jones, and Peter J. Klenow. 2019. "The Allocation of Talent and U.S. Economic Growth." *Econometrica* 87 (5): 1439–74.
Jones-Rogers, Stephanie E. 2019. *They Were Her Property: White Women as Slave Owners in the American South.* New Haven, CT: Yale University Press.

Logan, Trevon D., and Jonathan B. Pritchett. 2018. "On the Marital Status of U.S. Slaves: Evidence from Touro Infirmary, New Orleans, Louisiana." *Explorations in Economic History* 69 (1): 50–63.

Manjapra, Kris. 2018. "When Will Britain Face Up to Its Crimes against Humanity?" *The Guardian*, March 29. www.theguardian.com/news/2018/mar/29/slavery-abolition-compensation-when-will-britain-face-up-to-its-crimes-against-humanity.

Savali, Kirsten West. 2014. "Did You Know: US Gov't Paid Reparations . . . to Slave Owners." *NewsOne*, May 31. https://newsone.com/3012856/did-you-know-us-govt-paid-reparations-to-slave-owners/.

Steckel, Richard H. 1986. "A Peculiar Population: The Nutrition, Health, and Mortality of American Slaves from Childhood to Maturity." *Journal of Economic History* 46 (3): 721–41.

Swinton, David H. 1990. "Racial Inequality and Reparations." In *The Wealth of Races: The Present Value of Benefits from Past Injustices*, edited by R.F. America, 107–23. Westport, CT: Greenwood Press.

8

Reparations and Adult Education

Civic and Community Engagement for
Lifelong Learners

LISA R. BROWN

Central to the viability and relevance of the field of adult education are three aims: (1) basic education and literacy; (2) social justice, civic, and community engagement learning; and (3) workforce and human resource development—although the prominence of one or another of these aims in the field shifts around from time to time. Nevertheless, producing scholarship on adult education as an aspect of reparations is consistent with the field's historic role on the front lines in promoting social and economic justice for black people in the United States.

Yet the field of adult and continuing education has been relatively silent on the question of reparations for native black Americans. Except for a position paper written by Lisa Brown and William Darity (2020) for the American Association for Adult and Continuing Education (AAACE) at the time of this chapter's development, very little contemporary adult education literature advocates for making compensatory payments to citizens who are descendants of formerly enslaved people here in the United States.

Issues of poverty, police murders, and extrajudicial killings of unarmed blacks around the nation, combined with the disparate impacts of COVID-19 infections and deaths, have prompted the American Public Health Association and several state and local health departments to declare that racism in America is a twenty-first-century public health crisis (Benjamin 2020). Relatedly, this chapter presents the case for a true reparations project for black Americans described here as ethnic citizens of Ancestral Black American Lineage (ABAL; Darity et al. 2021)—to counter antiblack racism, especially in the domains of economics and psychosocial health.

The ABAL acronym, created by this author, identifies native black descendants of formerly enslaved people who were not voluntary immigrants and who subsequently formed a new black American ethnic identity in the United States. By definition, the parents and all four grandparents of an ABAL ethnic are native black citizens who are descended from American slaves. The ABAL term is like the term American Descendant of Slavery (ADOS), but an ADOS-identified black person may have one parent who is white or one parent who is of a foreign lineage (e.g., is a member of the African diaspora) whose family has voluntarily immigrated to the United States.

The field of adult education and lifelong learning has often been at the forefront of American social justice movements—from the Negro adult education literature produced during the mid-1930s under the leadership of Alain LeRoy Locke to the activism training at the Highlander Folk School, which provided community organizing tutelage for Martin Luther King Jr., Rosa Parks, and Septima Clark (Lisa Brown and Darity 2020; Hughes 1985). All three latter trainees used their preparation to help increase adult education and voter registration in the South (Hughes 1985). It would seem quite natural for those of us in the field of adult and continuing education to ally with the cause of reparations advocacy through our links to higher education, workforce development, and activities of civic and community engagement praxis for adults. This chapter draws upon a constructivist theoretical framework of adult developmental thinking and experiential learning (Bell and Bell 2020; Lisa Brown 2017, 2018; Lisa Brown, McCray, and Neal 2022; Piaget 1967) as a lens to explore and deconstruct the associated topics of black American reparations, racial terrorism, and eligible recipients for restitution. It is intended to provide insights into how coalition building around reparations might be advanced within the field and throughout the nation.

THE PAUCITY OF REPARATIONS LITERATURE IN ADULT EDUCATION

Reparations has long had a legal meaning as an instrument of criminal sentencing decision-making whereby a defendant is obliged to pay restitution to a victim. However, an interdisciplinary review of the literature on the reparations concept reveals a plethora of meaning-making. Merrall, Dhami, and Bird (2010) discuss reparations for victims of crime but make no explicit mention of race, lineage, or ethnic group affiliation as an associated condition for reparations. They also do not mention any form of direct payment to a crime victim as a function of the harm perpetrated.

One adult educator, Karen Charman (2015), a researcher in the new field of public pedagogy, or education outside formal institutions, has tangentially brought up reparations in her study of an Australian arts-based revitalization project called Memory Space in the suburb of Sunshine, Melbourne. Part of the project involved obtaining narratives from older adult residents adversely affected by the local impact of manufacturing and railways. The study examined the importance of memory preservation through oral histories and photos displayed as artifacts of the disruptive and sometimes tragic nature of industrialization in the Melbourne community. The older residents reflected on how industrial change had reshaped their workplace identities, particularly when privatization moved the railways from being government owned to privately held. The railways were a significant part of the Sunshine residents' heritage and memory. For older adults, the opportunity to offer photos in narrative reflections about the structures that had affected their ways of being in the community was described as cathartic and restorative. Charman (2015, 372) concluded that "the act of Nigel [one of the longtime residents] exhibiting his photos can be seen as *reparation*—to repair the damaged internal object in this instance the railways" (emphasis added).

However, a reparations project for black Americans must not center on the social repair of emotional damages. It must seek to provide external repairs as direct payments to the victims. Darity and Mullen (2020, 2) offer the acronym ARC to represent three critical elements necessary for a true reparations project for black Americans: acknowledgment, redress, and closure.

How central might adult education be in such a project? Suggestions emerge from John Tateishi's (2020) account of how the Japanese American Citizens League (JACL) conducted the campaign that succeeded in obtaining reparations for Japanese Americans' internment. The first part of the JACL's plan was a campaign to educate Japanese American adults about the racial injustice of the mass incarceration that had been imposed upon their community and about the federal government's role in directing the policies against Japanese Americans that had led to the mass incarceration and its accompanying harms. The JACL was instrumental in collecting testimony from members of the Japanese American community who had been interned, which was entered in the Congressional Record. The second part was to educate and engage the mainstream American public beyond the Japanese American community. Tateishi believed that until members of Congress could determine that voters, particularly in their own districts, supported the JACL campaign for redress, the more resistant Congress members would be under little obligation to draft redress legislation. The success of the Japanese Americans' reparations education campaign is instructive for contemporary reparationists—advocates for the payment of reparations—in their pursuit of national redress on behalf of native black Americans who are the descendants of slaves.

AN EARLY ERA OF NEGRO ADULT LEARNING SOCIETIES

The desire for literacy and adult education has always been strong within the black community. African Americans' initiative and desire to pursue adult education and learning is documented as early as 1673, when an ordained Puritan clergyman, Cotton Mather, attested to how a "company of poor Negroes came of their own accord" seeking his assistance and that of his church members to learn the Christian catechism and establish a Negro learning society for their group (Henschke 1997, 260). Hence, the creation of adult learning societies for blacks predates the Emancipation Proclamation—January 1, 1863—by nearly two hundred years, and such societies continued to multiply after the Civil War ended.

In the late eighteenth century, adult learning societies welcomed African American men and women. Among them were the African Union Society of Newport, Rhode Island, created in 1780, the Perseverance Benevolent and Mutual Aid Association of New Orleans (1783), the Free African Society of Philadelphia (1787), and the Boston African Society and the Benevolent Daughters of Philadelphia (1796). In the South such societies took much longer to emerge, and black churches were the most influential organizations for black adults' education (Stubblefield and Keane 1994).

In the Northeast, African Americans further sought to expand adult education opportunities by enlisting the aid of abolition societies and the American Conventions for Promoting the Abolition of Slavery, which began in 1794. Later, in 1853, other societies emerged in the West to provide education for blacks, such as the California Academy of Natural Sciences, the Historical Society, and the Negro San Francisco Athenaeum (Henschke 1997, 260).

However, educational programs such as the Quakers' evening schools for black adults began to "stir the prejudice" of whites against African Americans (Henschke 1997, 260). While some whites, particularly white abolitionists, saw adult literacy among blacks for purposes of daily functionality and work as acceptable, white supremacists feared that literacy would inspire blacks to seek equality with whites in life and opportunities via armed resistance. In the early nineteenth century, the enslaved Nat Turner learned to read and became inspired to lead a revolt against slavery. Turner may have read the work of a free black author named David Walker, who had penned *Appeal to the Coloured Citizens of the World*. In his writings, Walker called for armed resistance to slavery and the provision of land to black peoples (Darity and Mullen 2020, 88). Hence, among whites, blacks' acquisition of literacy became inextricably tied to fears about blacks resisting white supremacy theology and gaining their freedom.

THE FEDERAL GOVERNMENT'S ROLE IN ADULT EDUCATION

Access to education is not reparations but has been viewed as an asset that could increase black American prosperity. Historically, some federal actions have been initiated to support progress for black adults in America through the introduction of adult education and literacy legislation. Such efforts alone fall short of the economic repair and restoration necessary for a reparations plan that would include direct payments to all eligible recipients.

It can be argued that the federal government's significant role in adult education began with the expansive social welfare legislation introduced by President Lyndon Johnson's Great Society and War on Poverty in the early to mid-1960s (Rose 1991). Johnson believed these programs could uplift black Americans, but they did not close the black-white wealth gap, nor were they specifically designed as black reparations.

Johnson's predecessor, John F. Kennedy, had unsuccessfully sought to pass an education bill, including provisions for adult education, and after Kennedy was assassinated, Johnson presented a new version of that legislation, the Economic Opportunity Act of 1964, as a way of memorializing him (Eyre and Pawloski 2013, 10). Two years later, the adult education part of the bill was removed from Office of Economic Opportunity funding and transferred to the Office of Education under the 1966 Adult Education Act (AEA), partly because some legislators wanted to ensure that English as a second language (ESL) instruction would be provided even to individuals who were not low-income eligible.

For Johnson, education was a crucial antipoverty strategy (Rose 1991). During the mid-1960s, unemployment levels were generally dropping with recovery from the economic recession of 1960–61, but disproportionately high levels of unemployment remained for blacks, non-English-speaking adults, and the undereducated (Eyre and Pawloski 2013, 9). It became clear that their competitive disadvantage in the labor market could not be remedied by vocational programs alone, and the federal government consequently turned to adult education as a remedy. The AEA was a major turning point in the history of adult education: for the first time the federal government committed to funding adult basic education and ESL instruction, with the aim of enabling adults to obtain or retain employment and otherwise participate more fully as citizens.

Both the AEA and the 1964 Equal Opportunity Act provided means for the federal government to bypass the bureaucracies of states that lacked commitment to adult education and did not have legislation guaranteeing it, or whose dissimilar educational authority, operations, and funding could conflict with those of the federal government. Both pieces of legislation allowed the federal government to assume the major funding share (approximately 90 percent) for adult education. However, it was not uncommon to witness debates between states over the nature of the target population and appropriate nomenclature for the federally funded adult education programs, as well as conflicts due to limited administrative coordination among state agencies regarding questions of whose purposes were in best alignment to serve the adult learner population.

In 1991, the National Literacy Act (NLA), which included grants for workplace literacy, was passed and incorporated into the AEA. But in the 1990s an emphasis on promoting a competent workforce and individual economic self-sufficiency in the face of shrinking government resources led to the 1998 Workforce Investment Act (WIA). Introduced during the presidency of Democrat Bill Clinton and a Republican Congress led by Representative Newt Gingrich, Title II of this Act, the Adult Education and Family Literacy Act of 1998 (AEFLA), replaced both the AEA and NLA legislation. It promoted partnerships among adult education, labor, and training organizations, with the aims of enabling adults (1) to become literate and obtain the knowledge and skills necessary for employment and self-sufficiency; (2) to become full partners in the educational development of their children; and (3) to complete their secondary school education. It also heightened funded programs' accountability through the National Reporting System and annual performance measures.

During the early 1990s, the AEA integrated its services with other federal programs that provided special-needs services to immigrant populations, the institutionalized, and learning-disabled adults. Notably, there has been a historical pattern in which explicitly race-targeted federal initiatives and antidiscrimination programs, such as affirmative action, that were aimed at repairing injustices and providing equality and betterment for black Americans have encountered resistance from whites. Resentment toward race-preference programs for blacks in the twentieth century was pronounced, as was resentment toward reparations proposals—even when direct payments to eligible recipients were not included as part of the remedy (*Harvard Law Review* 2002).

To assuage white resentment about the active federal enforcement of race-preference affirmative action, an expansion of the law occurred to include the concept of equal employment opportunity and the hiring of antidiscrimination specialists. By becoming a part of broader equal employment opportunity and affirmative action programs that included non-ABAL ethnics, such as white women and other disadvantaged ethnic/racial classes, race-preference programs survived President Ronald Reagan's efforts in the early 1980s to enact cutbacks to their enforcement.

Subsequently, the rhetoric of diversity management was introduced as the instrument for ending discrimination, particularly in the areas of hiring (Kelly and Dobbin 1998) and higher education opportunities. However, organizational priorities and equal opportunity/affirmative action goals shifted for the antidiscrimination specialists, who began to tout diversity for achieving human resource efficiency and who newly articulated their previous race-preference mission as one of "increasing profits by expanding diversity in the workforce and customer base" (Kelly and Dobbin 1998, 962).

Currently, opponents continue to work to dismantle or weaken race-preference programs (Friedersdorf 2020) as American demographic trends are shifting in certain areas of the country, thereby introducing new levels of complexity to social justice advocacy in the field of adult education. Yet at the same time, the level of national public support is rising for reparations for black Americans who are the descendants of the formerly enslaved in the country.

THE ADULT EDUCATION TERRAIN FOR REPARATIONS WORK

Adult education is distinguished from the compulsory schooling that takes place in K-12 education (Parkay 2020) and from traditional undergraduate higher education. Typically, the field describes adult learners as aged twenty-five and over, as more mature, and as self-directed learners who require greater flexibility in their study schedules (evening/weekend classes). Often adult learners are characterized as being more technology averse than younger people or as having a lower tolerance for technology learning. They may be married or have parenting responsibilities, and they often hold full-time jobs.

Self-directed learning is a primary process and defining characteristic of adult education (Merriam and Bierema 2014). Under a self-directed learning model, pedagogical delivery is driven by learners who are *self-managing, self-monitoring,* and *self-modifying.* Theory suggests that adults' motivation to learn is based on the material's practicality to their lives and goals, with critical consideration given to what is worth knowing. Globally, most adult education occurs via three types of modalities—*formal, nonformal,* and *informal* learning.

Formal adult education is typically guided by a sanctioned curriculum that leads to a recognized credential such as a diploma, a certificate, or a degree. Instructors in the context of formal learning are usually trained (i.e., expert professionals) in pedagogical delivery. Service-learning curricula and community engagement projects are types of modalities for delivering formal civics education to undergraduates enrolled at many of the nation's colleges and universities.

Nonformal adult learning may or may not be guided by a formal curriculum and is loosely organized. It is typically led by a qualified teacher or by a leader-lecturer who possesses more experience. The learning objectives and goals do not result in a formal credential. Nonformal adult learning is highly enriching, builds skills and capacities, and is often considered more engaging because adult learners' interest is the driving force behind their participation (Rocco et al. 2020).

The lyceums of mid-nineteenth-century America exemplify this mode of learning. Named for a school in classical Athens conducted by Aristotle, lyceums were the first form of mass public education for adults in America (Merriam and Bierema 2014). They featured lectures, dramatic performances, and debates that moved from town to town and state to state. Some black celebrities went on the lyceum circuit, most notably Frederick Douglass, who used his rhetorical skills to encourage black freedmen to improve their condition and citizen standing through "social assimilation" and self-help (Ray 2002, 626). The lyceums created the space for nonformal mass public adult education in the realms of civic engagement and politics, particularly for black people.

Informal adult learning occurs when no sanctioned curriculum is used and no educational credits are earned. It also commonly takes place as self-directed learning. The knowledge is simply delivered by someone the learner might know on a more personal level who has more experience than the learner. Informal learning does not necessitate that the adult imparting new knowledge possess any level of formal expertise. Online social media is an emerging area of informal (especially political) adult education and learning.

CIVIC AND COMMUNITY ENGAGEMENT FOR ADULT LEARNERS

Building support for reparations among adult learners can occur under any of the previous three learning modalities. However, critiques of traditional K-12 education have repeatedly drawn attention to its failure to supply foundational civics instruction or adequate American history instruction given its neglect of black history or refusal to view black history as coequal. There is also a long tradition of "dismemory" campaigns: organized and systemic efforts to manipulate and distort the nation's racial history (Darity and Mullen 2020, 173).

After the Civil War, the United Daughters of the Confederacy (UDC) took a major role in this regard. Their propaganda campaign absurdly portrayed the traitorous rebel Confederate forces and their murderous actions during the war as heroic (Darity and Mullen 2020). School textbooks indoctrinated southern children in "Lost Cause" mythology (Lyman 2020, para. 6), particularly as it related to the details of the nation's founding. The UDC failed to reveal how the United States amassed its wealth from the exploitation of human chattel (i.e., slavery) and how white mobs orchestrated through violence the failures and sabotaging of black wealth creation before and after Reconstruction.

More specifically, cultural *memes* are behavioral units of culture that influence adult thinking (Lisa Brown 2016b, 103–15). Numerous memes in American culture can serve to perpetuate false narratives about the realities of slavery and American history within our traditional pedagogy, higher education, and textbooks. For example, a Texas textbook was challenged as recently as 2015 for describing blacks subjected to the atrocities of American chattel slavery as merely unpaid "workers" and as "immigrants" (Schaub 2015). Characterizing ABAL ethnics as *immigrants* downplays the cruel treatment inflicted on their enslaved ancestors and audaciously suggests that people who were bought and sold exercised some degree of agency through volunteering to accept a life of perpetual bondage for themselves and their children.

And the most extreme accounts gaslight ABAL ethnics, in some respects blaming them for becoming enslaved or for failing to succeed once freed. Such accounts ignore the ways that slavery, massacres of freed black people and seizures of their land and property, and ongoing exclusion of and discrimination toward black Americans have created and perpetuated a black-white wealth gap, and the ways the federal government's immoral policies, political handicapping, and legislative failures have made it complicit with these injustices.

During the early to mid-twentieth century, Dr. Carter G. Woodson and his colleagues established the Association for the Study of Negro Life and History (ASNLH), promoting academic research on black life and authoring several K-12 black history textbooks to counter memes and school-based instruction that "classified Black people as docile, uncivilized, and lazy" (King 2017, 14). But as Lyman (2020) notes, change has come slowly: "Textbooks that said Black southerners were content to be second-class citizens were in use in Virginia well into the 1980s," and in Mississippi, students were not required to learn about the civil rights movement until 2011.

As a result, for many black American adults who have little opportunity and limited resources to pursue formal higher education, nonformal and informal civic and community engagement activities are the most viable points of access for teaching about reparations in the public sphere free of charge (along with the use of social media). Building a better understanding of the importance and value of restorative justice and restitution for the debt owed to native black Americans is the starting point for developing reparationists, bolstering political advocacy, and promoting mass adult education in our communities about these topics.

REPARATIONS SKEPTICISM

In general, support for reparations has been increasing among both black and white Americans, with (unsurprisingly) significantly more support among black Americans (Dawson and Popoff 2004; Andrew 2019). Axelrod (2020, para. 2) found in a Reuters/Ipsos poll released in

2020 that one in five respondents said the US should use "taxpayer money to pay damages to descendants of enslaved people in the United States." But one of the most challenging and disheartening aspects of reparations advocacy among adults is the number of Americans who do not believe that such a project is even possible or who believe that black people do not deserve it.

The Issue of Defining Eligible Recipients

According to surveys, most blacks hold that direct payments to eligible recipients are necessary for the implementation of a fair and equality-driven reparations project. But what to make of the not-insignificant percentage of blacks who believe no such repair is warranted (AP/NORC 2019)?

This issue may turn on the question of what "eligible recipients" means. For Darity and Mullen (2020), one of the fundamental requirements of a *true reparations* plan for black Americans is a kinship connection to the once enslaved: at least one formerly enslaved ancestor who was at minimum subjected to US chattel slavery and subsequent phases of antiblack racial atrocities (e.g., government-sanctioned legal segregation and mass incarceration, and other forms of anti-ABAL ethnic oppression). The unique reality of slave bondage and enslavers' control over the sexual reproduction of human chattel prompted the authors to determine that employing a lineage standard *must complement the usage of a racial standard.*

Polls that register a lack of support among some black people for reparations as direct payments can be difficult to interpret, partly because race and ethnicity categories are often nebulously constructed when African American identity is not disaggregated by ethnic and cultural groups. For example, African immigrants are subidentified by tribes (George-Mwangi et al. 2017; Sharpe 2019), and Caribbean immigrants maintain distinct ethnic identities separate from native black Americans. Could such complexities of multiracial/multiethnic conditions of identity affect the levels of those who are polled under the umbrella grouping of "African Americans," yet oppose the project of government-funded reparations in the form of direct payments explicitly for native black Americans in the United States? There is currently a need for more empirical studies to address the complexity of black resistance to an ABAL reparations project.

Implicit Bias and Implicit Closeness

One perspective on attitudes toward reparations among whites is suggested by the research of Craemer (2014). It explores how the willingness of adults to accept pro-black policies (e.g., slavery reparations, affirmative action, government support for blacks, or voting for a person who is perceived to be black to the office of president) is based on two types of implicit associations: implicit bias, an *evaluative association*, in which a racial stimulus evokes race-unrelated target words (evaluation of blacks as the object of attitudes); and implicit closeness, a weaker *relational association*, in which a racial stimulus evokes feelings of self-other overlap (identification and empathy with blacks as people).

The persistence of antiblack *evaluative* bias in the United States has been described as hidden bias or essentially "aversive racism," even as Americans have become less willing to openly express explicit antiblack attitudes (Craemer 2014, 413). Moreover, a racial stimulus can evoke both types of association at the same time. For example, discussions of police brutality and mass incarceration in the black American community may evoke *relational associations* of empathy from whites even as those whites draw on negative antiblack attitudes and stereotypes of black criminality memes (i.e., *evaluative associations*). Such conflicts may lead non-ADOS to support the notion of reparations but not in the form of direct-cash payments—because of a meme believing that *blacks are lazy.*

Greenwald, McGhee, and Schwartz (1998) have also contributed to the scholarship on implicit bias via a popular measure of prowhite and antiblack evaluations in their Implicit Association Test (IAT). Almost two decades since its introduction, studies affirm the predictive validity of the IAT relative to measuring implicit biases between white and black subjects but in limited domains (Greenwald, Banaji, and Nosek 2014). The IAT's ability to detect racially discriminatory behavior is greater ($r = .236$) than the self-report measures ($r = .117$) of such biases. Oswald et al. (2013) have criticized the IAT's capacity to determine who will discriminate against whom when factors of consistency involving attitude-behavior or stereotype-judgment correlations are introduced. Nevertheless, a meta-analysis of the value of IAT concluded that it was empirically justifiable to use the test to "predict societally important discrimination" (Greenwald, Banaji, and Nosek 2014, 559) relative to black-white race attitudes.

However, the problem with such conclusive use of the IAT is associative criteria and visual assumptions about who is racially black or white. Such assessments are dependent upon the notion of racial intelligibility: the assumption that there is some innate capacity to determine race (with precision) using a set of commonly associated phenotypes. For example, it is very possible for a black American ABAL ethnic to visually look like a foreign-born member of the African diaspora or a continental African—a person of African Ancestry Foreign Lineage (AAFL). Racial intelligibility causes one to conveniently conclude that *all blacks are the same* even when they may possess strikingly dissimilar stories, tribal mores, and experienced psychosocial cultural realities and connections to American history. Such dubious assumptions underlie the suggested use of a simplistic *race-based* criterion for a native black American reparations project.

People of Color and the Stigma of Black American Self-Advocacy

The descendants of the formerly enslaved in America have been racially described by a plethora of names, most of them not self-authored; these have included *Negro, colored, black,* and subsequently *African American.* According to Rhonda Vonshay Sharpe (2019), more recently there has been a shift toward the term *people of color*, which aggregates African Americans with other nonwhite groups. This began in 1977, at the National Women's Conference in Houston, Texas. Black women activists and scholars attending the conference were concerned that its agenda did not adequately address black women's needs, so they drew up a Black Women's Agenda. "When other non-white women saw it, they wanted their concerns to be included—and they were—but that meant the name had to change to something more inclusive. Thus, the term 'women of colour' was born." Yet this change effectively reduced black women's power to self-advocate (Sharpe 2019, 1240).

Currently, more than forty years after the compromise, the term *people of color* (POC) is used to categorize and *minoritize* any non-white-identifying racial groups. We continue to see identity categories and groupings, such as "black and brown," "BIPOC," and (nonwhite) "minority," that generate antiblackness, racial oppression, or marginalization and are based upon *neo*-majoritarian realities (Love 2004). Such terms (i.e., memes) imply that a racial-ethnic sociopolitical alliance necessarily exists between these communities as it relates to the need for racial change proposals and responses to harms, though in some cases race-preference affirmative action at public and private universities has been legally challenged not only by whites but by other POC groups (Legal Information Institute 2012; Raymond 2021).

A historical pattern exists in America where whites attempt to thwart measures of group-specific or targeted self-advocacy on behalf of native black Americans. The POC term is among the latest memes used to decenter ADOS advocacy. The expectation has been that native black Americans should be inclusive in the establishment of their sociopolitical agenda sacrificially centering other groups' pushes for redress while decentralizing their own group-specific needs. It has been a socially stagnating phenomenon for ABAL citizens in America. This situation was eloquently described by Esolen (2018, 159), who wrote that "no one can behave unjustly toward others without harming himself in the act. . . . African Americans have been employed as ideological pack-mules. One group after another has heaped its luggage atop their backs, even while the injustice that the blacks did most grossly suffer has been elided. Their actual condition in the present is largely ignored by [the] right and left because it touches upon moral questions that we prefer not to address." Reparations, of course, is one such question, which some may oppose because it centers on native black Americans specifically.

Antireparations Arguments

Unsurprisingly, the most common challenges to reparations for black Americans come from adults who are not entitled to them, both whites and nonwhites. Some view a reparations project as moot because no persons who were themselves enslaved are still alive. Others have argued that race-conscious opportunities—that they have begrudgingly supported in the past—have already supplied the necessary framework for racial equality and generational restitution (Kaminer 2000); some even claim, offensively, that the debt has already been paid via the election of Barack Obama to the US presidency in 2008 (Barrett 2019). Still others believe that the contemporary black-white wealth chasm speaks more to the unindustrious nature of blacks than to the failure of government. They may embrace an ideology that American opportunity is based upon a system of meritocracy and that if one applies oneself through "self-invention" and diligence the American Dream is achievable (Kaminer 2000, 38). Such an ideology fails to consider the long-term detrimental impact of intergenerational barriers (Winship, Reeves, and Guyot 2018) and often amounts to memes suggesting that the poor should "pull themselves up by their bootstraps." Relatedly, some argue that reparations constitute a government "handout."

In their book *From Here to Equality,* Darity and Mullen (2020) have challenged such simplistic notions by tracing the history of the federal government's direct culpability for inequality. Their scholarship emphasizes the past and contemporary injustices against blacks who are the descendants of formerly enslaved blacks in America, highlighting how not only slavery but also subsequent denial of the promised forty-acre land grants to black families, atrocities targeting black Americans, and continued and systematic thwarting of wealth-building opportunities for blacks have all contributed to ABAL ethnics' ongoing position at the bottom of the economic ladder.

Notably, Winship, Reeves, and Guyot (2018) found that black American males born into poverty had the lowest income earnings mobility when compared to whites. Black women were at the highest risk of remaining in poverty as adults (62 percent), and they remained in the bottom quintile of individual earnings and family income when compared to black men, white men, and white women. The latter two groups had the economic bolstering effect of higher marriages, which served to increase their families' socioeconomic mobility and wealth when compared to black Americans.

Therefore, it is unwarranted to dismiss the importance of discriminatory economic disenfranchisement of ABAL ethnics as a mediating factor to lost familial hereditary wealth. A restitution project would insist that contemporary adults—who are the descendants of slaves—victimized by structural poverty that has been created and reinforced by the US government's actions and failures to act, be granted the direct payment owed to them (i.e., reparations) as an appropriate remedy. The federal government would not be providing a handout to black Americans. Rather, it would be meeting its long-overdue debt owed to a foundational group of people that has witnessed the progression and surpassing of ABAL citizens by not only whites but also aspiring immigrant groups as they collectively remain the largest nonwhite class of citizens in America perpetually tethered to the economic bottom.

USING A CONSTRUCTIVIST FRAMEWORK TO GUIDE REPARATIONS PLANNING

In earlier work (Lisa Brown 2016a, 2018), I examined the complexity of civic engagement among adults in South America and the United States using a constructivist adult development framework based on the stages of adult human development outlined in psychologist Clare W. Graves's (1970, 1974) Emergent Cyclical Levels of Existence Theory (ECLET). This chapter applies Graves's constructs to consider how adults might best be led, managed, instructed, and mentored for the cause of black American reparations.

My stage theory (Lisa Brown 2016a, 2018) offers a memetic taxonomy of types of adaptive worldview thinking that range from simplistic to higher-order cognition. These memetic ways of knowing and being and their associated deep-value systems are used to describe and deconstruct adult experiences on an individual, group, or societal level in response to existential dilemmas or life events (Beck and Cowan 2006; Beck et al. 2018). In the case of reparations, the stages can be used to understand which adults would be more inclined to support a black American reparations project (as well as those who would never do so) and how civic and community-engaged adult educators might influence and inform lifelong learners on this subject.

A FRAMEWORK FOR ADULT DEVELOPMENTAL THINKING

This section briefly describes various worldview constructs and those themes most relevant to civic and community engagement for reparations advocacy and coalition building. There are many life-stage models for adult development (Erickson 2007; Erikson 1959; Levinson 2016). Nevertheless, my elaboration of ECLET themes presents a deeper understanding of how these stages can be applied to adult developmental thinking theory and civic engagement research with adults (Lisa Brown 2018, 2016a; Lisa Brown and Sandmann 2013; Lisa Brown, Sandmann, and Bliss 2012), in turn raising possibilities for applications to a national black American reparations project.

To restate, memes are units of culture that are passed on from person to person via human imitation (Lisa Brown 2018; Dawkins 1976). They simply become how things (e.g., educational pedagogy, public policy, personal beliefs, or expressed values) have always been done, yet can evolve. The term *meme* in this chapter represents how adult learners problem-solve and interpret the surrounding world on the basis of their (often subconscious) values. Below is a clinical summary of established *value meme* systems (and developing definitions) associated with adult developmental thinking (Lisa Brown 2016b, 2018; Lisa Brown, McCray, and Neal, 2022; Graves 2005).

Basic Instinctive Worldview. Representative of a precultural exist-ence in which the individual possesses low self-awareness. Thinking is driven by physiological imperatives and the simple purpose of staying alive (Beck et al. 2018; Lisa Brown 2016b). Internal locus of control; individualistic thematic orientation.

Magical Mystical Worldview. Concerned with safety and security through kinship ties. This worldview system is characterized by a belief in obedience to the desires of magical-mystical spiritual beings and divine authorities (e.g., priests, shamans, tribe elders). Thinking is marked by tribalism and traditionalism. The individual desires to find protection within a dangerous and unpredictable world. Allegiance is given to the preservation of customs and clans. Sacred objects and spaces are preserved and protected, as tribal rituals are held in high esteem. External locus of control; collectivist thematic orientation.

Power Impulsive Worldview. Egocentric and often marked by imper-atives of domination by force. The individual perceives that life is a jungle with *haves* and *have-nots* and is motivated by a driving force to be among the *haves*. One aims to avoid shame and to defend one's reputation by demanding respect, even if it requires deadly force to do so. Thinking and actions are impulsive. The individual is remorseless about possible outcomes, as simplistic rationalizing suggests that conse-quences may or may not ever occur. Internal locus of control; individu-alistic orientation.

Purposeful and Saintly Living Worldview. Represents honor and a good-versus-evil memetic worldview. Thinking can be marked by dog-matic absolutism, urging calls for sacrifice to bring order and stability to a chaotic space. Responses to existential dilemmas require the use of guilt to enforce divine moral principles. The individual believes in indi-vidual assignments to specific places in life that are to be accepted as predestined. Problems are assessed by determining good versus evil, right versus wrong, and the most extreme versions of this worldview require dogmatic obedience. Thinking is often paternalistic and author-itarian, with the stated goal of obtaining the betterment of everyone. Rules are to be followed and are non-negotiable. External locus of con-trol; collectivist orientation.

Strategic Materialism Worldview. Marked by manipulation and a memetic worldview that privileges autonomy and independence. Win-ning and competition are prevailing values, with scheming and cunning strategies to obtain desired outcomes representing a driving force.

Achievements that bring praise and material possessions are optimal rewards. Scientific reliability and the use of technology are believed to offer the best competitive advantages that result in winning against an adversary. One is careful not to arouse the disfavor or suspicions of those in higher authority. Thinking is grounded in logic and a calculated reasonable certainty for success. More sophisticated than the prior Power Impulsive Worldview, strategic thinking means individuals do not seek to make open enemies. Internal locus of control; individualistic orientation.

Humanistic Consensus-Building Worldview. Believes in human dignity and consensus building in contrast to religious edicts. Features an effort to explore the personal *inner self* in cooperation with the inner self-discovery also being made by others. Prioritizes the life of community, unity, and harmony, as the group seeks to share societal resources for the benefit of all. Rejects notions of greed and dogmatic authoritarianism, as decision-making is based upon the concurrence of minds. Togetherness and acceptance replace the previous worldview of strategic materialism and privileging of scientific logic. Displays a more tempered acceptance of obedience and authority figures. External locus of control; collectivist orientation.

Creativity and Innovation Worldview. The first of the more complexity-oriented constructs (i.e., Tier 2 worldviews). Features flexible thinking that is open to change (Brown 2016). Represents a departure from the preoccupations of subsistence living found among the first six worldview constructs. Also features creative and innovative thinking, along with an attentiveness to *being* and a complex awareness of self and others. Problems typically associated with subsistence living are clearly understood even though they are not necessarily under control (Lisa Brown 2016b; Graves 2005). Adults with this worldview welcome paradoxes and uncertainty and appreciate the complexity of human nature and societies. Notions of individual competence, expertise, flexibility, and spontaneity are valued as instruments for creative thought, with a more *tempered individualism* than that of earlier stages. Adult learning primarily occurs through observation and participation (i.e., experiential learning) but also through the concept of *being* as an ethical expression rather than a moral or religious personhood expression. Internal locus of control; individualistic orientation.

Holistic Globalism Worldview. The second of the *being* typology constructs. Marked by its ability to more easily negotiate complexity and recognize patterns more immediately than prior worldview constructs. Believes in the pursuit of the good for all living things and views the world as a single dynamic organism possessing its unique type of independent and anthropomorphic energy of *mind*. Dichotomies are more easily accepted; adults use the physical and metaphysical ways of knowing in synergy to solve complex problems that adults experience in life and *being* (Dawlabani and Beck 2013). Holistic and intuitive; open to concepts of spirituality, morality, and embodied knowing (Tisdell 2003). External locus of control; collectivist orientation.

BECOMING AN ADULT REPARATIONIST

The field of adult education—with its attention to formal, nonformal, and informal learning styles and its unique pedagogy regarding delivery of knowledge to lifelong learners—is especially poised for the task of developing competent adult reparationists. To garner support for a federal reparations program, it is crucial to appeal to neighbors, family, associates, and friends in a way that speaks to their capacity to understand, problematize, and engage in praxis activities. Understanding the ways adults think in relation to their ways of making meaning and problem-solving can be instructive in efforts to advocate for reparations and build national coalitions.

Developing a critical mass of citizens who agree to a black American reparations project in conjunction with a congressional commitment to right the governmental wrongs committed over the three key phases of human atrocities in America (Darity and Mullen 2020) will be no easy task. Civic and community engagement requires foundational knowledge about the rights and duties of citizenship (i.e., civics). Being a citizen is not passive; it requires intentional and genuine activism.

PROFITEERING ACTIVISM VERSUS NOT-FOR-PROFIT ACTIVISM

The concept of *profiteering activism* is not new in America, but it has arguably made a memetic shift from the days of Ward Connerly, a self-identified black American who vehemently opposed affirmative action in California (Friedersdorf 2020). Connerly was able to spearhead his anti–affirmative action campaign because his political activism was highly resourced by funding from wealthy conservative families and support from right-leaning political think tanks (Nicol 2021). The contemporary exploitation of the black community that has emerged in America often occurs under the cover of nonprofit organizations and tends to be more liberal and politically left-leaning in its ideologies than Connerly's profiteering.

The grassroots activism of Black Lives Matter was sparked, most immediately, by a series of tragic events, widely publicized by social media, where unarmed blacks including Sandra Bland, and especially males—Trayvon Martin, Mike Brown, Tamir Rice, Freddie Gray, and Eric Garner—were brutalized or killed with impunity by police officers, and around instances of antiblack extrajudicial violence. But with the growth of the BLM movement and a groundswell of popular support came a flood of donations and the precipitous elevation of community activists such as DeRay Mckesson and Shaun King, who raised millions of dollars for private organizations and foundations that lacked transparency or accountability as to how the money was spent (Lee Brown 2021). Both have dedicated a predominance of their energy and amassed funds toward public protests, partisan advocacy, LGBTQIA policy advancement (Katz 2016), and immigration advocacy (A. Brown 2019).

But a primary accusation of black activists has been that only a fraction of the money raised around wrongful black deaths and stewarded by largely white foundations and board members has been used to support the local chapters of protesters whose communities are most victimized by the targeted violence and whose advocacy work most needed resources. "BLACK DEATH IS A BUSINESS," wrote Darren Seals in 2015. "Millions and millions flowing through the hands of these organizations in the name of Mike Brown yet we don't see any of it coming into our community or being used to help our youth" (quoted in Kendzior 2016). Some have described a phenomenon of profiting off black pain, similar to the "black trauma porn" of movies that have made millions by showing black suffering (Steven Cannon, telephone conversation with author, April 27, 2021). Shamefully, the co-opting of the BLM movement became an international phenomenon with the Black Lives Matter Global Network Foundation, which raised tens of millions of dollars in response to the deaths of George Floyd and Breonna Taylor in 2020 and is currently under investigation for mishandling of finances (Roberts 2022). We hold that reparations in the form of direct payments to native black Americans can better position them to defend against such physical and economic violence.

It is challenging to determine where public advocacy and social activism cross over into greed—greed that can thwart a reparations project or the repair of the collective black masses. Nevertheless, it is still possible to privilege the public good or a national reparations project for black Americans without schemes leading to the personal enrichment of scammers or community exploitation.

One example of what might be called not-for-profit activism is the movement to fund education through public television, which began with small donations but ultimately required a congressional appropriation to remain sustainable. Fred Rogers, creator of the children's program *Mr. Rogers' Neighborhood*, obtained that appropriation. His work demonstrates the type of collectivist worldview thinking that a reparationist would possess, devoid of the need to profiteer or to exploit a human tragedy.

Rogers was a longtime advocate for community-sponsored educational television. In his seven-minute testimony before Congress on May 1, 1969, he told the Senate Subcommittee on Communications how without their increased support for the just-established PBS network his program, which he also described as a vehicle for good mental health, would cease to operate and would no longer provide an uplifting and wholesome viewing option for children, their families, and neighborhoods (PBS 2019). Subsequent to his testimony, PBS was awarded the $20 million Rogers had requested.

One of Rogers's most memorable admonitions came from his mother. It was particularly comforting to families after the Sandy Hook massacre in Newtown, Connecticut, when Fred Rogers said: "When I was a boy and I would see scary things in the news, my mother would say to me, 'Look for the helpers. You will always find people who are helping.' To this day, especially in times of 'disaster,' I remember my mother's words, and I am always comforted by realizing that there are still so many helpers—so many caring people in this world" (Suarez 2012).

The importance of looking for "helpers" cannot be overstated in efforts to build a national coalition around reparations for black Americans. The meme of a constructivist framework of value can guide us to the helpers that Fred Rogers celebrated (Lisa Brown, McCray, and Neal 2022), for they will more likely be found in those institutions and communities where adults hold to a more pronounced collectivist worldview. Members of the helper group could be identified using value meme worldview constructs and subsequently be deemed amenable to becoming reparationists and joining a national coalition effort.

Recognizing and cultivating adult developmental thinking that values justice and equality would yield adults who are amenable to a reparations project—as a response to a historical, ethical, and moral wrong that must be met with an equal remedy of restitution. For example,

adults thinking from a Holistic Globalism worldview, one that is amenable to reparations, would believe that we are all interconnected and
that the earth must be managed effectively if all are to survive. Hence,
such adults and indeed any other adults who viewed the world from the
more collectivist worldview constructs outlined above would consider
unacceptable the extreme harm and poverty brought about by the infliction of slavery and human atrocities on black American ethnics.

Approaching civic engagement via the interpretive perspective of the Emergent Cyclical Levels of Existence Theory stages of adult developmental
thinking, we appreciate that adults can maintain varying worldviews that
may support or oppose reparations. Fortunately, when formal and informal education reduces some of the obstructions to higher-order thinking,
and makes new enlightenment possible, adult learners can support the
praxis and social activism that spark national reparations advocacy. Nevertheless, some adults may never support a national reparations project for
black Americans. We cannot be discouraged by such stumbling blocks in
our quest for justice. The call for reparations is just; the debt is past due.

It is the responsibility of every citizen to cease obstructing progress of
justice and equality for ABAL ethnics. An enormous debt is owed this specific lineage group. They and their ancestors have paid heavily in unrecom-
pensed blood, sweat, and tears. Native black Americans who are the
descendants of the enslaved in the United States do not petition the federal
government for a benevolent favor. Black Americans have witnessed, supported, and celebrated other racial and ethnic groups who have been harmed
when they received restitution through the dispensation of monetary payments for injustices suffered under the government's stewardship. Reparationists are calling the government to account as the appropriate debtor and
the only fiscal entity capable of paying the tremendous bill owed to black
American descendants of the formerly enslaved in the United States.

REFERENCES

Andrew, Scottie. 2019. "Nearly 75% of African Americans Support Repara-
tions for Slavery: Only 15% of White Americans Do, a Poll Says." CNN,
October 28. www.cnn.com/2019/10/28/us/reparations-poll-trnd.
AP/NORC (Associated Press / National Opinion Research Center). 2019. "The
Legacy of Slavery." Database. https://apnorc.org/projects/the-legacy-of-slavery/.
Axelrod, Tal. 2020. "1 in 5 Supports Reparations in New Poll." *The Hill*, June
25. https://thehill.com/homenews/news/504511-1-in-5-supports-reparations-
in-new-poll.

Barrett, Ted. 2019. "Mitch McConnell: Obama and I Are 'Both Descendants of Slaveholders.'" CNN Politics, July 9. www.cnn.com/2019/07/09/politics/mitch-mcconnell-obama-reparations.

Beck, Don E., and Chris C. Cowan. 2006. *Spiral Dynamics: Mastering Values, Leadership, and Change.* Santa Barbara, CA: Blackwell.

Beck, Don E., Teddy H. Larsen, Sergey Solonin, S. Rica Viljoen, and Thomas Q. Johns. 2018. *Spiral Dynamics in Action: Humanity's Master Code.* West Sussex: Wiley.

Bell, Robin, and H. Bell. 2020. "Applying Educational Theory to Develop a Framework to Support the Delivery of Experiential Entrepreneurship Education." *Journal of Small Business and Enterprise Development* 27 (6): 987–1004. https://10.1108/JSBED-01-2020-0012.

Benjamin, George. 2020. "Racism Is an Ongoing Public Health Crisis That Needs Our Attention Now." American Public Health Association (APHA), press release, May 29. www.apha.org/News-and-Media/News-Releases/APHA-News-Releases/2020/Racism-is-a-public-health-crisis.

Brown, Ann. 2019. "Shaun King's $34M Black Lives Matter Fundraising Audit Shows $63 1K for White Supremacy, $20M for Immigration." *Moguldom,* September 12. https://moguldom.com/224788/shaun-kings-34m-black-lives-matter-fundraising-audit-shows-631k-for-white-supremacy-20m-for-immigration/.

Brown, Lee. 2021. "Black Lives Matter Foundation Received over $90M in Donations Last Year." *New York Post,* February 24. https://nypost.com/2021/02/24/black-lives-matter-received-over-90m-in-donations-last-year/.

Brown, Lisa R. 2016a. "Civic Engagement Activities and Outcomes in Chilean Private For-Profit and Public Graduate Education." PhD diss., University of Georgia.

———. 2016b. "Spiral Dynamic Theory an Instrument for Praxis: Memetic Racism and Cultural Transfer." In *RIP Jim Crow: Fighting Racism through Higher Education Policy, Curriculum, and Cultural Interventions,* edited by Virginia Stead, 101–15. New York: Peter Lang.

———. 2017. "Using Spiral Dynamic Theory as a Guide to Examine Civic Engagement at For-Profit Universities." 2017 Annual American Educational Research Association (AERA) Online Paper Repository. www.aera.net/Publications/Online-Paper-Repository/AERA-Online-Paper-Repository/Owner/984244.

———. 2018. "Comparing Graduate Student Civic Engagement Outcomes among For-Profit and Public University Adult Learners in Chile." *Journal of Higher Education Outreach and Engagement* 22 (4): 81–112.

Brown, Lisa R., and William A. Darity Jr. 2020. "U.S. Reparations for Black American Descendants of Slavery (ADOS)." American Association for Adult and Continuing Education (AAACE), Position Paper, June 17. https://cdn.ymaws.com/www.aaace.org/resource/resmgr/advocacy/positionpapers/brown_l._r._darity_jr._w._a.pdf.

Brown, Lisa R., Pamela McCray, and Jeff Neal. 2022. "Creating Affective Collaborative Adult Teams and Groups Guided by Spiral Dynamic Theory." Paper presented at the Learning Ideas Conference, New York, June.

Brown, Lisa R., and Lorilee R. Sandmann. 2013. "Memes and Their Meaning for the Study of Adult Learners: Civic Engagement in Chilean For-Profit

Graduate Education." Paper presented at the 54th Annual Adult Education Research Conference (AERC), St. Louis, MO. https://newprairiepress.org /aerc/2013/roundtables/6/.

Brown, Lisa R., Lorilee R. Sandmann, and Anne Bliss. 2012. "Connecting Spiral Dynamic Theory to the Study of Civic Engagement in For-Profit Higher Education." Paper presented at the 12th Annual IARSLCE (International Association for Research on Service-Learning and Community Engagement) Conference, Baltimore.

Charman, Karen. 2015. "A Space for Memory." *Australian Journal of Adult Learning* 55 (3): 361–78.

Craemer, Thomas. 2014. "Implicit Closeness to Blacks, Support for Affirmative Action, Slavery Reparations, and Vote Intentions for Barack Obama in the 2008 Elections." *Basic and Applied Social Psychology* 36 (5): 413–24.

Darity, William A., Jr., and A. Kirsten Mullen. 2020. *From Here to Equality: Reparations for Black Americans in the Twenty-First Century.* Chapel Hill: University of North Carolina Press.

Darity, William A., Jr., A. Kirsten Mullen, Lisa Brown, and Gabriel Piemonte. 2021. "FHTE Reparationist Quick Guide—Volume 1, Issue 2." *Moguldom,* February 1, https://moguldom.com/333550/reparations-scholars-including-dr-sandy-darity-launch-free-from-here-to-equality-fhte-reparations-quick-guide-issue-2/.

Dawkins, Richard. 1976. *The Selfish Gene.* Oxford University Press.

Dawlabani, Said E., and Don Beck. 2013. *MEMEnomics: The Next Generation Economic System.* New York: Select Books Kindle.

Dawson, Michael. C., and Rovana Popoff. 2004. "Reparations: Justice and Greed in Black and White." In *Du Bois Review: Social Science Research on Race* (vol. 16, no. 2), edited by Lawrence D. Bobo, 47–91. Cambridge, MA: Harvard University Press.

Erickson, Diane M. 2007. "A Developmental Re-forming of the Phases of Meaning in Transformational Learning." *Adult Education Quarterly* 58 (1): 61–80.

Erikson, Erik H. 1959. "Identity and the Life Cycle: Selected Papers. *Psychological Issues* 1 (1): 5–165.

Esolen, Anthony. 2018. *Nostalgia: Going Home in a Homeless World.* Washington, DC: Regnery Gateway.

Eyre, Gary A., and Roberta Pawloski. 2013. "An American Heritage: A Federal Adult Education Legislative History, 1964–2013." US Department of Education, report. http://lincs.ed.gov/publications/pdf/Adult_Ed_History_Report.pdf.

Friedersdorf, Conor. 2020. "Why California Rejected Racial Preferences, Again: A Majority Voted against Repealing the State's Ban on Affirmative Action." *The Atlantic,* November. www.theatlantic.com/ideas/archive/2020/11/why-california-rejected-affirmative-action-again/617049/.

George-Mwangi, Crystal A., Nina Daoud, Shelvia English, and Kimberly A. Griffin. 2017. "'Me and My Family': Ethnic Differences and Familial Influences on Academic Motivations of Black Collegians." *Journal of Negro Education* 86 (4): 479–93. https://doi.org/10.7709/jnegroeducation.86.4.0479.

Graves, Clare W. 1970. "Levels of Existence: An Open System Theory of Values." *Journal of Humanistic Psychology* 10 (2): 131–55.

———. 1974. "Human Nature Prepares for a Momentous Leap." *The Futurist* 8 (2): 72–87.

———. 2005. *The Never Ending Quest: Dr. Clare W. Graves Explores Human Nature*. Edited by Christopher C. Cowan and Natasha Todorovic. Santa Barbara, CA: ECLET Publishing.

Greenwald, Anthony G., Mahzarin Banaji, and Brian Nosek. 2014. "Statistically Small Effects of the Implicit Association Test Can Have Societally Large Effects." *Journal of Personality and Social Psychology* 108 (4): 553–61. https://doi.org/10.1037/pspa0000016.

Greenwald, Anthony G., Debbie McGhee, and Jordan Schwartz. 1998. "Measuring Individual Differences in Implicit Cognition: The Implicit Association Test." *Journal of Personality and Social Psychology* 74 (4): 1464–80. https://doi.org/10.1037/0022-3514.74.6.1464.

Harvard Law Review. 2002. "Bridging the Color Line: The Power of African-American Reparations to Redirect America's Future." *Harvard Law Review* 115 (6): 1689–1712. https://doi.org/10.2307/1342564.

Henschke, John A. 1997. "Adult Education and Ethnic Minorities in the United States." In *Erwachsenenbildung und ethnische Minderheiten,* edited by Gundula Frieling, Klaus Raape, and Ulrike Sommer, 257–72. Munster: Agenda. www.umsl.edu/~henschkej/articles/Erwachsenenbildung.pdf.

Hughes, C. Alvin. 1985. "A New Agenda for the South: The Role and Influence of the Highlander Folk School, 1953–1961." *Python* 46 (3): 242–50.

Kaminer, Wendy. 2000. "Up from Reparations." *American Prospect* 11 (13): 38–40.

Katz, Emily T. 2016. "Black Lives Matter Activist DeRay Mckesson Endorses Hillary Clinton." CBS News, October 26. www.cbsnews.com/news/black-lives-matter-leader-deray-mckesson-endorses-hillary-clinton/.

Kelly, Erin, and Frank Dobbin. 1998. How Affirmative Action Became Diversity Management." *American Behavioral Scientist*, April, 960–84.

Kendzior, Sarah. 2016. "Meet Darren Seals. Then Tell Me Black Death Is Not a Business." *Correspondent*, October 1. https://thecorrespondent.com/5349/meet-darren-seals-then-tell-me-black-death-is-not-a-business/1512965275833-fe73c5b1.

King, LaGarrett J. 2017. "The Status of Black History in U.S. Schools and Society." *Social Education* 81 (1): 14–18.

Legal Information Institute. 2012. "Fisher v. University of Texas at Austin." Legal Information Institute. www.law.cornell.edu/supct/cert/11-345.

Levinson, David. 2016. "The Mid-life Transition: A Period in Adult Psychosocial Development." *Psychiatry* 4:99–122. https://doi.org/10.1080/00332747.1977.11023925.

Love, Barbara J. 2004. "*Brown* Plus 50 Counter-storytelling: A Critical Race Theory Analysis of the 'Majoritarian Achievement Gap' Story." *Equity and ExcellenceinEducation*37(3):227–46.https://doi.org/10.1080/10665680490491597.

Lyman, Brian. 2020. "Southern Schools' History Textbooks: A Long History of Deception, and What the Future Holds." *Montgomery Advertiser*,

December 2. www.montgomeryadvertiser.com/story/news/education/2020/12/03/southern-history-textbooks-long-history-deception/6327359002/.

Merrall, Elizabeth L. C., Mandeep K. Dhami, and Sheila M. Bird. 2010. "Exploring Methods to Investigate Sentencing Decisions." *Evaluation Review* 34 (3): 185–219. https://doi.org/10.1177/0193841X10369624.

Merriam, Sharan B., and Laura L. Bierema. 2014. *Adult Learning: Linking Theory and Practice*. San Francisco: Jossey-Bass.

Nicol, Donna J. 2021. "Activism for Profit: America's 'Anti-Affirmative Action' Industry." Al Jazeera, February 28. www.aljazeera.com/opinions/2021/2/28/activism-for-profit-americas-anti-affirmative-action-industry.

Oswald, Frederick L., Hart Blanton, Gregory Mitchell, James Jaccard, and Philip E. Tetlock. 2013. "Predicting Ethnic and Racial Discrimination: A Meta-analysis of IAT Criterion Studies." *Journal of Personality and Social Psychology* 105 (2): 171–92. https://doi.org/10.1037/a0032734.

Parkay, Forrest W. 2020. *Becoming a Teacher*. 11th ed. Hoboken, NJ: Pearson Higher Education.

PBS. 2019. "Mister Rogers Goes to Washington." MetroFocus, video clip, November 22. www.pbs.org/video/mister-rogers-goes-washington-ycjrnx/.

Piaget, Jean. 1967. *Six Psychological Studies*. New York: Random House.

Ray, Angela G. 2002. "Frederick Douglass on the Lyceum Circuit: Social Assimilation, Social Transformation?" *Rhetoric and Public Affairs* 5 (4): 625–48. https://doi.org/10.1353/rap.2003.0014.

Raymond, Nate. 2021. "Affirmative Action Opponents Ask U.S. Supreme Court to Take Up Harvard Case." Reuters, February 25. www.reuters.com/article/us-usa-court-harvard/affirmative-action-opponents-ask-u-s-supreme-court-to-take-up-harvard-case-idUSKBN2AP2FY.

Roberts, Nigel. 2022. "Report: BLM Foundation Has $42 Million In Assets, Tax Docs Reveal." BET, May 19. www.bet.com/article/pdodaq/blm-has-42-million-dollars-assets-irs-filing-reveal.

Rocco, Tonette. S., M. Cecil Smith, Robert C. Mizzi, Lisa R. Merriweather, and Joshua D. Hawley, eds. 2020. *The Handbook for Adult and Continuing Education*. Sterling, VA: Stylus.

Rose, Amy D. 1991. "Ends or Means: An Overview of the History of Adult Education Act." Center for Education and Training for Employment, Ohio State University. https://eric.ed.gov/?id=ED341875.

Schaub, Michael. 2015. "Texas Textbook Calls Slaves 'Immigrants' to Be Changed, after Mom's Complaint." *Los Angeles Times,* October 5. www.latimes.com/books/jacketcopy/la-et-jc-texas-textbook-calls-slaves-immigrants-20151005-story.html.

Sharpe, Rhonda Vonshay. 2019. "Disaggregating Data by Race Allows for More Accurate Research." *Nature Human Behavior* 3:1240. www.nature.com/articles/s41562-019-0696-1.

Stubblefield, Harold W., and Patrick Keane. 1994. *Adult Education in the American Experience: From the Colonial Period to the Present*. San Francisco: Jossey-Bass.

Suarez, Ray. 2012. "Words of Hope and Healing: Mr. Rogers Message Goes Viral." *PBS News Hour*, video clip, December 18. www.pbs.org/video/pbs-newshour-words-of-hope-and-healing-mr-rogers-message-goes-viral/.

Tateishi, John. 2020. *Redress: The Inside Story of the Successful Campaign for Japanese American Reparations.* Berkeley, CA: Heyday.

Tisdell, Elizabeth. 2003. *Exploring Spirituality and Culture in Adult and Higher Education.* San Francisco: Jossey-Bass.

Winship, Scott, Richard Reeves, and Katherine Guyot. 2018. "The Inheritance of Black Poverty: It's All about the Men." Brookings Institute, technical paper, March. www.brookings.edu/research/the-inheritance-of-black-poverty-its-all-about-the-men/.

9

The Children of Slavery

Genealogical Research and the Establishment of Eligibility for Reparations

EVELYN A. MCDOWELL

The English established their colony at Jamestown in 1618, introducing slavery in 1619 with the purchase of "20 and odd" individuals taken from a Portuguese ship called the *Sao Juan Baptista* by the captain of the *Treasurer*, sailing under Dutch authority. Slavery for an estimated ten million Africans continued across all thirteen colonies and in many states until it officially ended for nonincarcerated individuals with the passage of the Thirteenth Amendment in 1865. It took a bloody civil war to finally end slavery for at least 3.8 million individuals.

Today, more than 40.8 million people identify as black or African American, according to the 2016 US Census. However, not everyone with African ancestry has a forebear who was enslaved in the United States by the end of the Civil War, nor does everyone with an African ancestor identify as black or African American. Since the majority of individuals who fit this description arrived after the passage of the Civil Rights Acts of the 1960s, they are excluded from the scope of this chapter.

For purposes of reparations for American slavery, an individual must be a direct descendant to a person who was enslaved in the United States (Darity and Mullen 2020, 258; Darity 2019). Through these ties, a claimant can meet the lineage criterion for eligibility for black reparations for slavery. The claimant must establish a direct lineal descent from a qualifying ancestor. A qualifying ancestor is a man, woman, or child who was forced into enslavement within the jurisdiction of the

United States of America during the period from July 1, 1776, to the passage of the Thirteenth Amendment to the US Constitution and the passage of the Treaty of 1866.

The most expeditious way to establish lineal descent to a qualifying ancestor is to identify possible relatives and find evidence supporting enslavement. Genealogy is an essential tool for identifying family members across generations. Starting with the claimant, investigators can go back, meticulously, one generation at a time, noting all relatives' names, places and dates of births, deaths, and marriages, and finding supporting documentation for each entry until they identify possible ancestors who may have been enslaved. Genealogical standards provide a framework to evaluate data and the validity and reliability of supporting documentation.

This chapter lays out a two-part process for proving the lineal descent of an individual enslaved in the United States. The first part of the process is to create the family tree, and the second part is to gather evidence supporting the enslavement. There are many steps within each process; the overall procedure must be disciplined and systematic. A focused approach will yield the best outcome because many distractions and diversions are caused by discovering new information, which may or may not deliver results or progress.

In this chapter I first lay out the process of establishing lineal descent to a qualifying ancestor. Then I discuss the evidence needed to qualify the ancestor—evidence of enslavement. Also, I present a framework to understand the value of the evidence in documenting enslavement. I then present two case studies, one with an ancestor born in the South and the other with an ancestor born in the North. Last, I present some conclusions.

ESTABLISHING LINEAL DESCENT

There are many ways to trace one's lineage to an enslaved person. But first, the descendants must start with themselves and go backward, one generation at a time, noting the date and place of birth, marriage, and death for each person (and if applicable, the date and place of divorce) (Woodtor 2016).

A pedigree chart is an excellent way to gather generational information and to document the lineage of an individual. It starts with the individual and has spaces to document parents and the parents of the next generation, stretching back many generations. (An example of the form is included in Appendix B.)

Living relatives can be a fount of information for the pedigree chart. They can remember people who are long gone and can make connections to other generations. Therefore, it is essential to interview and record older relatives as soon as possible.

To validate and support each date and place it on the pedigree chart, the descendants should use vital records, if possible. These records are created at or near the time of the event, making them a primary source of information and more reliable than other sources. Vital records include birth, death, cohabitation, and marriage records. They are essential because they connect each generation to the next and provide dates, locations, and valuable clues if data are missing. A researcher can obtain these records from the Bureau of Vital Statistics in the city, county, or state where the event occurred, as well as from government archives.

Another essential document researchers should complete is a family group sheet (which also can be found in Appendix B). These sheets are used to collect information about the immediate family of the descendant's ancestors. They include data about parents and siblings of each ancestor. Researchers can use this information to find and confirm parents' names and other information. For instance, the death certificate of an uncle may have his parents listed and may therefore lead to the names of the parents of his sister or brother, who may be the targeted ancestor.

Using Census Records to Connect Generations

Since census enumerators collect information about entire households, they are an excellent resource to connect generations. Since 1790, the United States and many state governments have conducted censuses to enumerate the population. The federal government conducts the census every ten years. After seventy-two years, the federal census is made public. Unfortunately, the 1890 census was burned; however, fragments of certain states including Georgia, Alabama, the District of Columbia, and others remain. In addition, some portions of the 1810 and 1820 censuses also were lost for some states.

Both the federal and state governments conducted censuses, which collected names of the heads of household, their gender, their location, the number of individuals in the household, and their freedom status. Earlier censuses included less information than more current ones. Later censuses listed more detailed information about individuals in the household, including name, age, gender, race, and occupation. The

1870 census contained ancestors and their family members, including age, gender, race, birthplace, and occupation; after 1880, their relationship to the head of the household was included.

The censuses are best used by finding ancestors on the most recent census and working back one census at a time: that is, one should examine and collect all existing data on the individuals in question before going to the next census, being sure to include locations of residence, members of households, neighbors, and places of birth. Unfortunately, the African American population consistently has been significantly undercounted in federal censuses (Nguyen 1996; Reid 1995). Furthermore, names are often misspelled, and census takers' handwriting can be difficult to read. Nevertheless, gathering information about occupation, locations, literacy, the economic value of property, neighbors, and the whereabouts of other family members can help locate ancestors and provide clues to finding additional information.

Census data are widely available. Researchers can find census data at state libraries and archives. Records are also found in digital form and can be accessed on subscription-based and free genealogical databases like Ancestry.com, MyHeritage.com, and FamilySearch.com.

Using Other Federal Records to Connect Generations

Social Security records are another source to connect family members across generations. Although the Social Security Act of 1935 excluded nearly half of the American workforce—agricultural and domestic workers who were largely African Americans were explicitly excluded until 1960—the Social Security Administration began issuing Social Security numbers for all other workers in 1936 (Thompson 1975). Two kinds of records are available. One is the Social Security Death Index. The index includes deaths of individuals with Social Security numbers, reporting their birth year, death date and place, and the state in which the application was filed. These records are available only for individuals who were eligible for Social Security benefits, which did not apply to all workers.

The second record is the Social Security application (SS-5). This record shows the individual's name, birth date, birthplace, signature, and employment information at the time of the application, as well as parents' names with the mother's maiden name. A copy of the application can be obtained from the Social Security Administration in Baltimore, Maryland, through a Freedom of Information Act (FOIA) request.

Military records including draft records, muster rolls, payrolls, enlistment papers, official correspondences, court-martial case files, prisoner and casualty lists, burial records, "returns and ship logs," records of soldiers' homes for the elderly or disabled, and reports of engagements all contain important information for connecting generations and provide places and dates. After determining whether an individual served in the military, request the Compiled Service Record, detailed service information, and the pension records, if applicable.

Using Land Records to Connect Generations

Deeds can have important information about the family of an ancestor. Since multiple parties can own land, finding the deed can yield the name of family members. The husband and wife often purchase the land together, and if the land is passed down to multiple family members, the deed will list the name of each descendant.

Using Wills and Probate Information to Connect Generations

Probate records include wills, inventories and appraisals, annual returns, estate sales, and final distributions or settlements of estates. When an individual with sufficient property dies, a court proceeding is initiated to pay off outstanding debts and distribute the property of the deceased. When the property owner leaves assets to the heirs, often the descendants are identified. Probate records can be instrumental in finding evidence of enslavement.

Using Dawes Roll Cards to Connect Generations

Many African Americans have heard stories about American Indian ancestry. By working backward through one's lineage, the researcher may discover connections to American Indians. Individuals who were accepted as eligible for membership in the Five Civilized Tribes (Cherokee, Choctaw, Chickasaw, Creek, and Seminole) were included in the Dawes Rolls, also known as the "Final Rolls."

African Americans were also associated with the Five "Civilized" Tribes as enslaved people. In a practice that began in the late 1700s and intensified in the early 1800s, members of the Five Tribes used enslaved black women, men, and children as domestic and agricultural laborers.

The Dawes Freedmen Rolls were created to document the connections and lineage of these individuals.

The rolls contain more than 101,000 names from 1898 to 1914 (primarily from 1899 to 1906). They can be searched to discover the enrollee's name, sex, ostensible blood quantum, and census card number. The census card may provide additional genealogical information and may also contain references to earlier rolls, such as the 1880 Cherokee census. A census card was generally accompanied by an "application jacket." The jackets sometimes contain valuable supporting documentation, such as birth and death affidavits, marriage licenses, and other correspondences.

Using Church and Cemetery Records to Connect Generations

Many established churches have been in existence for hundreds of years. Church records can include details of marriages, christenings, baptisms, confirmations, and burials. These records include children's names, gender, date of birth, place of birth, and location of religious activities. Enslaved people often went to church with slaveholders. The information in these records could identify parents or other close relatives, enabling the researcher to connect generations. Also, many cemeteries are near churches attended by ancestors.

Cemetery records can also contain valuable information. Some cemeteries maintain interment files containing complete names with dates and places of births and deaths. Finding a death certificate can help the researcher locate family cemeteries, which also contain tombstones. They include birth and death dates, military and social club memberships, and parents' names. Also, since family members tend to be buried together, finding an ancestral cemetery can provide clues to the names of other relatives.

Using Other Family Trees to Connect Generations

Individuals have been creating and publishing family lineages for centuries. In recent times, some families have published their lineages in books, journals, and other publications. Published lineages can provide hard-to-find connections to other individuals and references to supporting documentation. However, there is a shortage of published genealogies for African American families. Unpublished genealogies exist on online family history sites such as FamilySearch.org and Ancestry.com, but they can be unreliable, since connections may be unsubstantiated. However, they can provide clues about linkages that can be supported with additional research.

Using Documentation from Newspapers and Other Sources to Connect Generations

Newspapers can also include stories about an ancestor. These stories can identify key family relationships, places, and dates that can lead to other clues to connect generations. For example, obituaries are often published in local newspapers and are extremely helpful to genealogists in providing information about families and their connections to each other. They can include the names of parents, children, siblings, and places of birth and death.

Newspapers can also publish other stories connecting parents to children or children to parents. Other examples include birth and marriage notices, court case summaries, and local news stories. Information from school notices, local business advertisements, and church activities can also lead to clues about connections.

Using DNA to Connect Generations

It is very possible to connect generations using DNA evidence; however, it is no substitute for a well-documented family tree. DNA can tell a potential claimant whether they share a common relative with another individual, but it cannot discern the individual's precise identity unless the DNA of the ancestral relative has been identified through DNA analysis and genealogical methods. At the time of this writing, the technology is unable to provide this level of exactness on its own. However, combining DNA with well-developed family trees of genetic relatives is a powerful way to connect generations (Bettinger 2019). (For an example of how DNA can be used to connect generations, see Garrett-Nelson 2020.)

QUALIFYING THE TARGETED ANCESTOR

To qualify the ancestor, one must identify him or her and find evidence to prove enslavement. In this section, I describe how to identify the targeted ancestor and gather the necessary evidence to document whether someone was enslaved.

Identifying the Qualifying Ancestor

Once the pedigree chart and the family group sheets are completed for each generation going back, at minimum, to the end of chattel slavery in December 1865, we are ready for the next step: identifying the qualifying ancestor. To find him or her, review each ancestor's date of birth and place of birth occurring after December 1865. Then check state laws ending slavery for the earliest ancestor's date and place. Slavery may not have been permitted in the location. For example, Ohio never formally accepted slavery. For ancestors born in "free states," researchers must extend the line as far as possible to identify a progenitor possibly born in a condition of enslavement. It may be necessary to go back to the late eighteenth and early nineteenth centuries.

Evidence of Enslavement

In this section, the evidence of enslavement is identified and described. First, the evidence is defined and is followed by the types of evidence generated by individuals, including the enslaver and the enslaved individual, government entities, news outlets, professional and social organizations, and business establishments.

Evidence Created by Enslaved Individuals

Sources of evidence created by enslaved individuals or their families include family stories, obituaries, narratives, and lost-relative advertisements. Enslaved people, of course, always maintained their own complete identities, though typically these were unknown or of no consequence to their enslavers. They referred to themselves using first and last names, as evident in the Works Progress Administration (later renamed Work Projects Administration; WPA) slave narratives and the research documented by many authors, including Herbert Gutman (1976). Consequently, the evidence they created for themselves is a precious information source regarding enslavement.

Enslaved individuals and their families preserved their history by passing down stories of their enslavement. Many of these stories survive today and are told by older family members. There are many individuals living today who saw and talked to a formerly enslaved person. Consider a child born in 1863, a few years before slavery ended, living to age eighty before passing away in 1943. Many individuals living today were born before 1943 and might recall meeting this person.

In addition, first-person narratives are an excellent source of information about enslaved individuals. Enslaved people often wrote about the pain and struggle of being subjected to one of the most horrendous institutions the world has ever known. These writings make up a genre known as the slave narrative. There are more than six thousand autobiographical narratives. Since many were published near the end of slavery or immediately after 1865, these works are now in the public domain and widely available on the internet.

One of the most significant sources of slave narratives has been the seventeen-volume *Slave Narratives: A Folk History of Slavery in the United States from Interviews with Former Slaves,* created by the Federal Writers' Project (FWP) in the 1930s and published in 1941 in microform (FWP 1941). This series has since been digitized as the collection *Born in Slavery: Slave Narratives from the Federal Writers' Project, 1936–1938* and can be widely found online, including at the Library of Congress website. It contains more than 2,300 first-person accounts of slavery and five hundred black-and-white photographs. Other sources of slave narratives are the transcribed interviews of formerly enslaved persons compiled by Fisk University and published as a series of volumes called *The Unwritten History of Slavery* (1968), as well as interviews compiled by Southern University in the collection *Opinions Regarding Slavery: Slave Narratives,* which have been digitized and are available on their website (Cade 1935).

Enslaved people created other evidence. Newspapers published some of the information they generated. As stated elsewhere in this chapter, formerly enslaved individuals generated ads looking for relatives lost during slavery and the aftermath of the Civil War. Bible and journal entries and letters to loved ones are other examples of evidence generated by enslaved people.

Evidence Created by Enslavers

Enslavers created evidence of their enslavement of individuals through various means. Since enslaved people were held as property, slaveholders created many types of documents to prove ownership and to account for them, including probate records, deeds, account books, manumission records, runaway ads, and bills of sales/receipts.

Manumission is the formal act of freeing someone from slavery. Freeing enslaved people became more difficult as slave societies, particularly in the South, became entrenched. For example, by 1820, in South Carolina, laws were passed that allowed the emancipation of enslaved people only by a legislative act. When emancipation was legal, enslavers filed formal manumission records in courthouses. Many of these records still exist today.

As mentioned earlier, deeds can be used to connect generations. In addition, deeds may contain detailed information about enslaved individuals. Since enslaved people were considered and treated like subhuman property, buying and selling them was often transacted in deeds. Often, the sale of land included the enslaved people who worked it. Therefore, such deeds often will include the enslaved individuals' first names and ages.

In special collections of libraries all over the country, there are documents created by slaveholders to account for the activities of their slave operations. Enslavers allocated slaves' labor from task to task, monitored their productivity, and calculated depreciation on human lives (Rosenthal 2019). Planters' records included "inventory lists" with names, ages, purchase dates, and sale dates. These records can be used to identify enslaved people and to determine whether someone was an enslaver.

Finding the Slaveholder

To access the documents created by enslavers and unlock information leading to details about additional generations, finding the names of the enslavers is vital. Since enslaved individuals were treated as property, slaveholders and other parties (including taxing authorities, insurance companies, creditors, and courts) maintained documents tracking and accounting for them. These records were usually tied to the slaveholder. Consequently, by identifying the slaveholder, the researcher may discover data to connect enslaved individuals to their families and provide evidence and details of enslavement.

An important clue in discovering the slaveholder is the last name carried by the freed ancestors. A common assumption is that most freed people took the surnames of the most recent slaveholders. However, the surname may have belonged to an earlier slaveholder, may have been taken from a famous individual, or may have been passed down from a father or other relative (Gutman 1976; Smith and Croom 2008). Some individuals did indeed take the last name of the most recent enslaver. These names could lead to clues to find evidence of one's ancestor's enslavement or evidence extending one's family tree.

Enslaved people were enumerated in the US Federal Census in 1850 in a separate census called slave schedules, and these also can prove to be a useful resource. Unfortunately, most were not listed by name but instead were numbered by age, sex, and color (e.g., black or mulatto) from the oldest to the youngest, by slave owner's name. In addition, the schedules reported individuals who were manumitted (freed) fugitives, as well as individuals who were deaf, blind, "insane," or "idiotic."

The US conducted a second slave census in 1860 that included the same information. The 1860 slave schedule was taken in the following states: Alabama, Arkansas, Delaware, Florida, Georgia, Kentucky, Louisiana, Maryland, Mississippi, Missouri, New Jersey, North Carolina, South Carolina, Tennessee, Texas, and Virginia (Dollarhide 2001). Both schedules included location information (state, county) and date.

Researchers should search near the area where the newly freed ancestor lived to find enslavers. For ancestors born in a slaveholding state, one can identify the individuals living near them on the 1870 census, especially wealthy white landowners with the same surname. In addition, one can review land tax records, plat books, or county deed records to find landowners near the family in the 1870 census.

After identifying possible slaveholders, it is imperative to review the slave schedules and tax and land records for evidence of slaveholding. Land records (deeds and property records) can include transfer of titles and mortgage collateral containing information of enslaved people. In addition, creating the family tree of possible slaveholders will help identify documents generated to purchase, hold, and sell their human property.

Evidence Created by Government Agencies

At all levels, the US government was instrumental in establishing and maintaining the nation's slave society. Consequently, it generated significant evidence of enslavement. It established the laws that created and maintained the system of slavery. The federal government created tax records and the federal census, which included slave schedules. It made federal court records involving enslaved people and maintained federal pension applications, which documented evidence of enslavement by freed pensioners.

The federal government also ran certain agencies for newly freed individuals, which generated documents about enslavement, including the Freedmen's Bureau, which was created in 1865 by an act of Congress to aid newly freed individuals who faced hunger and deprivation. Field offices existed in Alabama, Arkansas, District of Columbia, Florida, Georgia, Kentucky, Louisiana, Mississippi, North and South Carolina, Tennessee, Texas, and West Virginia. The National Archives is the repository for these records (see www.archives.gov/research/african-americans/freedmens-bureau), but some of them are accessible online at Family Search.org.

On the state and local levels, documents of enslavement were created in many ways. Evidence was generated by court cases involving enslaved people, tax records, slave births, indentured servants, and other labor contracts. A significant piece of evidence includes laws created by state and local governments.

As noted earlier, both the federal and state government conducted censuses that documented freedom status, and the 1850 and 1860 censuses included a slave schedule that listed slaveholders and enslaved people by age, sex, and race.

We have compelling evidence of enslavement when the census is used with state slave laws. Many state laws were passed to maintain slavery by calling for the removal of free people of color. Consequently, any black or "mulatto" individual remaining, by default, must have been enslaved. In addition, since free people were enumerated on the census, if individuals were on the 1870 census and cannot be located on previous censuses, despite their ages, then the logic of negative evidence tells us these individuals must have been enslaved.

Another source of evidence is employment contracts registered with state or local governments. For example, newly freed enslaved individuals in certain states were required to be employed to avoid vagrancy charges. Many of these labor contracts were registered with the local government. In addition, indentured contracts for individuals enslaved for a "term" were registered with the local municipality.

Tax records and the revenue for fees, fines, and sales of enslaved people held in settlement of fines can be found and used as support for enslavement. Enslaved people were identified as taxable property or income in many state and local governments. Tax tables listed the slaveholder's name and the number of enslaved people in many places. This information can be used with more direct data to bolster or corroborate other evidence. Federal, state, or local court cases against or cases brought on behalf of or by enslaved individuals are other sources of evidence of enslavement. Court transcripts can be invaluable if a descendant can find an ancestor listed as a plaintiff or defendant.

Evidence Created by Media Companies

Newspapers and early magazine articles contained substantial evidence of enslavement. News articles were written about slaveholders and enslaved individuals. In many cases, the reporter used full names, locations, and descriptions when referring to enslaved people and slaveholders. In addition, as stated previously, newspapers often ran runaway advertisements and, after the end of slavery, "lost friend" advertisements—ads placed by newly freed individuals seeking family members who had been sold or had run away from slavery. After emancipation, many freed people used newspaper advertisements to try to contact their family members. These advertisements provided an important stopgap measure to help separated families reunite during Reconstruction in the absence of help from the federal government (Williams 2016). A searchable database can be found at www.informationwanted .org/research.

Evidence Created by Ancillary Organizations

More and more evidence connected to slavery is being gathered from ancillary sources, organizations, and corporations that supported the institution of slavery. For example, slaveholders took out mortgages on the lives of enslaved people. Many records from ship manifests are available online. In addition, many copies still exist of the insurance policies taken out to insure the lives of these individuals.

Evidence Provided by Third-Party Organizations

Some organizations have hired professional genealogists to identify the descendants of enslaved individuals connected to an individual slaveholder or place. One example of this type of organization is the GU272 Descendants Association, which has traced and notified descendants of the 272 individuals sold by Jesuit priests of Georgetown University in 1838. Another is the Montpelier Descendants' Project, which seeks to identify and work with descendants of individuals enslaved at Montpelier and elsewhere in Orange County, Virginia.

To become a member of a hereditary organization, like Sons & Daughters of the United States Middle Passage (SDUSMP), applicants must document their lineage to a qualified ancestor. For SDUSMP, which was established in 2011, the qualifying ancestor is one who was enslaved in the United States, including its colonial period. The applicants must include documentation supporting each generation and evidence of enslavement. A board-elected registrar(s) who is a genealogist verifies the applications, and the board of directors approves each application.

Enslavement Evidence Evaluation Framework

There is an abundance of evidence indicating whether a person was enslaved. Unfortunately, much of the evidence was created in a system that identified enslaved African Americans as subhuman property without full names, the ability to purchase property, or, in many cases, the ability to keep and form families. However, researchers are attempting to match this information to people living as fully human. The data are inconsistent with the two realities. Consequently, much evidence cannot be used to directly answer the straightforward research question "Was my ancestor enslaved?"

To evaluate the usefulness of certain evidence of enslavement, I propose the framework of three levels detailed below (see table 9.1). Such an evaluation is necessary because time is finite and trying to match questionable documents created under the assumption that humans are subhuman property can be extremely inefficient. In the following framework, evidence is categorized by who/what created it (the enslaved person, the slaveholder, government entities, ancillary or supporting organizations, or the written media) and its ability to substantiate enslavement.

Level I evidence, the most direct and useful, leaves no doubt about whether a person was enslaved. Not only are the data complete, but the evidence also refers to a human being as a human being. Examples of Level I evidence are slave narratives, because their inclusion of the full name of the individual leaves little doubt about enslavement.

Level II evidence indirectly proves enslavement but does not specifically refer to one individual. It is relevant to an entire group. Examples include state and federal laws and immigration patterns of groups.

TABLE 9.1   EVALUATION FRAMEWORK FOR ENSLAVEMENT EVIDENCE

Evidence Created by:	Evidence Level		
	I	II	III
Enslaved people	Slave narratives, lost-friends ads, obituaries, Bible entries, DNA		
Slaveholders	Manumission records		Bills of sale, wills, diaries, account books, inventories, deeds
Government	Criminal court cases, pension files, Freedmen's Bureau records, WPA narratives, indentured contracts, freedmen Dawes Rolls, other court records	Slave laws, negative evidence, census demographic data	Mortuary schedules (1850–60), slave schedules, slave birth records, Confederate slave payroll, tax records, deed and property records
Ancillary/ supporting organization/ other	Membership rolls of descendant legacy groups, hereditary societies for descendants of enslaved people		Ship manifests, insurance policies
Media/authors (created in temporal proximity to events)	Newspaper articles/ observers		Runaway ads, estate sale ads

Level III evidence would normally be classified as direct because it documents enslavement; however, it refers to enslaved individuals without surnames and describes them in crude and dehumanizing terms: for example, as having a "muddy" complexion and a scar on the face, or as wearing certain clothing. This evidence must be combined with other evidence to make it useful.

The framework helps individuals new to this type of research understand the failures of this extraordinary evidence when applied to ordinary contexts. The institution of American slavery created an artificial world in which people could be property and subhuman, leaving modern-day researchers the unenviable task of considering and weighing appalling evidence like a bill of sale for a human being. It helps us understand why much of this evidence cannot be used on its own but may be helpful when combined with other evidence. Level II evidence can stand on its own, but it is not as compelling as Level I evidence. Level II is based on deduction from strong evidence. For many claimants, it may be the only evidence available to them, given that finding Level III documentation, such as bills of sale or slave schedules, without knowing the slaveholder would be difficult and would take countless hours of going through the data with a low chance of payoff. In addition, because the evidence was born in a context based upon a discriminatory belief system (i.e., enslaved Africans and their descendants are less than human), the data, in many cases, cannot provide exact proof of enslavement. For purposes of qualifying an ancestor, Level I and II evidence should be sufficient, and Level III evidence, although highly prized, should not be required or sought.

CASE STUDIES

To demonstrate how to find an enslaved individual, we will use two cases, one from a family with southern roots and another in a family from the North. These cases were obtained from members of Sons & Daughters of the United States Middle Passage (SDUSMP), a hereditary organization for descendants of Africans enslaved in the United States and Colonial English America.

Case 1: Family Lineage Includes Ancestors Living in the South before 1865

Boston Lincoln Aniton, a relative, listed in the pedigree chart of an SDUSMP member, was born in Oneonta, Alabama, on January 24, 1889, and died on October 19, 1967. The Alabama Center for Health Statistics began filing birth and death certificates in 1908 for persons who were born and died in Alabama. With no birth certificate and no Bible entries, the claimant consults with other family members to create a family group sheet that includes known brothers and sisters of Boston. Using a genealogical database, we search for Boston Aniton and his brothers and sisters. We find family members listed in the census, the expected location, under the last name of "Anderton."

The census answers many questions. It connects the generations and confirms the age of Boston, gives us the original family name, and gives us his parents' names and birthplaces. The 1900 census also includes

TABLE 9.2 INFORMATION REPORTED ON 1870 AND 1880 CENSUSES

Dwelling and Family	Name	Age	Sex	Color	Birthplace	Father's Birthplace	Mother's Birthplace	Implied Year of Birth[c]
				1870 Census[a]				
764	Jack Staton	54	M	B	Alabama	NR	NR	1816
	M. Staton	43	F	B	Alabama	NR	NR	1827
				1880 Census[b]				
89	Jack Staton	63	M	B	Alabama	Virginia	Virginia	1817
	Lucinda M. Staton	53	F	B	Alabama	North Carolina	Tennessee	1827

NR—Information was not a question on the census.

[a] 1870 US Census, East Half, Blount, Alabama, p. 97, Jack Staton household, Roll: M593_3; Page: 334A; Family History Library Film: 545502.

[b] 1880 US Census, Blount, Enumeration District: 005, Alabama, p. 404B, Jack Staton household, Roll: 2; Family History Film: 1254002.

[c] Calculated field based on the reported age and the census year.

the names, dates, and places of birth of Boston's parents. Consequently, we are now able to extend the pedigree chart with two more names. (Some of these findings are summarized in table 9.2; Appendix B contains the completed pedigree chart and the family group sheet.)

Boston's mother, Easter Anderton, and his father, William Anderton, were both born during the time of slavery. Easter was born in 1852, and William was born in 1854 in Blount County, Alabama. Upon reaching ancestors who were born before the end of slavery, we are now ready to determine whether they were born into slavery. Since the 1890 census was burned in a fire, we search the 1880 census for William and Easter Anderton, living in Blount County, Alabama. We review the information to determine whether the name stayed the same and to identify any new information. In the 1880 census, we see William and Easter using the "Anderton" last name. However, we note two new pieces of data: Easter's father was born in Georgia, and William's race is listed as "mulatto." The years of birth for Easter and William are also different: 1855 and 1860, respectively.

Because William and Easter were both born in Alabama, it is very likely they were enslaved. The 1833 Slave Codes of Alabama forced all "free persons of color" to leave the state before February 1, 1833 (Akin 1833). Consequently, any "mulatto" or black person born after this date can be presumed to be enslaved, with very few exceptions.

Our next step is to find a marriage certificate to determine Easter's maiden name. We find it using an online genealogy database. It indicates that Easter and William were married on January 9, 1876, in Blount County, Alabama, and that Easter's maiden name is Staton. We also obtain the death certificate of Easter Anderton, which identifies her mother as Menerva Bynum and her father as Jack Staton. Next, we move to the 1870 census to find Easter Staton. We assume she should be around fifteen years old. On the census, we find a female named "E. Staton," seventeen years old, living in the East Half of Blount County, Alabama, with her family. Her mother is listed as M. Staton, and her father as Jack Staton. We can confirm we have found Easter, since the names of her parents, her age, and the residence all agree with prior information. We also have two more possible enslaved individuals to research.

Using Level II evidence, we can make a very strong case that Easter was enslaved. As indicated previously, Alabama expelled free people of color in 1833. The law effectively kept the population of free people to below 2,700 individuals from 1840 to 1860 (US Bureau of the Census 1860, 603–4). During the same period, the population of enslaved people in Alabama grew from 41,879 in 1820 to 435,080 in 1860, according to census records (see US Bureau of the Census 1860, "Classified Population"). According to "Classified Population of the States and Territories, by Counties," of the June 1, 1860, census, there were only 2,690 free people of color in the entire state of Alabama out of a total population of 526,271. Only six free people of color were living in Blount County, Alabama, all under the age of thirty.

Since Easter was born between 1853 and 1855, she and her family would almost certainly have been pressured to leave. In addition, if the family were free, they would probably be enumerated in the 1850 census. However, they do not appear in the 1850 census, and Jack Staton, her father, does not appear in the 1850 or 1840 censuses. Consequently, Easter and her mother, father, and siblings born before 1865 were most likely enslaved. For many families, the search for an enslaved ancestor could end here.

To provide evidence that this conclusion is valid, we will demonstrate how to find confirmation of enslavement using Level III evidence. To access Level III evidence, you must know the name of the enslaver. The case analysis demonstrates how to obtain this information. For purposes of this case study, we will focus on Easter's mother, Menerva Staton.

The next step is to learn as much as we can about Menerva Staton. From the 1870 census, we determine that Menerva was born in 1827 in

Alabama. We go back to the 1880 census to obtain more information about her. In the 1880 census, Menerva is listed with her husband Jack as Lucinda M. Staton. She indicates that her mother was born in Tennessee and her father was born in North Carolina.

Since we know her maiden name is Bynum, we scan the 1870 census a few pages before and after to record the names of white people living near them, looking for any Bynums, since Bynum could be the enslaver's last name. Going forward to the 1860 slave schedule, we look for Bynums living in Blount County and find Solomun Bynum listed near Thomas Staton, the last name of Menerva's husband.

The slave schedule shows an enslaved female in her thirties listed under the slaveholder name of Solomun Bynum. On the 1850 slave schedule, we find a black female in her twenties. Next, we create the family tree for Solomon Bynum to determine if it is possible he "inherited" Menerva Bynum. In doing so, we determine that Solomun Bynum died after the end of slavery; however, his father, Asa Bynum, was born in North Carolina in 1781 and died in 1833 in Alabama. Since Lucinda indicated her father was from North Carolina in the 1880 census, Asa Bynum may have been the original enslaver.

The next step is to find the will of Asa Bynum to determine if Lucinda is listed as "property." Using FamilySearch.org, we find Asa Bynum's will and we see a Lucinda listed, just above the hogs and furniture, valued at $350.00—a jarring discovery for any descendant. We believe Lucinda Menerva Bynum is the young girl named Lucinda on the will. She would have been six or seven years old when Asa Bynum died. This matches the information we found for Lucinda before finding the will. It is possible the young girl on the will may not be an ancestor in question; however, the evidence makes a very compelling case.

Finding the enslaver or slaveholder can unlock the rich confirmatory information contained in Level III evidence. With the will, we have very compelling evidence that Lucinda and her children were enslaved. But for purposes of qualifying an ancestor for a reparations claim, Level III information is overkill. In addition, such data are not available to every claimant (e.g., if the slaveholder died after December 1865).

Case 2: Family Lineage Includes Ancestors Living in the North before 1865

Thousands of individuals were enslaved in the North, but finding evidence of their enslavement is complicated by the fact that different states

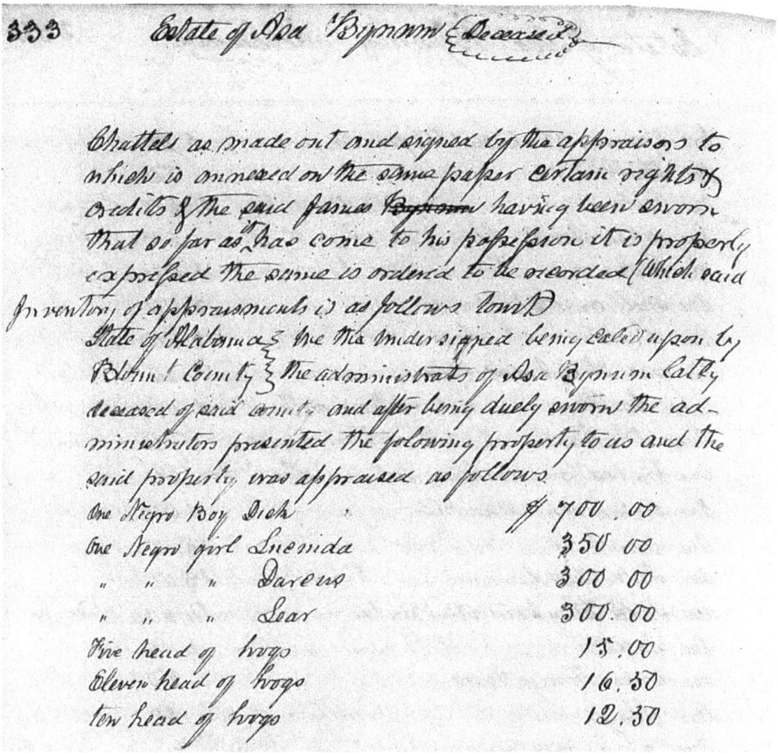
333 Estate of Asa Bynum {Deceased}

Chattels as made out and signed by the appraisors to
which is annexed on the same paper certain rights &
credits & the said James ~~Bynum~~ having been sworn
that so far as it has come to his possession it is properly
expressed the same is ordered to be recorded (Which said
Inventory of appraisements is as follows towit)
State of Alabama } We the undersigned being called upon by
Blount County } the administrators of Asa Bynum lately
deceased of said county and after being duely sworn the administrators presented the folowing property to us and the
said property was appraised as follows

One Negro Boy Dick				$ 700.00
One Negro girl Lucinda				350 00
"	"	"	Dareus	300 00
"	"	"	Lear	300.00
Five head of hogs				15.00
Eleven head of hogs				16.50
ten head of hogs				12.50

FIGURE 9.1. Transcription Excerpt of the Will of Asa Bynum. Lucinda is named in the second line item (thirteenth line down). Source: Alabama, Blount County, "Alabama Probate Records, 1809–1985. Minutes 1829–1852," Orphan Court Minutes 1829–1841, Image 183 of 734. FamilySearch, July 18, 2022, county courthouses, Alabama. www.familysearch.org/search/collection/1925446.

Inventory of appraisement is as follows to wit [?]
State of Alabama } [?], the undersigned, being sealed upon by
Blount County } the administrat[or?]s of Asa Bynum lately
deceased of said county, and after being duly sworn the ad-
ministrators presented the following property to us, and the
said property was appraised as follows

One Negro Boy Dick				*$700.00*
One Negro girl Lucinda				*350.00*
"	"	"	*Dareus [?]*	*300.00*
"	"	"	*Lear*	*300.00*
Five head of hogs				*15.00*
Eleven head of hogs				*16.50*
ten head of hogs				*12.50*

TABLE 9.3 A SUMMARY OF THE 1790 US CENSUS

Districts	Free People of Color	Enslaved
Vermont	255	16
New Hampshire	630	158
Massachusetts	538	0
Maine	5,463	0
Rhode Island	3,407	948
Connecticut	2,808	2,764
New York	4,654	21,324
New Jersey	2,762	11,423
Pennsylvania	6,537	3,737
Delaware	3,899	8,887
Maryland	8,043	103,036
Virginia	12,866	292,627
Kentucky	114	12,430
North Carolina	4,975	100,572
South Carolina	1,801	107,094
Georgia	398	29,264
South Western Territory	261	3,417

abolished slavery at different times and did so according to a variety of Gradual Abolition Acts passed before 1810 (see table 9.3).

This next case follows a claimant with an ancestor enslaved in the North, specifically in New Jersey. The New Jersey state legislature was the last of those in the North to abolish slavery, passing the Gradual Abolition Act in 1804. African Americans born to enslaved mothers after July 4, 1804, had to serve an "apprenticeship" to the owners of their mothers. The legislation freed women at age twenty-one, but men were not emancipated until twenty-five. New Jersey passed another law to end the forced indentured contract for African Americans in 1846. However, slavery did not truly end in the state until it was ended nationally, in 1865, after the American Civil War, with the passage of the Thirteenth Amendment to the US Constitution.

The claimant is a descendant of Annie Scott, who was born in New Jersey on November 16, 1933, and died on April 7, 2013. The Social Security Death Index verifies her date and place of birth. The researcher can also verify this information by reviewing her birth and death certificates. To connect Ms. Scott to her parents, we locate her on the 1940 census. We find her living in Trenton, Mercer County, New Jersey, with her father, Daniel Scott, age thirty-two; her mother, Myrtle

Scott, age twenty-five; and several siblings. We calculate her parents' years of birth as 1908 and 1915 for Daniel and Myrtle, respectively. We also note that Daniel Scott was born in Georgia and Myrtle Scott was born in New Jersey. Since Myrtle Scott was born in New Jersey, we will focus on her lineage for this example.

To connect Myrtle Scott to her parents, we must determine her maiden name. There are many ways to accomplish this. First, we can obtain her marriage, birth, or death certificate to discover her maiden name. Then, using the Social Security Death Index, we determine her maiden name to be Nixon. We find Myrtle on the 1930 census living with her parents, Charles and Dora Nixon, and her siblings. Dora Nixon was fifty years old, making her estimated year of birth sometime around 1880. Her parents were both born in New Jersey.

Next, we locate the Social Security Claims Indexes for two of Dora's children, Beatrice Nixon Miller, and Dorothy Nixon. Both daughters indicated their mother's (Dora Nixon) maiden name to be Jones. We locate her on each census, starting with the last census (1930) in which we find her, noting new information and updating family groups. On the 1910 census, Dora indicated that she had been married for thirteen years, making 1897 the year of marriage. On the 1900 census, she was living with her husband in Freehold, Monmouth, New Jersey.

To connect Dora M. Jones to her parents, we look for her by searching for a "black" Dora Jones, born around 1880 and living in the Upper Freehold area. We find Dora lived with her parents Ellis Jones, born in 1854, and Sarah Jones, born in 1855, both born in New Jersey. Ellis and Sarah indicate that their parents as well were all born in New Jersey. We also search for and find Ellis Jones's marriage license. He married Sarah S. Conover on April 21, 1877. The date seems correct since Ellis is absent from his parents' household in 1880. The New Jersey Marriage Record, 1670–1965, also lists Ellis's parents as Stephen and Sara Jones. Following the family to the 1870 census, Ellis is listed with his parents and siblings. His mother, Sara Jones, is forty-three years old, making 1827 her inferred year of birth; his father, Stephen Jones, is age fifty-one, with an implied birth year of 1819.

To get more information about Stephen and Sara Jones, we go back to the 1850 census. On this census, Stephen is thirty-nine years old, which updates his year of birth to 1811. The census takers list his wife as age twenty-two and her year of birth as 1828, consistent with the 1870 census. The family list includes Charles Henry Jones, who also appears on the 1870 census. The family was living in Upper Freehold,

Monmouth, New Jersey. Unfortunately, the 1820 census for New Jersey was lost.

Looking for Level I evidence of enslavement, we review Monmouth County, New Jersey, manumission records. We find nothing. To access Level III evidence, such as Monmouth County slave birth records, we need the slaveholder's name. For ancestors enslaved in the North and granted freedom by legislation, it is more challenging to locate the slaveholder. The earlier census records only include the names of heads of households. No federal slave schedules were generated as they were in 1850 and 1860. For states like New Jersey, earlier census records were lost or burned, leaving interested parties to spend hours looking through Level III evidence hoping for a match.

As with the Alabama example, we can use Level II evidence to prove enslavement. We can consider the year and place of birth for these individuals to conclude where they were enslaved. Since the Gradual Abolition Act did not grant automatic freedom to children of enslaved mothers, it is very possible that both Sara and Stephen were born forced into an indentured servant agreement because their mother was enslaved at the point of their birth.

Despite being in a state of "unfreedom," they could have been enumerated on the census as "free." Consequently, we cannot use the absence of a person or family on a census before the law was enacted to denote slave status. However, since more than 78 percent of the black people living in Monmouth County were enslaved (Wright 1989), and since it is possible they both were born under the Gradual Abolition Act (i.e., before 1846), we can surmise they were mostly likely enslaved or had parents who were enslaved.

Immigration patterns of free Africans and individuals of African descent further bolster the claim of enslavement, or the claim of having descended from those who were enslaved, for black people in the country before a certain time. There was very little immigration from Africa and the West Indies before 1846 (see table 9.4). Just nine thousand "Free People of Color" in the United States were born in Africa or the West Indies in 1850 and 1860. Consequently, for a claim of reparations, anyone identified as black or "mulatto" who was born in New Jersey before 1846 should be identified as enslaved or a descendent of an enslaved individual.

Using this logic, we can further extrapolate that, given that during this period there was little immigration to the United States of non-

TABLE 9.4 NATIVITIES OF FREE POPULATION

Region	US Census		Total
	1850	1860*	
Africa	4	526	530
West Indies	1,244	7,353	8,597
Total	1,248	7,879	9,127

SOURCE: 1850 Census, table LXXI (US Bureau of the Census 1853), and 1860 Census, Recapitulation: Nativities of Free Population (US Bureau of the Census 1864, 620).

*In 1860, most of the West Indians settled in New York, Florida, and Louisiana. Africans primarily settled in Massachusetts (126) and New York (69).

enslaved Africans or their descendants, to establish a claim for lineage-based reparations based on a reasonable assurance of slave ancestry a claimant may need only to find an ancestor who identified as black and was born before December 1865. Nevertheless, tracing one's lineage to 1865 and before may still prove a formidable task and will require knowledge of the information sources described in this chapter.

This chapter has provided claimants for reparations with information about how to establish a direct line to a qualifying ancestor, using genealogical techniques. I describe the process of identifying an enslaved ancestor and then lay out a framework to analyze evidence. The process consists of establishing lines, one generation at a time, going back as far as possible, and gathering documents along the way. Upon completing that process, the claimant should identify which ancestor to qualify. If the claimant has many ancestors to choose from, as is the case for most African Americans, they may want to choose an ancestor enslaved in the South, since the Level II analysis of the evidence of enslavement is often easier to find. In any case, they should start by researching the laws governing the lives of enslaved and free persons of color in the state where their potential qualifying ancestor(s) was born. The next step is to find the enslaver to access Level II evidence, if necessary.

The work outlined here of tracing the connection to enslaved ancestors for millions of people could be conducted and funded by genealogists. This option should prove valuable for many cohorts: those who could conduct this research themselves but who would still need to have their research vetted, those who could not conduct the research themselves, and those who could not afford to hire a professional to do it for them.

REFERENCES

Akin, John G. 1833. *A Digest of the Laws of the State of Alabama—1833*. Montgomery: Alabama Department of Archives and History.

Bettinger, Blaine T. 2019. *The Family Tree Guide to DNA Testing and Genetic Genealogy*. Cincinnati, OH: Family Tree Books.

Cade, John Brother. 1935. *Opinions Regarding Slavery: Slave Narratives*. http://7008.sydneyplus.com/final/Portal/SouthernUniversity.aspx?lang=en-US.

Darity, William A., Jr. 2019. "The Case for Reparations: Is the Nation Ready to Give African Americans Reparations?" *Crisis* 126 (3): 12–17. https://lsc-pagepro.mydigitalpublication.com/publication/?i=608868&ver=html5&p=14.

Darity, William, A., Jr., and A. Kirsten Mullen. 2020. *From Here to Equality: Reparations for Black Americans in the Twenty-First Century*. Chapel Hill: University of North Carolina Press.

Dollarhide, William. 2001. *The Census Book: A Genealogist's Guide to Federal Census Facts, Schedules and Indexes: With Master Extraction Forms for Federal Census Schedules, 1790–1930*. North Salt Lake, UT: Heritage Quest.

Fisk University. 1968. *The Unwritten History of Slavery*. Washington, DC: Microcard Editions.

FWP (Federal Writers Project). 1941. *Slave Narratives: A Folk History of Slavery in the United States from Interviews with Former Slaves*. 17 vols. Microform. Washington, DC: Library of Congress Work Project.

Garrett-Nelson, LaBrenda. 2020. "Parents for Isaac Garrett of Laurens County, South Carolina: DNA Corroborates Oral Tradition." *National Genealogical Society Quarterly* 108 (2): 85–111.

Gutman, Herbert G. 1976. *The Black Family in Slavery and Freedom, 1750–1925*. New York: Pantheon Books.

Nguyen, Phung. 1996. "Census Undercount and the Undercount of the Black Population." *Western Journal of Black Studies* 20 (2): 96–103. https://eric.ed.gov/?id=EJ548401.

Reid, Richard. 1995. "The 1870 United States Census and Black Underenumeration: A Test Case from North Carolina." *Social History / Histoire Sociale* 28 (56): 487–99. https://hssh.journals.yorku.ca/index.php/hssh/article/view/16645/15503.

Rosenthal, Caitlin. 2019. *Accounting for Slavery: Masters and Management*. Cambridge, MA: Harvard University Press.

Smith, Franklin Carter, and Emily Anne Croom. 2008. *A Genealogist's Guide to Discovering Your African-American Ancestors: How to Find and Record Your Unique Heritage*. Baltimore: Genealogical Publishing.

Thompson, Gayle B. 1975. "Blacks and Social Security Benefits: Trends, 1960–73." *Social Security Bulletin* 38(4): 30–40. https://www.ssa.gov/policy/docs/ssb/v38n4/v38n4p30.pdf.

US Bureau of the Census. 1853. *The Seventh Census of the United States: 1850*. Washington, DC: Robert Armstrong. https://www2.census.gov/library/publications/decennial/1850/1850a/1850a-01.pdf.

————. 1864. "Recapitulation of the Tables of Population, Nativity, and Occupation." In *Population of the United States in 1860, Compiled from the Original Returns of the Eighth Census.* Washington, DC: Government Printing Office. https://www2.census.gov/library/publications/decennial/1860/population/1860a-46.pdf.

Williams, Heather Andrea. 2016. *Help Me to Find My People: The African American Search for Family Lost in Slavery.* Chapel Hill: University of North Carolina Press. www.vlebooks.com/vleweb/product/openreader?id=none&isbn=9781469601687.

Woodtor, Dee Parmer. 2016. *Finding a Place Called Home: A Guide to African-American Genealogy and Historical Identity.* Salt Lake City: Digitized by the Genealogical Society of Utah.

10

On the Black Reparations Highway

Avoiding the Detours

WILLIAM A. DARITY JR. AND A. KIRSTEN MULLEN

Some actions taken recently by ostensible supporters of reparations threaten a movement that is gaining unexpected momentum.[1] In 2000, a national survey on American attitudes toward reparations found that a tiny 4 percent of white Americans agreed with the statement "The federal government should pay monetary compensation to African Americans whose ancestors were slaves," while 67 percent of black Americans agreed with the same statement (Dawson and Popoff 2004). By 2019, a Gallup poll found the proportion of whites endorsing "cash payments to black Americans who are descendants of slaves" had reached 16 percent. Simultaneously, more than 70 percent of black Americans supported the same policy (Younis 2019). By April 2021, more than a year into the COVID-19 pandemic and after the international outcry over the police murder of George Floyd, a University of Massachusetts at Amherst national poll found that 28 percent of white Americans supported black reparations, while 86 percent of black Americans did (Sharpe 2021).

Growth in support for reparations of black American descendants of US slavery, in a climate of national reckoning, has meant a rush of Americans calling for racial redress. Unfortunately, several of their presumably well-intentioned efforts can undercut the pursuit of true reparations and create dangerous off-ramps from the comprehensive, national program of reparations that our country so desperately needs to enact.

There are four key off-ramps produced by reparations advocates: (1) local or piecemeal reparations, (2) House Bill 40 (H.R. 40), (3) the claim that reparations must be "more than just a check," and (4) the promise and priority ascribed to indirect and/or universal programs as a means of closing the racial wealth gap. Rather than creating an infrastructure to support black reparations, these detours are becoming obstacles to true reparations and are worth interrogating in greater detail.

"LOCAL REPARATIONS"

Critical to the position we take throughout this volume is the emphasis we place on the elimination of the racial wealth gap as the central aim of a reparations plan. Reparations undertaken by state or local governments or by individuals or other private organizations simply cannot meet the goal. As discussed in our opening chapter, neither state and local governments nor other organizations, individually or collectively, have the financial wherewithal to eradicate the difference in black and white net worth.

To illustrate this, we assume conservatively that the average payout per individual needed to bridge the racial wealth disparity is $300,000.[2] Moreover, we assume that 90 percent of a city or state's black population will be eligible for reparations.

Evanston, Illinois, a city parading an ordinary housing voucher program as a reparations plan, cannot approach generating the funds needed to address the racial wealth gap for its residents. If Evanston has about eleven thousand eligible black recipients, it would need $3.3 billion, while its annual budget is $300 million, less than 10 percent of the total bill.

The city has placed a cap on the housing voucher plan of $10 million to be financed by a marijuana tax. That amount, less than .04 percent of the $3.3 billion needed to eliminate the racial wealth gap for Evanston's black residents, is woefully insufficient.

Amherst, Massachusetts, making overtures to replicate Evanston's program, has a smaller eligible black population of about two thousand persons. Even so, it would need $600 million to erase the racial wealth gap while having a current town budget of $85 million.

St. Louis, Missouri, with a considerably larger eligible black population of approximately 120,000 persons, would have to make an impossibly large $36 billion expenditure out of a $1.2 billion annual budget.

Los Angeles, California, with an eligible black population of about three hundred thousand persons, would need to spend $90 billion, nearly nine times its $11.2 billion budget.

The state of California, which established a reparations task force scheduled to issue a final report to the State Assembly in mid-2023, has an eligible black population of about two million. The $600 billion needed to close the racial wealth gap is more than double the state's current $270 billion budget.

Durham, North Carolina, has an eligible black population numbering one hundred thousand. The $30 billion needed to erase the wealth gap is sixty times the city's $50 million budget.

Austin, Texas, would require an expenditure of at least $21 billion to meet the demands of a true reparations effort. Its annual budget is closer to $4.2 billion.

We estimate that the state of Texas would have to make an outlay of at least $660 billion to eliminate the racial wealth gap for its black residents. The state's total budget is $250 billion.

Some cities and states where the black presence is a miniscule share of the total population constitute the exceptions that prove the rule— but they still would find it difficult to make the payments. Salt Lake City has a black resident population of about 4,500 persons who would be eligible for reparations. Elimination of the wealth gap for them would mean an expenditure of $1.35 billion, while the city's budget is about $2 billion.

Similarly, Utah has a total eligible black population of about thirty-three thousand. A $10 billion tab still would be almost half of the state's $22 billion budget.

In 2019, Telluride, Colorado, had *no* recorded black residents. Clearly, it could pay $300,000 to its first black resident without breaking its $4.5 million budget. Nevertheless, the single $300,000 outlay would be more than 5 percent of the town's annual budget.

Local reparations are an impossibility, a virtual oxymoron. But to the extent that these initiatives crop up everywhere, were a direct claim to ever be set before Congress for a national reparations program, opponents could conveniently argue that it had already happened, since so many cities and states have adopted "reparations." These varied local and state acts of atonement will not eliminate the racial wealth gap and should not be labeled "reparations." We have suggested they refer to these steps as racial equity initiatives.

US HOUSE OF REPRESENTATIVES BILL 40 (H.R. 40)

H.R. 40 (S. 40 in the Senate), congressional legislation that would establish a study commission to provide Congress with proposals for African American reparations, has taken on near-mythical (and mystical) proportions. Although widely deemed a harbinger of reparations, we have learned that many of its champions—including legislators who are its sponsors—have not read it. First introduced by Congressman John Conyers in 1989, the bill has served as a legislative placeholder for the reparations movement for more than thirty years.

The bill has been revised multiple times—not necessarily for the better. In fact, H.R. 40 is another detour from true reparations. The most recent revision took place immediately before the bill finally came out of the Judiciary Committee for consideration on the floor of the House in April 2021. While the original version of H.R. 40 hardly was a model of perfection, the version reported out of the Judiciary Committee is deeply flawed.

The bill's weaknesses take two forms: flaws in intent and flaws in structure.

H.R. 40's flaws in intent involve failure of the legislation to ensure that the commission it activates will produce a report that supports true reparations. The bill gives no directives to the commission about the content of the proposals it develops.

The commission's charge is entirely open-ended with respect to the reparations plans it ultimately delivers to Congress. It could recommend nothing more than a new apology for slavery and legal segregation, in addition to the apologies issued by the House in 2008 and the Senate in 2009. It could recommend a black housing voucher program, bringing the Evanston plan to a national scale. It could propose a program of black American repatriation to the African continent or any number of other approaches to African American reparations.

The bill should direct the commission to design a proposal based on the four pillars of true reparations described in the first chapter of *From Here to Equality*: The proposal should identify black American descendants of US slavery as eligible recipients; it should target elimination of black-white wealth differences; it should prioritize direct payments to eligible recipients; and it should indicate that reparations will be financed by the federal government.

The National African American Reparations Commission (NAARC), the Institute of the Black World (IBW), and the National Coalition on

Black Reparations in America (N'COBRA) have played an important role in the revision of H.R. 40 over the years, and they have done so with an eye toward producing a plan for restitution that departs sharply from true reparations (N'COBRA 2017).

NAARC's ten-point plan for reparations calls for *all* persons of African descent to be eligible for reparations, not specifically those who are black and who have ancestors enslaved in the United States. The NAARC plan does not give preeminence to eradication of the black-white wealth gap as the core objective of a black reparations plan. Nor does the NAARC plan emphasize that black reparations should be conducted primarily or exclusively by the federal government (NAARC 2021).

NAARC in fact seeks to funnel reparations monies through a variety of newly created intermediate institutions under unspecified supervision and management. These include an African American Housing and Finance Authority, a Black Business Development Bank, a National Board of Education of African Ancestry, and, perhaps most significantly, a National Reparations Trust Authority with funds "to develop an infrastructure of [black] strategic financial, commercial, industrial, agricultural and technology-oriented business/economic enterprises." In short, NAARC's approach takes reparations funds out of the control of the presumed beneficiaries.

Flaws in structure involve peculiarities in H.R. 40 that will produce a defective commission. Our concerns about structural flaws appeared in a 2021 Actify Press report:

1. The bill, as currently written, specifies that the Federal Advisory Committee Act does not apply to this Commission. The Federal Advisory Committee Act ensures that all advisory groups engage in transparent deliberations, e.g. hold hearings, hold public meetings, and provide ongoing reports of their activities prior to delivery of the final report.

2. The bill, as currently written, provides each member with pay at a daily rate of up to Executive IV level on the federal salary scale, which is up to $172,000 per annum. The Commission now has a timeline of at least 18 months. This means pay could run as high as $253,000 per member. [We]'ve long said it is inappropriate for members of a Commission with this type of mission to receive pay. They should receive compensation for their expenses, and there should be a paid professional staff to support commissioners'

efforts—but the members of the Commission themselves should not receive salaries. The presence of the paid professional staff should enable them to maintain their normal lines of employment and to also serve. We should not want members of this Commission who only will serve if they receive substantial pay.

3. Originally the bill had provisions for 7 members appointed by the President (3), the Speaker of the House (3), and the President Pro Tempore of the Senate (1). Between 2015–16 and 2017–18 sessions of Congress, NAARC/NCOBRA rewrote the bill to expand the number to 13, adding six members who would be representatives of organizations with a legacy of promoting reparations. At the time, there were no specifics about how the six would be selected or appointed. The version of the bill that came out of markup now specifies 15 members (!): nine members, three each appointed by the President, the Speaker, and the President Pro Tempore and the additional six selected by the (administrative) director of the Commission who will be appointed by the Chair and Vice-Chair. [This] is a very odd internal selection [process for] the additional six members [who are to be chosen] "from the major civil society and reparations organizations that have historically championed the cause of reparatory justice."

4. The bill, as currently written, says a quorum is seven members, less than half of the total membership of the Commission.

5. The bill, as currently written, says no elected official or public employee can be a member of the Commission. It's interesting to note that federal law would make any of these persons unable to receive payments. Consequently, the bill as currently written ensures that every member will be eligible to receive a salary. (Graham 2021)

We view the assignment of authority to the administrative director of the commission, who will not be a member, to select six of the commissioners and the constitution of a quorum by a minority of the members as highly unusual arrangements. The exclusion of elected officials and public employees from the commission will limit its potential credibility and influence. The highly effective Commission on Wartime Relocation and Internment of Civilians that developed the reparations plan for Japanese Americans included both contemporary and formerly elected officials. Regrettably, support for H.R. 40 will derail African American reparations.

"IT NEEDS TO BE MORE THAN A CHECK"

The oft-made assertion that reparations should be "more than a check" trivializes the life-changing effects of each black household having an additional $840,900 in resources measured in 2019 dollars (or each black individual claimant having an additional $357,000 in resources). As we have said before, "Reparations will not solve all problems that confront Black Americans. For example, the recent national (and international) wave of protests against anti-Black police violence triggered by the highly visible execution of an unarmed and prostrate George Floyd brings to the fore a seemingly eternal problem of atrocities associated with law enforcement practices. Reparations payments alone are unlikely, automatically, to alter those practices. However, an [$840,900] increase in net worth per Black household could have a dramatic impact on Black health outcomes, homeownership, education, economic security, and more" (Darity and Mullen 2020).

Indeed, monetary payments will not end American racism—although for a redress plan for black American descendants of US slavery to be enacted, American racism will have to decline sufficiently for a solid majority of citizens to support it. However, substantially greater resources will enable black families to cope more effectively with the manifestations of racism. These coping mechanisms can encompass expanded political participation, leading to the adoption of policies that penalize discriminators severely and mitigate the effects of antiblack attitudes.

A "check" of this amount per eligible recipient would be powerfully transformative. At last it will give black Americans with enslaved ancestors in the United States the material conditions for full citizenship. If black reparations were "just a check" of this order of magnitude, it would greatly alter the American political and social landscape—for the better.

Nevertheless, we do advocate an additional key component of a reparations plan going beyond the essential element of monetary payments. Because the history we have been taught is distorted and dishonest, especially with respect to slavery, the Civil War, and the Reconstruction Era, an effective reparations plan must include an educational and instructional component for Americans of all ages to correct the record. Such a plan must be kept in place for at least three generations. This arm of the reparations movement would actively promote de-Confederatization.

However, we implore readers not to devalue nor dismiss the significance of the "check." It matters for both symbolic and substantive reasons.

INDIRECT AND UNIVERSAL PROGRAMS

Some who advocate elimination of the racial wealth gap do not share the desire for black-specific reparations. Instead, they argue for alternatives that either avoid making direct payments to eligible recipients or avoid providing resources exclusively to black American descendants of slavery. Under both schemes, the nation ducks making race-specific monetary payments to its black population with a lineage connection to US slavery.

This growing array of indirect and universal programs stacked one upon another have become an additional obstacle to true reparations, if only because of the time consumed in establishing their inadequacies.

Indirect approaches to closing the racial wealth gap include the provision of scholarships for higher education for black Americans, financial support for Historically Black Colleges and Universities (HBCUs), subsidies for black-owned businesses, and subsidies for black homeownership (as in Evanston). These policies certainly have desirable features, but it is a major overstatement to claim that separately or together they will have much of an impact on black-white differences in wealth.

The following fact undercuts the higher education scholarships gambit as a means of narrowing the racial wealth gap: black heads of household with a college degree have two-thirds of the net worth of white heads of household *who never finished high school*. Greater black educational attainment hardly offsets the inherited advantages in wealth transmission held by white Americans (Hamilton et al. 2015).

To the extent that the objective of improving the financial status of HBCUs is motivated by the expectation that it will improve black educational attainment, the problem remains that greater educational attainment among black Americans does not have much effect on racial differences in wealth. Furthermore, there seems to be an assumption that HBCUs permanently will serve primarily black students, but there are a growing number of cases where that, evidently, is not true.

In West Virginia, both Bluefield State College and West Virginia State University, institutions established to serve black students under the regime of segregated higher education, have white student populations that exceed 70 percent of their total enrollments. Lincoln University in Missouri is a third HBCU that now has a majority white student body. In fact, estimates now indicate one in four students at HBCUs are white (Butrymowicz 2014). Therefore, there is no assurance that more financially stable HBCUs even will be serving mostly black students in the future.

Will closing the black-white business ownership gap via subsidies close the difference in black and white wealth? There is a gulf in rates of business ownership by race. While the white business ownership rate of 72 percent is virtually identical with their population share, black American descendants of US slavery constitute 12 percent of the nation's population but own a mere 5.6 percent of all American businesses.

Bringing the black share of businesses owned into conformity with the black population share still will not address the mammoth difference in the scale of black- versus white-owned enterprises. Consider that in 2020 there were twenty-one black-owned banks with a combined level of assets slightly under $5 billion. JP Morgan Chase had assets valued *in excess of $3 trillion.* Even the 250th-ranked white-owned bank, the Bryn Mawr Trust Company, had assets valued at $5.4 billion, a sum greater than the total assets of the nation's black-owned banks.

Before the pandemic, the combined annual retail sales of all black-owned businesses amounted to about $270 billion, approximately half of Walmart's annual retail sales taken alone. Even if an allocation of $30 billion was given to black-owned businesses that enabled them to expand annual retail sales by a multiple of five, their sales still would fall short of Walmart's by $100 billion (Sanford School of Public Policy 2021).

The conventional view of the wealth-business nexus is to presume that building black enterprise will build black wealth. However, reverse causation might be more pertinent here: build black wealth, via reparations, to build black enterprise. With greater initial wealth, black entrepreneurs would have more opportunities to start new businesses, expand existing businesses, acquire existing businesses from other owners, and maintain the continuity of their businesses. The latter consideration takes on added weight amid the challenges posed by a pandemic where 40 percent of black-owned businesses ceased operation between February and April 2020 (Washington 2021).

There is also a glaring discrepancy in black (47 percent) and white homeownership (73 percent) rates. Home-buying subsidies could contribute to narrowing that gap, but the average level of equity that whites hold in their homes is $216,000; for blacks the average level is $94,000 (Ross 2020). Raising the black homeownership rate to the white rate would not address the discriminatory component in the racial spread in equity values in homes: "Differences in home and neighborhood quality do not fully explain the devaluation of homes in Black neighborhoods. Homes of similar quality in neighborhoods with similar amenities are worth 23 percent less ($48,000 per home on average, amounting to $156 billion in cumulative losses) in majority Black neighborhoods, compared to those with very few or no Black residents" (Perry, Rothwell, and Harshbarger 2018).

Moreover, the focus on homeownership overlooks substantial racial disparities in the ownership of other assets. There is a wide difference in the possession of other types of assets by race. Sixty percent of white households have retirement accounts but only 34 percent of black households. Fifteen percent of white households have family-owned business equity but a mere 7 percent of black households. Sixty percent of white households have publicly traded stocks but only 31 percent of black households (Ross 2020).

There is a general tendency to overemphasize homeownership as the primary route toward asset building. Stated plainly, equity in a home is the core asset for households in the middle of the wealth distribution. However, for persons in the upper quarter of the wealth distribution, homeownership is markedly less important in comparison with retirement accounts, nonresidential land ownership, business ownership, and stocks and other financial assets.

On average, overall primary residences amount to no more than 35 percent of household net worth. The combination of business interests, financial assets, and retirement accounts constitutes more than 60 percent of household net worth (Swanson 2018).

Universal policies advertised as closing the racial wealth gap include, most prominently, student debt relief and "baby bonds." Student debt relief as an avenue to eliminating the black-white wealth differential assumes that the debt side of the net worth ledger dominates the asset side in shaping the racial wealth gap. This assumption is incorrect.

The fundamental reason for black-white differences in wealth is not high black indebtedness, inclusive of student loan debt. The fundamental reason is low black asset holdings.

A Prosperity Now study in 2019 reported that median black household liabilities were $30,800, while median white household liabilities were more than twice as large at $73,800. However, white households had a median level of assets valued at more than $260,000 in contrast with the median black households' assets valued at $55,900 (Nieves 2019). The median black household had 40 percent of the debt of the median white household but only 20 percent of the assets. Correspondingly, the ratio of assets to debts for black households was 1.6 versus 2.8 for white households, both measured at the median.

Once we account for differences in enrollment rates in colleges and universities between blacks and whites—whites have higher rates—it is apparent that elimination of student loan debt will reduce the racial difference in wealth between individuals by an average of slightly less than $2,000.

"Baby bonds" is a policy that provides each newborn infant with a publicly funded trust account—a good idea, but, again, not a policy that will eliminate racial differences in net worth.[3] Under this policy, each child will receive an account calibrated in size to their parents' wealth position.

Children from the wealthiest families will receive a token $50 account, but children from the most net-worth-poor families will receive an account ranging from $50,000 to $60,000. The accounts would earn a guaranteed 1 percent real rate of interest per annum. Recipients will be able to access their accounts when they reach young adulthood, giving them an asset to launch them on a lifetime path toward opportunity and economic security.

The reason a "baby bonds" policy will be insufficient to close the racial wealth gap is that it sets as its target median wealth for all American households, rather than median white household wealth, never mind mean white household wealth. Black youth would receive an average of $29,038, and white youth would receive an average of $15,790 (both at age eighteen). Under a fully executed, multiple-cohort program, the racial wealth gap would fall by $13,248 for recipients of the trust accounts (Cassidy et al. 2019). This would amount to approximately a 20 percent reduction in the racial wealth gap at the median, but a far less impressive 4 percent reduction at the mean.

Each of these offramps uniquely fails to provide the necessary acknowledgment, redress, and closure to black American descendants of persons enslaved in the US. Moreover, they all pose a similar risk in that they threaten to alleviate the growing, uncommon, and—for at least the past 150 years—unprecedented pressure that exists for reparations, and would alleviate this pressure in exchange for a return that is grossly insufficient for this population's needs. To squander this momentum for the pitiful half measures these avenues offer would be tragic.

We conclude that it is high time to go full bore on the implementation of a comprehensive program of black reparations. If American society is to meet an outstanding justice claim and become an authentic democracy, including bringing its black citizens fully into the nation's life, it must, at least, do away with the immense chasm in wealth between blacks and whites. Nothing less than reparations can do this, and if America is to ever finally lay the foundation for a racially equitable society, nothing less will do.

NOTES

1. Conditions and strategies for building greater support for black reparations are considered in chapters 7 and 8 of this volume.

2. More precise estimates of the per-person payout needed to eliminate the black-white wealth gap run closer to $360,000. See the essay in chapter 2 of this volume.

3. In the interest of full disclosure, one of the authors of this chapter is an architect of the baby bonds idea and hence very enthusiastic about it, while still recognizing its limitations.

REFERENCES

Butrymowicz, Sarah. 2014. "Historically Black Colleges Are Becoming More White." *Time*, June 27. https://time.com/2907332/historically-black-colleges-increasingly-serve-white-students/.

Cassidy, Christa, Rachel Heydemann, Anne Price, Nathaniel Unah, and William Darity Jr. 2019. "Baby Bonds: A Universal Path to Ensure the Next Generation Has the Capital to Thrive." Insight Center for Community Economic Development and Samuel DuBois Cook Center on Social Equity, Duke University, December. https://socialequity.duke.edu/wp-content/uploads/2019/12/ICCED-Duke_BabyBonds_December2019-Linked.pdf.

Darity, William, and Kirsten Mullen. 2020. "Black Reparations and the Racial Wealth Gap." Brookings, *Up Front* (blog), June 15. www.brookings.edu/blog/up-front/2020/06/15/black-reparations-and-the-racial-wealth-gap/.

Dawson, Michael C., and Rovana Popoff. 2004. "Reparations: Justice and Greed in Black and White." *Du Bois Review: Social Science Research on Race* 1 (1): 47–91. https://doi.org/10.1017/s1742058x04040056.

Graham, Michael. 2021. "Benign Neglect, Reparations, and Juneteenth." Actify Press, September 1. https://actifypress.com/benign-neglect-reparations-and-juneteenth/.

Hamilton, Darrick, William Darity Jr., Anne E. Price, Vishnu Sridharan, and Rebecca Tippett. 2015. "Umbrellas Don't Make It Rain: Why Studying and Working Hard Isn't Enough for Black Americans." Insight Center for Community Economic Development, New School, and Samuel DuBois Cook Center on Social Equity at Duke University, April 1. https://insightcced.org/wp-content/uploads/2015/08/Umbrellas_Dont_Make_It_Rain_Final.pdf.

NAARC (National African American Reparations Commission). 2021. "NAARC Rolls Out Preliminary 10 Point Reparations Plan." Institute of the Black World 21st Century, September 20. https://ibw21.org/initiative-posts/naarc-posts/naarc-rolls-out-preliminary-10-point-reparations-plan/.

N'COBRA (National Coalition of Blacks for Reparations in America). 2017. "Congressman John Conyers Introduces New HR40 Reparations Bill." Press release, January 9.

Nieves, Emanuel. 2019. "What We've Learned about Debt in Black Communities." *Prosperity Now Blog*, February 7. https://prosperitynow.org/blog/what-weve-learned-about-debt-black-communities.

Perry, Andre M., Jonathan Rothwell, and David Harshbarger. 2018. "The Devaluation of Assets in Black Neighborhoods." Brookings, November 27. www.brookings.edu/research/devaluation-of-assets-in-black-neighborhoods/.

Ross, Jenna. 2020. "The Racial Wealth Gap in America: Asset Types Held by Race." *Visual Capitalist*, June 12. www.visualcapitalist.com/racial-wealth-gap/.

Sanford School of Public Policy, Duke University. 2021. "The Tulsa Massacre, Racism and the Black-White Wealth Gap." March 28. https://sanford.duke.edu/story/tulsa-massacre-racism-and-black-white-wealth-gap.

Sharpe, Jared. 2021. "UMass Amherst/WCVB Poll Finds Nearly Half of Americans Say the Federal Government Definitely Should Not Pay Reparations to the Descendants of Slaves." UMass Amherst, News, April 29. www.umass.edu/news/article/umass-amherstwcvb-poll-finds-nearly-half.

Swanson, Jann. 2018. "How Homeownership Affects Household Wealth." *Mortgage News Daily*, March 26. www.mortgagenewsdaily.com/03262018_homeownership.asp.

Washington, Kemberley. 2021. "Covid-19 Has Had a Disproportionate Financial Impact on Black Small Businesses." *Forbes*, December 15. www.forbes.com/advisor/personal-finance/covid19-financial-impact-on-black-businesses/.

Younis, Mohamed. 2019. "As Redress for Slavery, Americans Oppose Cash Reparations." Gallup.com, News, July 29. https://news.gallup.com/poll/261722/redress-slavery-americans-oppose-cash-reparations.aspx.

List of Documented Massacres and Instances of Mob Violence Perpetrated against Black Individuals, Civil War through 1950

Year	Locations
1863	Detroit, MI
	New York, NY
1866	Memphis, TN
	New Orleans, LA
1868	Albany, GA
	Millican, TX
	Opelousas, LA
	St. Bernard Parish, LA
1870	Eutaw, AL
1871	Meridian, MS
1873	Colfax, LA
1874	Barbour County, AL
	Coushatta, LA
	Vicksburg, MS
1875	Clinton, MS
1876	Charleston, SC
	Ellenton, SC
	Hamburg, SC

1887	Thibodeaux, LA
1888	Danville, VA
	Fort Bend, TX
1891	Omaha, NE
1896	Polk County, AR
1898	Phoenix, SC
	Wilmington, NC
1900	New Orleans, LA
1901	Pierce City, MO
1903	Evansville, IL
	Whitesboro, TX
1908	Springfield, IL
1910	Little Rock, AK
	New York, NY
	Norfolk, VA
	Shreveport, LA
	Slocum, TX
	Uvalda, GA
1912	Forsyth County, GA
	Oscarville, GA
1917	Chester, PA
	East St. Louis, IL
	Houston, TX
1919	Austin, TX
	Baltimore, MD
	Bisbee, AZ
	Blakeley, GA
	Bogalusa, LA
	Cadwell, GA
	Charleston, SC
	Chicago, IL
	Corbin, KY

Dublin, GA
Elaine, AK
Ellisville, MS
Garfield Park, IN
Hattiesburg, MS
Hubbard, OH
Jacksonville, FL
Jenkins County, GA
Knoxville, TN
Lexington, NE
Longview, TX
Macon, MS
Memphis, TN
Millen, GA
Montgomery, AL
Morgan County, WV
New London, CT
Norfolk, VA
Omaha, NE
Orono, ME
Philadelphia, PA
Putnam County, GA
Syracuse, NY
Texarkana, TX
Vicksburg, MS
Washington, DC
Wilmington, DE

1920	Hurtsboro, AL
	Ocoee, FL
1921	Denton, TX
	Tulsa, OK
1922	Perry, FL

1923	Catcher, AK
	Rosewood, FL
1926	Benson, AL
	Susanna, AL
1943	Beaumont, TX
	Detroit, MI
	Los Angeles, CA
	Mobile, AL
1946	Chicago, IL
	Columbia, TN
1947	Chicago, IL
1948	Vanport, OR
1949	Peekskill, NY
	Washington, DC

Sample Pedigree Chart and Family Group Sheet from Sons & Daughters of the United States Middle Passage

Pedigree Chart

Chart No. ___1___

No. 1 on this chart is the same person as No. ___10___
On Chart No. ___2___

1
Boston Lincoln Aniton
Born 24 Jan 1889
Place Oneonta, Blount, Alabama
Married 17 Dec 1918
Place Blount Co, Alabama
Died 19 Oct 1967
Place Cleveland, Cuyahoga, Ohio

Irene Polk
NAME OF SPOUSE

2
William Anderton/Aniton ("Mulatto")
Born About 1856
Place Blount Co, Alabama
Married 09 Jan 1876
Place Blont. Co. Alabama
Died 15 Dec 1934
Place Blount Co, Alabama

3
Easter Staton (Enslaved)
Born About 1853
Place Alabama
Died 07 Dec 1934
Place Oneonta, Blount, Ala

4
Artimissy Anderton (White)
Born About 1838
Place Alabama
Married Unknown
Place Unknown
Died Jul 1870
Place Blount Co, Alabama

5
Unknown (Enslaved)
Born
Place
Died
Place

6
Lucinda Menerva Bynum (Enslaved)
Born About 1827
Place Alabama
Married Unknown
Place Alabama
Died About Jun 1891
Place Blount Co, Alabama

7
Jack Staton (Enslaved)
Born About 1871
Place Blount, Alabama
Died Before 1891
Place Unknown

8
Ruth Blakely Anderton (White)
CONT. ON CHART

5 John W. Anderton (White) Enslaver
CONT. ON CHART

10 Unknown (Male) presumed enslaved
CONT. ON CHART

11 Unknown (Female) presumed enslaved
CONT. ON CHART

12 Unnamed Male (Enslaved) b. NC
CONT. ON CHART

13 Unnamed Female (Enslaved) b. Tenn
CONT. ON CHART

14 Unnamed Male (Enslaved) b: Virginia
CONT. ON CHART

15 Unnamed (Female) Enslaved b: Virginia
CONT. ON CHART

FIGURE B.1. Sample Pedigree Chart. Source: Sons & Daughters of the US Middle Passage (SDUSMP).

Family Group Sheet

Husband		William Anderton/Aniton		# 2	Occupation(s)	Farm Laborer
	Date	Place		Immigration	N/A	
Born	About 1856	Blount Co, Alabama		Naturalization	N/A	
Christened				Military Service	None	
Died	15 Dec 1934	Blount Co.Alabama		Cause of Death	Pnuemonia	
Buried		Old Liberty Cemetery, Oneonta, AL		Date of Will		
Married	09 Jan 1876	Blount, Oneonta, AL.		Other Marriages	N/A	
Father	Unknown #5					
Mother		Artimissey Anderton, Blount, Alabama #4		Other Information		

Wife (maiden name)		Easter Staton		# 3	Occupation(s)	Keep House
	Date	Place		Immigration	N/A	
Born	About 1853	Alabama		Naturalization	N/A	
Christened				Military Service	None	
Died	Before	1891		Cause of Death		
Buried		Old Liberty Cemetery, Oneonta, AL		Date of Will	N/A	
Father	Jack Staton #6			Other Marriages		N/A
Mother	Lucinda Menerva Bynum #7			Other Information		

Other Information/Records (ie. Census, Passports, etc…)	
Various Census Records	
Marriage Certificates	
Death Certificates	

- Represents number on the Pedigree Sheet (or other numbering system, if applicable)
Sons & Daughters of the United States Middle Passage

www.sdusmp.org

	Sex	Name	Birth		Date of first marriage	Date of Death/ Cause
#	M/F		Date	Place	Name of Spouse	Place
	F	Mary L. Anderton	abt 1882	Blount, Alabama	Unknown	Unknown
					Unknown	Unknown
	M	Raphus Anderton	abt. 1884	Blount, Alabama	Unknown	Unknown
					Emma Graves	Unknown
	M	Greeley Aniton	1887	Blount, Alabama	Unknown	after 1925
					Hattie Mayberry/Freddie Buchanan 2nd Marriage	Cleveland, Cuyahoga, Ohio
	M	Boston Lincoln Aniton	24 Jan 1889	Blount, Alabama	17 Dec 1918	19 Oct 1957 Heart attack
					Irene Polk	Oneonta, Blount, Alabama
	M	Henry Clifton Aniton	24 May 1892	Blount, Alabama	Unknown	07 Nov 1948
					Georgia Edwards	Oneonta, Blount, Alabama
	F	Dora Anderton	1894	Blount, Alabama	22 June 1931	1974
					Elijah Carethers	Alabama
	F	Nellie Z. Aniton	22 Nov 1895	Blount,Alabama	21 April 1912	25 June 1895
					Elbert Roy Robinson	Oneonta, Blount, Alabama

FIGURE B.2. Sample Family Group Sheet. Source: Sons & Daughters of the US Middle Passage (SDUSMP).

The Reparations Planning Committee

ROBBIE AKHERE-CHANDLER, Carolinas Educate4Reparation

BERNARD E. ANDERSON, University of Pennsylvania

MEHRSA BARADARAN, University of California-Irvine

WESLEY BELLAMY, Virginia State University

KEISHA L. BENTLEY-EDWARDS, Duke University

MARY FRANCES BERRY, University of Pennsylvania

KENDRA BOZARTH, Liberation in a Generation

LISA R. BROWN, University of the Incarnate Word

TRESSIE MCMILLAN COTTOM, University of North Carolina at Chapel Hill

THOMAS CRAEMER, University of Connecticut

WILLIAM A. DARITY JR., Duke University

MALIK EDWARDS, North Carolina Central University

WALTER D. GREASON, Macalester College

BRIANNA HARRISON, University of Memphis

LUCAS HUBBARD, Duke University

TREVON D. LOGAN, The Ohio State University

EVELYN A. MCDOWELL, Rider University, Sons & Daughters of the United States Middle Passage

A. KIRSTEN MULLEN, Artefactual

RODNEY PIERCE, Nash County Public Schools

KATHY L. POWERS, University of New Mexico

TREVOR SMITH, Black Liberation—Indigenous Sovereignty

Index

AAFL (African Ancestry Foreign Lineage), 159

ABAL (Ancestral Black American Lineage), 147–168; definition of, 148

abolition of slavery: failure of governments to invest in, 65; failure to institute, and US moral debt for colonial slavery, 27–28; reparations paid to slave owners for, 18, 142; state laws, varying dates for, 181; George Washington's voluntary abolition scheme, 28

abolition societies, and black adults' education, 150, 151

acknowledgment, redress, and closure (ARC, objectives of reparations): adult education and achievement of, 149–150; apologies in acknowledgments, generally, 41, 101, 114; closure not possible without an end to racial discrimination, 58; closure not possible without reparations, 22; definition of, 103n1, 111; detours from reparations (ideas to avoid) all failing to provide, 210; health and wellness disparities and, 95, 103

Adenauer, Konrad, 114–115, 130

ADOS (American Descendants of Slavery), 65, 148

adult developmental thinking: civic and community engagement and, 162, 165, 168; as constructivist framework (ECLET), 161–162, 167; and the helper group, finding, 167; profiteering activism vs. not-for-profit activism, 165–167; and reparations advocacy and coalition building, 162, 165, 167–168; stages of worldview constructs in terms of individualistic and collectivist thinking, 163–165; stage theory, overview, 162; value meme systems, 162, 167

adult education: overview, 147–148; adult learning societies for blacks, 150–151; celebrities on the circuit of, 154; definition of, 154; employment as focus of, 152–153; English as a second language (ESL), 151, 152; federal funding of, 152; federal programs and legislation for, 151–153; formal, 154; informal, 155; and Japanese internment and reparations by the US government, 149–150; literacy as focus of, 151–153; the lyceums of mid-nineteenth-century America as, 154–155; nonformal, 154–155; public pedagogy field, 149; reparations taught to students in, 156, 165, 167–168; self-directed learning as basic to, 154, 155; and social justice movements, 147, 148. See also adult developmental thinking

Adult Education Act (AEA, 1966), 151, 152–153

Elaine, AR, 49

electoral politics. *See* voting rights

eligible recipients must be black Americans whose ancestors were enslaved in the United States: overview as pillar of true reparations with two criteria, 17–18; identity standard as criterion for, 17, 140; lineage standard as criterion for, 17, 140, 174–175; logistical support to identify all who qualify, 140, 142, 143; racial standard rejected, 157, 159. *See also* exclusion from eligibility of blacks whose ancestors were not enslaved in the United States; genealogy research to prove lineage

elimination of the black-white wealth gap. *See* black-white wealth gap elimination

emotional distress: as omitted in estimations of reparations bill, 138–139; September 11th Victim Compensation Fund awards for, 121

employment. *See* labor-market discrimination

English as a second language (ESL), 151, 152

enslaved persons: childbearing, childrearing, and family structure harms, 139; identity as a whole person maintained by, 181; medical experimentation performed on, without informed consent or proper care, 96–97, 100, 102–103, 103nn2–3; mortgages and life insurance taken on, by slaveholder, 186; names used by, first and last, 181; oral histories, 181; personhood of, defined in the Constitution, 29; slave narratives, 181–182; as working harder than white ancestors, 25–26. *See also* eligible recipients must be black Americans whose ancestors were enslaved in the United States; estimation of historic economic losses for the purposes of black reparations; labor of enslaved ancestors

Esolen, Anthony, 160

estimation of historic economic losses for the purposes of black reparations: and the amounts required to pay a free individual to submit to permanent slavery, 26, 39; colonial slavery (1619–1775), 27–28; historical records used from the perspective of the enslaved, 33; Jim Crow era, 49–50; land-based estimation, 30–31; New Deal era housing discrimination, 50–51; New Deal era labor-market and labor rights

discrimination, 50–51; price-based estimation, 32–33; Reconstruction period and lack of, 48; white terrorist violence, 49–50. *See also* comprehensiveness in the range of historical injustices considered; conservatism in model parameters; formulas to calculate costs; interest rates chosen in estimating total economic losses; lost freedom, compensation for; wage-based estimation of economic losses

Evanston, IL, "local reparations" plan, 201

exclusion from eligibility of blacks whose ancestors were not enslaved in the United States: overview, 174; double counting concerns addressed, 58–59; false characterization of the argument, as based in a claim of lack of experience of US racism, 17, 20n2; not descendants of the unfulfilled promise of forty-acre land grants, 17–18; parallel reparations claims exclude black Americans and vice versa, 18, 20–21n3; voluntary migration to a racist country as issue, 17; wealth position upon arrival not a product of US policies, 17. *See also* African diaspora and claims for reparations

Executive Order 8802 (defense industry integration, 1941), 55

Executive Order 9066 (Japanese internment), 119

Fair Labor Standards Act (1938, FLSA), 51

FamilySearch.com, 177, 179, 192

family structure, 139

farmworkers, New Deal programs explicitly excluding, 50–51

Federal Advisory Committee Act, 204

Federal Emergency Relief Administration (1933, FERA), 51

federal government: Medicare Act as intervention for desegregating medical facilities, 4, 99–100, 103. *See also* federal government must finance black reparations; federal public policy as creating and sustaining the black-white wealth gap; New Deal; Supreme Court

federal government must finance black reparations: overview, 19–20; as the capable party, 19–20, 140, 168; companies that profited from enslavement adding funds to, 140, 142, 143; the COVID-19 pandemic as demonstrating the ability to mobilize and spend

Omnibus Diplomatic Security and
Anti-Terrorism Act (1986), 125
*Opinions Regarding Slavery: Slave
Narratives* (1935, Southern University),
182
opposition to black reparations: overview,
160; blacks in opposition, 157; implicit
bias vs. implicit closeness and, 158;
Barack Obama's election held to be
sufficient, 160; race-conscious
opportunities held to be sufficient, 160;
the stigma of black American self-advocacy and, 159–160. *See also* opposition
to black reparations, rebuttals to
opposition to black reparations, rebuttals
to: overview, 24; "Civil War to end
slavery is sufficient," 30; "heirs not
eligible for reparations," 29–30; "it
needs to be more than a check," 206;
"it's a handout," 160–161; "poor
whites disadvantaged," 132n14; "the
living aren't responsible," 29; "too
complicated," 29
Orfield, Gary, 80, 83, 84, 90
Orlando, FL, 16–17
Oswald, Frederick L., 158

pain and suffering: and determination of the
amounts required to pay a free
individual to submit to permanent
slavery, 26; in the formula to compute
costs, 27; as omitted in estimations of
reparations bill, 46, 58, 138–139;
September 11th Victim Compensation
Fund awards for, 121
Paret, Marcel, "Law, Race, and Education
in the United States," 85, 86–87
Parks, Rosa, 148
past experiences with reparations: overview,
113, 126–130, 141–142; acknowledgment, redress, and closure (ARC) as
objectives for reparations, 111;
Americans held hostage in Iran (US
embassy), 124–126, 130; former slave
owners paid reparations for abolition of
slavery, 18, 142; heirs awarded in,
29–30, 114, 125, 131–132n12, 142;
Kerner Commission and report
(1967–68), 75, 115–117, 127, 130; the
murderers must not inherit, 114,
128–129; public support enhanced by
prompt delivery of report, 128; public
support increased with critical work on
the nature of the nation's historical

memory, 127–128, 133n19; public
support may or may not be necessary
for success of, 115, 122, 126–127,
133n18; "special master" administrator
and, 121, 131–132n12; study commissions as the customary format for design
of programs, 113; uniform payments,
with additional support based on need,
123, 128; the value of having a powerful
ally or allies, 114–115, 120, 130. *See
also* German reparations to Holocaust
victims; Japanese internment and
reparations by the US government; local
black reparations programs; September
11th Victim Compensation Fund
PBS funding, 167
Penn Central Court, 88
people of color (POC), as term, 159–160
Perry, Jule, 129
Perseverance Benevolent and Mutual Aid
Association of New Orleans, 150
Philadelphia, PA: adult learning societies for
blacks, 150; investment in legacy of
Benjamin Franklin, 65
physician-patient racial concordance, 102
Pittsburgh Courier, 55
Pittsburgh, PA, 67
Plessy v. Ferguson (1896), 78–79, 80, 81,
91n16, 99
police, benefits for families of officers killed,
122
police murders of unarmed black people:
Black Lives Matter movement arising
from, and financial exploitation by
outsiders, 166; black reparations will
not end police violence, but black
families would have greater resources
for coping with it, 206; impunity of
police in, and hostile climate in black
communities, 57; and increase of public
support for black reparations, 1, 127,
200; and racism declared a public health
crisis, 147; and War on Drugs
disparities, 57. *See also* police violence
against black people
police violence against black people:
ancestry of black victims as no
protection against, 17, 20n2; and black
soldiers in World War II, 54; and white
terrorist violence, 47
poor whites: benefits of slavery to, 132n14;
denial of education to, 76; Freedmen's
Bureau providing education and medical
care to, 76, 104n4

Popoff, Rovana, 127
population of black Americans whose
ancestors were enslaved in the United
States: estimated number of, 40; federal
censuses as consistently undercounting,
177; as percentage of black population
(90%), 13; as percentage of the nation's
population vs. percentage of business
ownerships, 208; as percentage of the
nation's population vs. percentage of
wealth held, 13, 111–112
population of enslaved persons: formula
for, 36; table of, 35; total number of,
174; as uncertain during the Civil War
period, 34, 36, 41
Portland, OR, 71
Portuguese slave traders at Jamestown, 174
postindustrial economy: and economic
instability of cities, 67; as global
informational economy, 63; Great
Recession and further increase of the
black-white wealth gap, 67; and income
inequality, 75; predatory inclusion of
black people as sabotaging policies
designed to promote black inclusion and
equity, 66–68; stratification of, and
increasing segregation of schools,
75–76
poverty: blacks born into, having the lowest
income earnings mobility, 161;
education as crucial strategy against,
152; Obama-era self-help programs, 67;
and postindustrial income inequality,
75; "pull themselves up by their
bootstraps" meme and ignorance of
realities of, 160–161; and racism
declared a public health crisis, 147;
Reconstruction and denial of education
to those in, 76; War on Poverty
(Johnson), 151. See also poor whites
Powell, Adam Clayton, 70
predatory inclusion, 66–67, 71
President's Commission on Hostage
Compensation, 124–125
price-based estimation of economic losses,
32–33
Prince George's County, MD, 68
private donors, incapability of paying the
reparations debt, 19
profiteering activism vs. not-for-profit
activism, 165–167
property taxes: deduction for, disparities in,
57; and school funding as dependent on
wealth, 89

Provident Hospital and Training School
(Chicago), 99, 104n7
public health, racism declared to be a crisis
of, 147
public housing: overview of the New Deal
ambition for federal government to
reduce the worst problems of the nation,
63–64; federal agenda for reparations
and, 68–69; New Deal interventions,
63, 68; public funding slashed for (after
1970), 68
Public Safety Death Benefits Law, 122
public support for reparations in the past:
increased with critical work on the
nature of the nation's historical
memory, 127–128, 133n19; Japanese
internment and reparations by the US
government, 119–120, 126, 133n18,
149–150; may or may not be necessary
for success of reparations, 115, 122,
126–127, 133n18; prompt delivery of
report as enhancing, 128
public support increasing for black
reparations: overview, 1, 156–157; by
blacks, 156–157, 200; by conservatives,
22; the COVID-19 pandemic and, 1,
200; Democratic presidential contenders
(2019), 1; despite continued white
opposition to race-preference programs,
153; and detours from reparations
(ideas to be avoided), 200, 210;
educating the public by building a
national historical narrative of the racial
atrocities, 144; by millennials, 127;
police murders of unarmed black people
and, 1, 127, 200; powerful political
allies, 1, 138; by whites, 127, 200
Public Works Administration (PWA), 51

Quakers, evening schools for black adults,
151

race as social construction: and increasing
residential segregation, 65; and race
correction (race norming) in medical
care, 103
racial discrimination. See discrimination
racial intelligibility, 158–159
racism: critique of lineage standard for
reparations based on false claim about,
17; as experienced by black people of all
ancestries, 17, 202n2; health outcome
disparities resulting from systemic
racism, 102; the Kerner Commission

Founded in 1893,
UNIVERSITY OF CALIFORNIA PRESS
publishes bold, progressive books and journals
on topics in the arts, humanities, social sciences,
and natural sciences—with a focus on social
justice issues—that inspire thought and action
among readers worldwide.

The UC PRESS FOUNDATION
raises funds to uphold the press's vital role
as an independent, nonprofit publisher, and
receives philanthropic support from a wide
range of individuals and institutions—and from
committed readers like you. To learn more, visit
ucpress.edu/supportus.